SOUTHERN CALIFORNIA
Golden Gate Baptist Theo...
12311 Chapman Avenue...
Garden Grove, California 92640

YO-DCE-320

Witnesses to the Holy Spirit

Warren Lewis

Witnesses to the Holy Spirit

An Anthology

Judson Press® Valley Forge

WITNESSES TO THE HOLY SPIRIT

Copyright © 1978
Judson Press, Valley Forge, PA 19481

All rights reserved. No part of this publication may be reproduced, stored in a retrieval system, or transmitted in any form or by any means, electronic, mechanical, photocopying, recording, or otherwise, without the prior permission of the copyright owner, except for brief quotations included in a review of the book.

Unless otherwise indicated, Bible quotations in this volume are in accordance with the Revised Standard Version of the Bible, copyrighted 1946, 1952, 1971, 1973 © by the Division of Christian Education of the National Council of the Churches of Christ in the United States of America, and are used by permission.

Also quoted in this book:
    The Holy Bible, King James Version.

Library of Congress Cataloging in Publication Data

Main entry under title:
Witnesses to the Holy Spirit.
    Includes bibliographical references.
    1. Holy Spirit—Addresses, essays, lectures.
I. Lewis, Warren.
BT121.2.W57   231'.3   78-7546
ISBN 0-8170-0809-8

The name JUDSON PRESS is registered as a trademark in the U.S. Patent Office. Printed in the U.S.A.

for Lynne, Vi, Jenette, and Judee
and the "ecclesia spiritualis"
at West Islip, Long Island

Contents

INTRODUCTION
Toward a Theology
of the Holy Spirit

We are living in apocalyptic times. Eschatology (the understanding of "last things"), once thought to be little more than a troublesome though negligible oddity of New Testament biblical mythology, has now become a part of everyone's theology. Whether in fear or hope, we all are watching the onrush of the future. The Holy Spirit is both part of that biblical-eschatological perspective and also part of the perspective of the new eschatologists. In the language of the mystic wise men from the East, for example, the new astrological "Year of the Water Man," dawning with the turn of the millennium, is a time when He pours out the flood of His aquarian Spirit upon us, immersing us and giving us to drink. Or, in the language of the planners of a Christian utopia, we are soon to arrive at global consciousness, establish a utilitarian system of worldwide justice, and begin to sense the earthly presence of God-with-us in an international, public way. Or, in the language of the rabbinic-prophetic Joachite tradition, the Third World Age of the Holy Spirit is upon us.

Consciousness III, the Third Reich, the messianic millennium of the Spirit, the time of the Lord of the Second Advent, the Omega Point of the ultimate evolutionary stage of creation's Sixth Day—whatever currently available phrase one uses to describe it, we are said to be coming to perfection in the spiritualization of humankind and the hominization of the earth. Tomorrow morning the Seventh Day will dawn, the Sabbath rest of the heavenly Guest, who through his Holy Spirit from heaven to earth removes his blest abode and makes his home with people.[1]

In order for our Day of the Lord to come in final shalom and ultimate delight rather than as penultimate holocaust, we need to find a way to keep totalitarians and leaders of false starts from usurping the momentum of the ages in the meantime for their own finite ends. This is the work of common repentance. Neither by the power of old-style politics nor by the force of military arms does the latter reign (reign/rain—pentecostal pun intended; see Joel 2:23) of the Spirit come. Those who wear the Ring of Power, even for a good cause, even Hobbits, are corrupted by it, as J. R. R. Tolkien has said.[2] Rather, through personal indwelling, friendly charismation with simple gifts, and Mother's love do peace and joy most surely come. This anthology of texts is intended to lighten our path toward an understanding of the Holy Spirit for the twenty-first century.

Three main concerns are represented:

(1) The *orthodox-catholic development* of the traditional theological affirmation of the divine Third-Personhood of the Holy Spirit is the main line of Christian reflection which secures for us the full, objective personality of the Spirit as a distinct person within the Godhead. The development of orthodoxy is traced in sections 8, 9, 11, 12, 14-22, 23, 25, 27, 31-33, 40, 47, 48, 50-52. This tradition stands in opposition to two prevalent ideas: the notion that the Holy Spirit is

[1] For the current discussion of eschatology and the Spirit, see Wolfhart Pannenberg, ed., *Revelation As History* (New York: Macmillan, Inc., 1968); "The Working of the Spirit in the Creation and in the People of God," in *Spirit, Faith, and Church,* W. Pannenberg, Avery Dulles, and Carl E. Braaten (Philadelphia: The Westminster Press, 1970); see also Carl E. Braaten, "Spirituality of Hope," in *Christ and Counter-Christ: Apocalyptic Themes in Theology and Culture* (Philadelphia: Fortress Press, 1972), pp. 82-100; Jürgen Moltmann, fountainhead of the "theology of hope" school, has now applied his eschatological perspective to questions concerning the Holy Spirit in *Kirche in der Kraft des Geistes. Ein Beitrag zur messianischen Ekklesiologie* (München: Kaiser, 1975). Theodore Roszak, *The Unfinished Animal: The Aquarian Revolution and the Evolution of Consciousness* (New York: Harper & Row, Publishers, 1975), see especially the chart, pp. 26-29, describes a sociology of spirituality that runs the gamut from devoutly pious religionists to radically secular consciousness hawkers, all standing on what Roszak calls the "Aquarian Frontier" of the future and of the Spirit.

[2] J. R. R. Tolkien, *The Lord of the Rings,* 3 vols. (New York: Ballantine Books, Inc., 1965), the title page of each volume repeats the apocalyptic foreboding of doom which awaits the denizens of Middle Earth should they attempt to wear the Ring of Power.

merely the impersonal "power" or "subtle influence" of God; and the too-immanentist identification of the Holy Spirit with the human spirit, which is allegedly realized through "meditation" or some other inner or parapsychological path. According to the catholic tradition, the Holy Spirit is affirmed to be of the same substance with the Father and the Son. The Holy Spirit has always existed with the Father and the Son and with them is to be glorified and worshiped with the same worship and glory which they receive. The orthodox-catholic line of thought will culminate in a future dogmatic definition by Ecumenical Council that the Holy Spirit is "one person indwelling many persons."[3]

(2) The next tradition represented is the often *"heretical" but perennial corrective* of the orthodox-catholic development as urged by the charismatic pentecostals of whatever stripe, in whatever century. This continuing tradition is traced in sections 1, 2, 3, 5-7, 11-13, 20, 21, 26, 28-30, 34, 36, 37-46. The ecclesiastical main line (1) has tended to describe the person and work of the Holy Spirit in terms of the person and work of Jesus Christ, who is the Second Person of the Godhead and who became the God-Man. But it has been the work of the charismatic tradition to focus upon the unique and particular activities of the Holy Spirit, who is the Third Person of the Godhead and who is the person of God indwelling many persons. The religion of experience, reception of the charismatic gifts, and direct leading are some of the hallmarks of this tradition, evident in every century of the church's life, for those who have eyes to see it.[4] The most fruitful times of the Spirit have been those occasions when the orthodox-catholic, traditional perspective, and the charismatic, heretical-pentecostal experience have cross-fertilized each other.

[3] For an American statement in this direction, see Herbert Richardson, *Toward an American Theology* (New York: Harper & Row, Publishers, 1967), pp. 108-160; the work of Heribert Mühlen, *Der Heilige Geist als Person* (Münster: Aschendorff, 1966) and *Una Mystica Persona* (München, Paderborn, Wien: Schöningh, 1968) should prove contributory to the future conciliar definition.

[4] The best overview of this tradition now available is by George Huntston Williams and Edith Waldvogel, "A History of Speaking in Tongues and Related Gifts," in *The Charismatic Movement*, ed. Michael P. Hamilton (Grand Rapids: William B. Eerdmans Publishing Company, 1975), pp. 61-113, including bibliographical references to the works of the founders of Holiness Pentecostalism, and the longest list to date of those known to have spoken in tongues. See also the classic by Ronald Knox, *Enthusiasm* (Oxford: University Press, 1950). James L. Ash, Jr., "The Decline of Ecstatic Prophecy in the Early Church," *Theological Studies*, vol. 37, no. 2 (June, 1976), pp. 227-252, has traced and discusses the supposed quenching of the Spirit in the ancient church.

(3) The last concern represented is the tradition which has stressed the *femaleness and divine motherhood of the Holy Spirit.* See especially sections 1, 2, 7, 10, 12, 13, 14, 24, 26, 29, 30, 35, 42, 43, 48 and 51. This primitive Christian experience of the Holy Spirit as the feminine dimension in the Godhead was suppressed by the emerging male-dominant Christian establishment. But the Spirit's femininity has prevailed in the prophecies of women charismatics, hidden in the quiet hysteria of convents, emerged in the tough minds of female doctors of the church, and has been intimated in the Roman identification of Mary as the mediatrix of grace and mother of the Church. [5] Among these people, the other third of the truth about the nature of God has been upheld: the Spirit is woman. Created in her image and according to her likeness, we become aware of our receptivity before God and to one another: She is God the True Mother (not the Earthmother of ancient and modern paganisms, dominating and devouring her children and lovers!) who comforts us by pouring out her Mother love in our hearts. She is God the Matron of honor, who prepares us as brides for the coming of the Son, our bridegroom. She is God the Midwife, who stands by us, as she both prepared and stood by the virgin Mary, while Christ is formed within us and is born from our suffering, happy bodies. She is God the Mediatrix of God and of all grace, whether of the finalization of creation or of the gifts of charismation. She is God the Girlfriend, who personally indwells us, delights us, touches us with her love in every way we let her, ravishes us at all levels of our being, and calls forth the best that lies within us. Mary Baker Eddy, mother of Christian Science, hinted at this tradition in her prayers to "Father-Mother God." Johann Conrad Beissel, the founder of Ephrata Community, similarly spoke of "God our Father, Christ our Brother, and the Holy Ghost our Mother." [6] Certain rabbis and the Jewish cabalistic tradition interpreted the feminine personification of wisdom to refer to the female depths within God (Prov. 8, Ecclesiasticus 1; 4:11; 24:1). Jesus may also have understood Wisdom, or the Holy Spirit, in this way (Luke 7:35; 11:49; Matt. 11:19).

[5] The paragraph headings of the article on Mary in the *New Catholic Encyclopedia,* vol. 9, pp. 347-364, would make an adequate outline for a systematic theology of the Holy Spirit if one were only to substitute the word "Spirit" for "Mary" in each instance; compare Leon Cardinal Suenens, *A New Pentecost?* (New York: The Seabury Press, Inc., 1975).

[6] See Walter Klein, *Johann Conrad Beissel, Mystic and Martinet* (Philadelphia: University of Pennsylvania Press, 1942), pp. 194-197.

The latest contribution comes from the Christian Orient in the form of the eschatologically motivated Holy Spirit Association for the Unification of World Christianity (or Unification Church) of the Korean, Reverend Sun Myung Moon, who in his *Divine Principle* says:

> God is the absolute subject, who exists with His dual characteristics of positivity and negativity. . . . Jesus and the Holy Spirit came as the True Parents in place of Adam and Eve to give rebirth to mankind. . . . A father alone cannot give birth to children. There must be a True Mother with the True Father, in order to give rebirth to fallen children as children of goodness. She is the Holy Spirit. . . . There are many who receive revelations indicating that the Holy Spirit is a female Spirit; this is because she came as the True Mother, that is, the second Eve. Again, since the Holy Spirit is a female Spirit, we cannot become the "bride" of Jesus unless we receive the Holy Spirit. Thus, the Holy Spirit is a female Spirit, consoling and moving the hearts of the people (I Cor. 12:3). She also cleanses the sins of the people in order to restore them, thus indemnifying the sin committed by Eve. Jesus, being male (positivity), is working in heaven, while the Holy Spirit, being female (negativity), is working on earth.[7]

I have arbitrarily decided to excerpt no living author; therefore, contemporary charismatics and theologians of the Holy Spirit are not included.[8] The biblical material is readily available to anyone with the patience to run the proper references in a concordance.[9] A

[7] Sun Myung Moon, *Divine Principle* (Washington: HSA-UWC, 1973), pp. 24, 118, 215.

[8] See Williams and Waldvogel, *op. cit.;* Walter J. Hollenwegger, *The Pentecostals* (London: SCM Press, 1972), especially the appendix of original Pentecostal texts, pp. 513-522, and the best bibliography on worldwide contemporary Pentecostalism, pp. 523-557; Frederick D. Bruner, *A Theology of the Holy Spirit: The Pentecostal Experience and the New Testament Witness* (Grand Rapids: William B. Eerdmans Publishing Company, 1970), pp. 323-341, also contains a selection of original statements. Some forerunners of this anthology are these works on the history of the Holy Spirit: Henry B. Swete, *The Early History of the Doctrine of the Holy Spirit* (Cambridge, 1873); *The Holy Spirit in the New Testament* (London, 1909); *The Holy Spirit in the Ancient Church* (London, 1912); H. Watkin-Jones, *The Holy Spirit in the Medieval Church* (London, 1922); *The Holy Spirit from Arminius to Wesley* (London, 1929); George Barton Cutten, *Speaking with Tongues: Historically and Psychologically Considered* (New Haven: Yale University Press, 1927); a similar assembly of texts: Yolande d'Ormesson Arsène-Henry, *Veni Sancte Spiritus: Die schönsten Texte über den Heiligen Geist* (Luzern: Räber & Cie, 1959); see also M. F. Toal, ed., *The Sunday Sermons of the Great Fathers,* vol. 3 (Chicago: Henry Regnery Company, 1959).

[9] Two pieces of outstanding exegetical work are those of G. Hasenhüttl, *Charisma: Ordnungsprinzip der Kirche* (Freiburg: Herder, 1969) and J. D. Dunn, *Baptism in the Holy Spirit: A Reexamination of the New Testament Teaching on the Gift of the Spirit in relation to Pentecostalism* (London: SCM Press, 1970); see also B. Lindars and S. S. Smalley, *Christ and the Spirit in the New Testament* (Cambridge: University Press, 1973).

number of persistent pneumatological issues have been slightly touched upon in deference to a more thorough representation of the three traditions mentioned above. See sections 17, 22, 23 (Constantinople [381] in particular), and 32 in regard to the "Filioque." [10] For the relationship of "Spirit" and "letter," see especially sections 4, 21, 23, 28, 31-33, 37, and 41.

These three traditions correspond in some way to three outstanding words for the Holy Spirit which we find in Scripture, two from the New Testament, one from the Old: *Paraklete* is masculine. "He" is the Counselor, the indwelling Spirit of Christ, who has come in the place of the Ascended One as second advocate and intercessor, defense attorney for the elect and state's attorney to bring the world to justice. *Pneuma* is neuter. "It" is the Spirit, the programmer and systems analyst of the gifts, of spiritual cybernetics, and of the technology of sanctification. It is the medium and synapse between us and the spirit-world of angels and the "spirits of just persons made perfect." It is the ultimate trip. *Ruach* is feminine. "She" is the Wings over creation, the Love of our True Mother, the Power of receptivity, the Playmate of the soul, proud and careful Perfection, and the beloved Lover of Love's Body.

Warren Lewis
Pentecost, 1977

---

[10] See Anselm of Canterbury, *On the Procession of the Holy Spirit* (trans. H. Lee Gibbs and Warren Lewis) in *Anselm of Canterbury: Theological Treatises* (vol II), ed. Jasper Hopkins and Herbert Richardson (Cambridge: Harvard Divinity School Library, 1966), pp. 1-61; reprinted *Anselm of Canterbury: Trinity, Incarnation and Redemption: Theological Treatises,* ed. Jasper Hopkins and Herbert Richardson (New York: Harper & Row, Publishers, 1970).

NONCANONICAL
SCRIPTURE

1

Testament of Job

(c. 100)

Early Christians wrote not only "New" Testament literature but also produced "Old." The Testament of Job seems to have been originally a Jewish document in Aramaic which was translated into Greek and reworked by a Christian editor. In this selection Job's three virgin daughters gird themselves with special belts, which probably represent celibacy, so that they no longer have sexual desires. As a result, they are enabled to speak and sing in the tongues of three of the orders of angels: angels, rulers, and cherubim. Nereus, the brother of Job and the women's uncle, who is telling the story, describes the urging of the Lord and the Holy Spirit in the house-church setting. The texts may either have been influenced by, or could be a source of, the thought of two New Testament texts: 1 Corinthians 13:1 (KJV), "Though I speak with the tongues of men and of angels . . ." and Acts 21:9 (KJV), "[Philip] had four daughters, virgins, which did prophesy."

In this way, furthermore, Job's first daughter, the one called Hemera, stood up and wrapped a belt around herself, just as her father had said. And she took upon herself another heart, no longer to think the things of the earth. She thus expressed herself in the angelic dialect, sending up a hymn to God according to the angelic style of hymn singing. And the Spirit permitted the hymns which she emitted to be inscribed on her own garment.

And then Cassia [the next daughter] girded herself with a belt; and she got a changed heart, the kind that no longer desires worldly things. And then her mouth took up the dialect of the angelic rulers, and she glorified the work of the High Place. Wherefore, if anyone wants to know the work of the heavens, they would be able to find them out in the hymns of Cassia.

And then the other daughter, the one called Amaltheiakera, girded herself with a belt, and she got the tongue for speaking in the dialect of those in the Highest. And after that, her heart was changed, being separated from worldly things; for she spoke in the dialect of the cherubim, glorifying the Master of the virtuous by showing their glory. And whoever wants to get hold of the remaining proof of the Father's glory, they will find it written down in the prayers of Amaltheiakera.

Now after the three hymn singers had ceased, the Lord was still urging—and I, Nereus, the brother of Job—and also the Holy Spirit was still urging. I sat down near Job on my bed. I listened to the great things, making careful notes one after the other. And I wrote down an entire scroll of the great signs of the hymns of my brother's three daughters—this being salvation, that these things are the great things of God.[1]

[1] J. Armitage Robinson, "Testament of Job" in *Texts and Studies* (Cambridge University Press, 1899), vol. 5, pp. 135-136, author's translation.

2

Fragments
from Other Gospels
and Acts

(First to Fifth Centuries)

The four canonical Gospels and the one book of Acts of the Apostles contained in our New Testament are but a fraction of the literary output of the first Christian centuries. In addition, other "biblical forms" were also produced—revelations, epistles, and isolated sayings of Jesus. Several of these were once read in some churches as Scripture; some of them still are. Some of them are wildly fantastic, representing nothing much more than the early Christian romantic literary mind at work, embroidering the central theme; yet others, for example, the Gospel of Thomas, *represent very early forms of biblical material and contain authentic sayings of Jesus which have as much claim on our interest as the sayings included in the canonical Gospels and Acts. This latter group of writings was produced during the late first and early second centuries in and by churches whose spiritual pedigree goes back as far as the churches which produced the canonical writings, even if their theological perspectives differ somewhat. The authenticity of the now accepted twenty-seven book canon (first listed by Bishop Athanasius of Alexandria, Egypt, in his thirty-ninth Paschal letter in the year 367) is a moot point in terms of our purpose in this section to assemble an anthology of texts which create an impression of what the earliest Christians believed about the Holy Spirit.*

Luke 3:22

In Luke 3:22, according to the Western Text, the Itala, Justin Martyr, Gospel of the Ebionites, Clement of Alexandria, Origen, and Methodius, as well as others, the Spirit says of Jesus: "You are my Son; this day have I begotten you."

The Gospel of the Ebionites

The Ebionites, a group of Jewish Christians who fled east of the Jordan River after the destruction of Jerusalem, understood this text to mean that the man Jesus was adopted to become the Son of God when the Holy Spirit descended upon him at his baptism, at which time "the Christ" came to him, making him divine. Epiphanius of Salamis (c. 315–403), a native of Palestine, quotes from The Gospel of the Ebionites *in his* Refutation of All Heresies, *chapter 30:*

After the people were baptized, Jesus also came and was baptized by John; and as he came up from the water, the heavens were opened, and he saw the Holy Ghost in the likeness of a dove that descended and entered into him, and a voice from heaven saying: Thou art my beloved Son, in thee am I well pleased: and again; This day have I begotten thee. And straightway there shone about the place a great light.

Epiphanius goes on to say that the Ebionites teach that Jesus was born a mere man and then was chosen by God, and so by the choice *of God* he was called the Son of God from the Christ that came into him from above in the likeness of a dove.[1]

The Gospel of the Nazarenes

The Gospel of the Nazarenes *or* Gospel of the Hebrews, *now no longer extant, was an Aramaic version of the Gospel of Matthew with some additional peculiarities of its own. It was used by another group of Jewish Christians who lived in Syria. Jerome (c. 342–420), the scholarly translator of the Vulgate, saw, copied, and translated this Gospel and commented that Origen (c. 185–254) had also used it. In the Gospel of the Nazarenes, the Holy Spirit is referred to as the mother of Jesus. This identification was a natural one for a Hebrew- or Aramaic-speaking person since the word for Spirit (ruach) is*

[1] Translated by M. R. James in *The Apocryphal New Testament* (Oxford: Clarendon Press, 1924), pp. 9-10. Reprinted by permission of publisher.

feminine. Origen, commenting on the Gospel of John 2:12, says:

And if any accept the Gospel according the Hebrews, where the Saviour himself says, "Even so did my mother, the Holy Spirit, take me by one of my hairs and carry me away to the great mountain Tabor," he will be perplexed.[2]

Jerome, commenting on Isaiah 11:9 and Ezekiel 16:13, quotes Jesus from this Gospel to have said: "My mother, the Holy Spirit."[3]

In another place, the Gospel of the Nazarenes describes the Spirit at her descent upon Jesus at his baptism as the one who speaks to him (as opposed to the canonical Gospels in which the voice is that, presumably, of God the Father), thus allowing for the motherhood of the Spirit in her act of adoption of Jesus to divine sonship:

And it came to pass when the Lord came up out of the water, the whole fount of the Holy Spirit descended upon him and rested on him and said to him; My Son, in all the prophets was I waiting for thee that thou shouldest come and I might rest in thee. For thou art my rest; thou art my first-begotten Son that reignest for ever.[4]

The understanding of the female, motherly quality of the Spirit was easy not only for the Aramaic-speaking person but fitted as well into the systems of emanations of the heavenly aeons which the Christian Gnostics devised. The usual idea was that the Holy Spirit was the feminine counterpart in the syzygy *(pair) of aeons of which Christ was the masculine half. For example, in the Valentinian system of Ptolemaeus (c. 160), Achamoth, the aborted Desire of Sophia, the impetuous aeon who lusted after Forefather, is described to have a certain aroma of imperishability which had been left her by Christ and the Holy Spirit. For this reason she* [Achamoth] *is called by both names: Sophia* [Wisdom] *after her mother (for her mother was called Sophia) and Holy Spirit from the Spirit with Christ.*[5]

[2] *Ibid.,* p. 2.

[3] *Ibid.,* p. 5.

[4] Edgar Hennecke and Wilhelm Schneemelcher, eds., *New Testament Apocrypha,* English translation edited by R. McL. Wilson (Philadelphia: The Westminster Press, 1963; Copyright © 1959, J. C. B. Mohr, Paul Siebeck, Tübingen, English translation © 1963, Lutterworth Press), vol. 1, p. 164. Used by permission. *The Nag Hammadi Library in English,* ed. James M. Robinson (San Francisco: Harper & Row, Publishers, 1977), is now the best source of Christian Gnostic writing, being a one-volume collection of the Coptic sources found in Egypt in 1945.

[5] R. M. Grant, ed., *Gnosticism* (New York: Harper & Row, Publishers, 1961), p. 170. Copyright © 1961 by Robert M. Grant. Reprinted by permission of Harper & Row, Publishers, Inc.

In the "Hymn of the Pearl," a Gnostic poem, the soul of man is said to have descended from a trinity of royal persons:

> From thy Father, the King of kings
> And thy Mother, the mistress of the East
> And from thy Brother, our next in rank,
> To thee our son, who art in Egypt, greeting![6]

Gospel of Truth

In the Gospel of Truth, *one of the documents from Nag-Hammadi, the Spirit is described variously as the tongue of the Father, by which the Father is mutually joined to the Truth (the Logos), and as a means of knowledge of the Father and the revelation of his Son, of refreshment and sensation of things divine:*

And happy is the man who comes to himself and awakens. Indeed, blessed is he who has opened the eyes of the blind.

And the Spirit came to him in haste when it raised him. Having given its hand to the one lying prone on the ground, it placed him firmly on his feet, for he had not yet stood up. He gave them means of knowing the knowledge of the Father and the revelation of his son. For when they saw it and listened to it, he permitted them to take a taste of and to smell and to grasp the beloved son.[7] The Father is sweet and his will is good.... For there are no nostrils which smell the aroma, but it is the Spirit which possesses the sense of smell and it draws for itself to itself and sinks into the aroma of the Father.[8]

But in another place, the Spirit is described in the Gospel of Truth *as the Mother counterpart to God the Father:*
Thus the Logos of the Father goes forth into the all, being the fruit of his heart and expression of his will. It supports the all. It chooses and also takes the form of the all, purifying it and causing it to return to the Father (and) to the Mother, Jesus of the utmost sweetness! The Father opens his bosom, but his bosom is the Holy Spirit.[9]

Acts of Thomas

A final example of the motherhood of the Spirit from an extra-canonical source is contained in three hymns of epiclesis and two

[6] *Ibid.,* pp. 119-120.
[7] *Ibid.,* p. 154.
[8] *Ibid.,* p. 156.
[9] *Ibid.,* p. 151.

doxologies from the Acts of Thomas *which, with the* Gospel of Thomas, *give us an indication of the style of Christianity experienced in and around Edessa, Syria, during the first two or three hundred years of the Christian era.*

Come, holy name of Christ *that is above every name;*
Come, power of the Most High and perfect compassion;
Come, thou highest gift: [charisma]
Come, compassionate mother;
Come, fellowship of the male;
Come, thou feminine that dost reveal the hidden mysteries;
Come, mother of the seven houses, that thy rest may be in the eighth
    house;
Come, elder, messenger of the five members, understanding,
    thought, prudence, consideration, reasoning,
Communicate with these young men!
Come, Holy Spirit, and purify their reins and their heart
And give them the added seal in the name of the Father and
    Son and Holy Spirit.[10]

(Come, gift of the Most High;)
Come, perfect compassion;
Come, fellowship of the male;
(Come, Holy Spirit;)
Come, thou that dost know the mysteries of the Chosen;
Come, thou that hast part in all the combats of the noble athlete;
(Come, treasure of glory;)
(Come, darling of the compassion of the Most High;)
Come, silence
    That dost reveal the great deeds of the whole greatness;
Come, thou that dost show forth the hidden things
    And make the ineffable manifest;
Holy Dove
    That bearest the twin young
Come, hidden Mother
Come, thou that art manifest in thy deeds and dost furnish joy
    And rest for all that are joined with thee;
Come and partake with us in this Eucharist
    Which we celebrate in thy name

[10] Hennecke-Schneemelcher, *op. cit.,* vol. 2, pp. 456-457.

And in the love-feast
In which we are gathered together at thy call.[11]

The third, quasi-baptismal epiclesis found in the Acts of Thomas *does not betray an interest in the femininity of the Spirit but does give further evidence of Christian Gnostic language, here brought together with a sacramental understanding of healing according to which the presence of the Spirit fills the waters themselves of a partial baptism with the gift of the Spirit gained through baptism:*

Come, waters from the Living Waters [cf. John 7:38-39], the existent from the existent and sent to us; rest that was sent from the Rest; power of salvation that comes from that Power which conquers all things . . . that the gift of the Holy Spirit may be perfectly fulfilled in them![12]

The first doxology comes at the end of a song which the apostle Thomas sings in allegorical praise of a Hebrew flute-girl who represents the heavenly Bride. At the end of the song, the wedding party

. . . glorified and praised, with the living Spirit,
the Father of Truth and the Mother of Wisdom.[13]

The other doxology comes at the close of a burst of praise in honor of Christ from the Apostle in response to a message given him by a talking donkey. Thomas says: "we glorify and praise thee [Jesus Christ] and thine invisible Father, and thy Holy Spirit and the Mother of all creation."[14]

Simon the Magician

According to a different sense of the word "Spirit," in which "God is Spirit," an androgynous being comprising both male and female is envisioned. According to Hippolytus of Rome, Simon Magus of Samaria (cf. Acts 8:9-24), whom Irenaeus named in perhaps not entirely legendary terms as the "father of all heresies," proclaimed God to be a "Power at once male and female." Hippolytus is quoting Simon's writing:

There are two stems of all the Aeons, having neither beginning nor end, from one root, which is Power-Silence, unseen and incompre-

[11] *Ibid.*, p. 470.
[12] *Ibid.*, p. 472.
[13] *Ibid.*, p. 446.
[14] *Ibid.*, p. 465.

hensible. One of them appears on high, who is a great power, the mind of the universals, who orders all things and (is) a male. And the other, below, is a great Thought, a female giving birth to all things. These, then, being set over against each other form a pair and show forth the middle space, an incomprehensible air having neither beginning nor end. In this (space) is a Father who upholds all things and nourishes those which have a beginning and end. This is He who Stood, Stands and will Stand, being a masculo-feminine power after the likeness of the pre-existing Boundless Power which has neither beginning nor end but exists in oneness. For the thought which came forth from the power in oneness was two. And that was one. For he when he contained her within himself was alone, nor was he indeed first, although he existed beforehand, but having himself appeared from himself, a second came into being. But he was not called Father until she named him Father. Just as then he, drawing himself forth from himself, manifested to himself his own thought, so also the thought having appeared did not create him; but beholding him, hid the Father—that is Power—within herself; and there is a masculo-feminine Power-and-Thought when they are set over against each other. For Power does not differ at all from thought, they being one. From the things on high is discovered Power; from those below, Thought. Thus then it is that which appeared from them being one is found to be two, a masculo-feminine, having the female within it. This is Mind-in-Thought, for they being one when undivided from one another are yet found to be two.[15]

Simon identifies these two halves of the male/female original androgyne: he is himself the masculine half, as Jerome in his commentary on Matthew 24:5 says Simon stated: "I am the Word of God, I am the Paraclete, I am the Almighty, I am all that is God's."[16] *Or, as Irenaeus relates it, Simon allowed himself to be glorified as a god, somewhat modalistically teaching that he himself had* "appeared among the Jews as the Son, but descended in Samaria as the Father, while he came to other nations in the character of the Holy Spirit."[17]

[15] Hippolytus, *Philosophoumena or Refutation of All Heresies* 6:18, trans. F. Legge (London: SPCK, 1921), vol. 2, pp. 14-15.
[16] Henry B. Swete, *The Holy Spirit in the Ancient Church* (London: Macmillan, 1912), p. 51.
[17] *Ante-Nicene Fathers,* ed. J. Donaldson (rev. American edition, A. C. Coxe) (Oxford, 1885; republished in Grand Rapids: William B. Eerdmans Company), vol. 1, p. 348.

The female half of the pair was Simon's girl friend Helen, whom Irenaeus describes in this way:

Simon . . . led about with him a certain Helen, after he had redeemed her from a life of prostitution in Tyre, a city of Phoenicia. He said she was the first conception of his mind, the Mother of All, through whom in the beginning he had the idea of making angels and archangels. This Thought, leaping forth from him and knowing what her father willed, descended to the lower regions and generated angels and powers, by whom this world was made.

She was in that Helen because of whom the Trojan war was undertaken.

Transmigrating from body to body, and always enduring humiliation from the body, she finally became a prostitute; she was the "lost sheep" (Luke 15:6). For this reason he came, in order to rescue her first and free her from her bonds, then to offer men salvation through his knowledge.

Therefore the priests of their mysteries live promiscuously and perform magic, in so far as each is able to do so. They employ exorcisms and incantations and are constantly occupied with love-philtres, love-magic, familiar spirits, dream-inducers and other abstruse matters. They have an image of Simon made in the likeness of Zeus and one of Helen in the likeness of Athena, and they worship these.[18]

Secret Book of John

The femininity and motherhood of the Spirit is evident also in the Christian Gnostic Apocryphon *or* Secret Book of John, *composed in the middle of the second century by the Ophites or Barbelognostics on the basis of earlier Jewish Christian material and rediscovered with the other Gnostic books at Nag Hammadi. In one place, Jesus— who is revealing himself to a perplexed John in order to answer some hard questions—in a rather Sabellian, patripassionist fashion identifies himself as all the persons of the Godhead, including "the Mother" in the place of the Holy Spirit:*

He said to me: "John, why do you doubt? . . . Do not be of little faith; I am the one who is with you always. I am [the Father], I am the Mother, I (am the Son). I am the eternally Existent, the unmixable."[19]

[18] Grant, *op. cit.*, pp. 24-25. Hippolytus, *Philosophoumena* 6:19, *op. cit.*, vol. 2, p. 15, describes Helen in much the same way.

[19] Grant, *op. cit.*, p. 70.

In another place, the Spirit is called "Life, the Mother of All." [20] *But in one particular context, "Spirit" is a vast, theologically potent term and is given a more systematic treatment here than possibly anywhere else in primitive Christian writing:*
The Spirit is a Unity, over which no one rules. It is the God of Truth, the Father of the All, the Holy Spirit, the invisible one, the one who is over the All, the one who exists in his imperishability, the one who exists in pure light into which no sight can look.

One must not consider the Spirit as god or as of a specific quality, for it is more excellent than the gods. It is a Beginning that none precedes, for no one existed before it and it has no need of them. It does not need life, for it is eternal; it needs nothing, for it is not perfectible, since it has no deficiency which might be perfected, but is beyond all perfection. It is light. It is illimitable because no one is before it to give it limits; undifferentiated, because no one is before it to differentiate it; immeasurable, because no one has measured it as though existing before; invisible, because no one has seen it. It is the eternal which always exists, the indescribable because no one has apprehended it so as to describe it, the one whose name no one can tell, because no one existed before it to name it.

It is the immeasurable Light, the holy and pure purity, the indescribable, perfect and imperishable. It is not perfection or beatitude or deity, but something far more excellent. It is not boundless nor are limits set to it; it is something more excellent. It is neither corporeal nor incorporeal, not great, not small, not a quantity, not a creature; no one can think it. It is not anything existent, but something prior—not as if in itself it were prior, but because it is its own. It has no part in an Aeon. Time does not belong to it, for one which participates in an aeon has been formed by others. Time is not allotted to it, since it receives nothing from any other which allots. It makes use of nothing. In short, there is nothing before it. It seeks only itself in the perfection of Light, and comprehends the pure Light. The immeasurable greatness, the eternal, the giver of eternity, the Light, the giver of light, the life, the giver of life, the blessed one, the giver of blessedness, the knowledge, the giver of knowledge, the eternal good, the giver of good, the benefactor; that which is not of such a kind because it is such, but it

[20] *Ibid.*, p. 75.

gives (qualities); the merciful mercy, the grace-giving grace, the immeasurable Light.

What shall I say to you of It, the incomprehensible—the vision of the light—corresponding to what I shall be able to comprehend? For who will ever comprehend It as I can discuss It with you? Its Aeon is imperishable existing in rest and reposing in silence. It existed before the All. It is the head of all Aeons. If another were with It—for no one among us has recognised that which belongs to the immeasurable one except the one who dwelt in it. He told this to us (cf. John 1:18), he who alone understands himself in his own light which surrounds him, he who is the fount of the water of life, the light full of purity.

The fount of the Spirit flowed out of the living water of light (cf. John 7:38). And It supplied all Aeons and all worlds in every way. It understood Its own image, when It saw it in the pure water of light which surrounds It. And Its Thought became operative and revealed herself. She stood before It out of the splendour of the Light, which is the Power which is before the All, the Power which has revealed itself and is the perfect Forethought of the universe, the Light, the copy of Light, the image of the invisible. She is the perfect Power, the Barbelo, the perfect Aeon of glory. She praises It because she appeared through It and understands It. She is the First Thought, Its Image; she became a First Man , i.e., the Virginal Spirit, the thrice-male one, which has three powers, three names, three acts of generation; the Aeon which does not age, the male-female which came out of Its Forethought.[21]

Through the intervention of a heavenly aeon, sexual intercourse is discovered by the mortals who then commence to practice on earth by imitation what they now know takes place in the heavenlies among the syzygies of aeons:

Adam knew his nature and begot Seth. And as in the generation which is in heaven under the Aeons, so the Mother sent the (Spirit) which belongs to her. The Spirit descended to her [to Eve] in order to awaken the nature which is like it, after the model of perfection, in order to awaken them from lack of perception and from the wickedness of the grave. So It remained for a time and worked for the seed, so that when the Spirit comes from the holy Aeons, it may place them outside deficiency in the arrangements of the Aeon; so that it

[21] *Ibid.*, pp. 70-72.

may become holy perfection, so that deficiency may no longer be with it. . . . Those upon whom the Spirit of Life descends, when they are bound together with the power, will be saved and will become perfect and they will become worthy to rise upward to that great light.[22]

The Apocryphon of John closes with this doxology:
The One to be praised, the Father-Mother, the One rich in mercy, takes form in her seed . . . .

The Mother once descended before me. But these are the things which she effected in the world; she raised up her seed.[23]

Gospel of Mani

From another direction, the Hebrew Christian identification of the Spirit as the Mother had influence among the Manichees, an eclectic sect of archheretics deplored by every ancient Christian author who knew about them. From a Gospel ascribed to Mani (c. 215–275), the founder of the rigorously dualistic religion, the following doxology may be approximately restored:

Praised is, and praised may he be, the dear son of Love, the life-giver Jesus, the chief of all these gifts. Praised is and praised shall be the Virgin of Light, the chief of all excellences. Praised is and praised shall be the holy religion (the pure totality of the holy religion) through the power of the Father, through the blessing of the Mother and through the goodness of the Son (Jesus). Salvation and blessing upon the sons of salvation and upon the speakers and the hearers of the renowned word (or, of the commandment of the Holy Ghost)! Praise and glory be to the Father and to the Son and to the elect Breath, the Holy Spirit, and to the creative (or, holy) Elements! . . . .[24]

Wisdom of Jesus Christ

In the Sophia *(Wisdom) of Jesus Christ, another of the Christian Gnostic gospels found at Nag Hammadi, Jesus, after his resurrection, is answering questions put to him by Mary and the apostles. At the end, he summarizes in this fashion, intimating once again the idea that "Mother" refers to the Holy Spirit whereas "Spirit" is somehow a larger term, referring to God-Father (though not exclusive of femininity and motherhood):*

[22] *Ibid.,* p. 82.
[23] *Ibid.,* p. 85.
[24] Hennecke-Schneemelcher, *op. cit.,* vol. 1, p. 359.

Behold, I have taught you the name of the Perfect One, the whole will of the holy angels and of the Mother, that the manly host may here be made perfect, that they may appear in all aeons from the Unlimited up to those which have arisen in the unsearchable riches of the great invisible Spirit, that they all may receive of his goodness and of the riches of his place of rest above which there is no dominion. . . .

Thus said the blessed Redeemer and vanished from their sight. But they fell into great and indescribable joy in the Spirit. From that day on his disciples began to preach the gospel of God, the eternal Father of him who is immortal for ever.[25]

Pistis Sophia

The Pistis Sophia *("faith-wisdom") is a Gnostic account of instructions given by Jesus after his resurrection. It was produced in Egypt by someone in the Valintinian tradition of Christian Gnosticism and includes the following Gospel story of Jesus as a youth communing with his twin brother, the Holy Spirit. It is significant that in this version of the Christ/Spirit emanation, the Spirit is not thought to be feminine, but is, rather, more or less an alter-ego to Jesus, or, itself a masculine being and another Son of God. Mary tells the tale:*

When thou [Jesus] wast little, before the Spirit came upon thee, the Spirit came from the height whilst thou wast in a vineyard with Joseph, and came unto me in mine house in thy likeness, and I knew it not, and I thought that it was thou. And the Spirit said unto me: Where is Jesus my brother, that I may meet with him? And when it spake thus unto me, I was in perplexity, and thought that it was a phantom come to tempt me. I took it therefore and bound it to the foot of the bed that was in mine house, until I should go forth unto thee and Joseph in the field and find you in the vineyard, where Joseph was staking the vineyard. It came to pass then, that when thou heardest me tell the matter unto Joseph, thou understoodest the matter, and didst rejoice, and say: Where is he, that I may behold him? otherwise I will tarry for him in this place. And it came to pass, when Joseph heard thee speak these words, he was troubled: and we went together and entered into the house and found the Spirit bound to the bed. And we looked upon thee and upon it, and found that thou wert like unto him: and he that was bound to the bed was loosed, and

[25] *Ibid.*, p. 247.

embraced thee and kissed thee, and thou also kissedst him, and ye became one. [26]

Although Jesus, according to John 3:34, is said to have received the Spirit in a measureless way, he is not reported in any of the canonical Gospels to have manifested that charisma of the Spirit which was so important at least for some segments of primitive Christianity: speaking in tongues. In chapter 136 of the Pistis Sophia *however, the worldwide reach of his cosmic prayer is formulated in untranslatable Greek syllables (except for the last word "sabaoth"). And since an interpretation of part of the glossolalia shortly follows, it seems to be a fair reading of this text to suggest that here the charismatic Jesus is praying in the Spirit:*

Now it came to pass, when our Lord Jesus was crucified and on the third day was risen from the dead, then his disciples gathered round him, and entreated him, saying: Our Lord, have mercy on us, for we have forsaken father and mother and the whole world and have followed thee. Then Jesus stood with his disciples by the water of the ocean and called aloud this prayer, saying: Hearken to me, my Father, thou Father of all Fatherhood, thou boundless Light: *aeēiouō iaō aōi psinōther thernōps nōpsiter zagourē pagourē nethmomaōth nepsiomaōth marachachtha thōbarrabau tharnachachan zorokothora ieou sabaōth.*

But while Jesus was saying this, Thomas, Andrew, James and Simon the Canaanite were in the west, with their faces turned towards the east, but Philip and Bartholomew were in the south turned towards the north, but the other disciples and the women disciples stood behind Jesus; but Jesus stood beside the altar.

And Jesus cried out, turning towards the four corners of the world with his disciples, who were all clothed in linen garments, and said: *iaō, iaō, iaō.* This is its interpretation: Iota since the All is gone forth—alpha, since it will turn back again—Omega, since the perfection of all perfections will take place.

But when Jesus had said this, he said: *iaphtha iaphtha mounaēr mounaēr ermanouēr ermanouēr,* i.e.: Thou Father of all Fatherhood of the Infinite, hearken unto me for my disciples' sake; whom I have brought before Thee, that they may believe on all the words of Thy truth, and grant all whereof I cry to Thee, for I know the name of the Father of the treasure of light. [27]

[26] James, *op. cit.,* p. 66.
[27] *Ibid.,* pp. 258-259.

Gospel of the Hebrews

In the Gospel of the Hebrews there is this brief saying of Jesus:
If your brother has sinned by a word and made thee amends, seven times in a day receive thou him. Simon his disciple said to him: Seven times in a day? The Lord answered and said unto him: Yes, I say unto thee, unto seventy times seven. For in the prophets also, after they were annointed by the Holy Spirit, the sinful word was found.[28]

Ascension of Isaiah

The Ascension of Isaiah is a Jewish-Christian-Gnostic composite book, some parts of which date from as early as the first part of the second century (if not earlier), but the whole as we now have it may have been finally edited in the fourth century. The Spirit is referred to as "the angel of the Holy Spirit" who, along with "my Lord" worships God the Father. This is a picture of the Holy Spirit of prophecy as it was effective in the life of the Christian's favorite Old Testament prophet; the "singing in the tongues of angels" in which Isaiah participates is a reflection of early Christian charismatic worship "in the Spirit."

Isaiah prophesies the resurrection of Christ through the angelic power of Michael the Archangel and the Holy Spirit:

Beloved, from the seventh heaven had been revealed . . . the descent of the angel of the church which is in the heavens, whom he will summon in the last days; and that the angel of the Holy Spirit and Michael, the chief of the holy angels, would open his grave on the third day.[29] . . . and that many who believe in him will speak in the Holy Spirit, and that many signs and wonders will take place in those days. . . . And there will be much slandering and boasting at the approach of the Lord and the Holy Spirit will depart from many. And in those days there will not be many prophets nor such as speak reliable words, except a few here and there. . . . And they will set aside the prophecies of the prophets which were before me and also pay no attention to these my visions, in order to speak from the torrent of their heart. . . .[30]

And while he was speaking by the Holy Spirit in the hearing of all, he became silent and his consciousness was taken from him and he

---

[28] J. Jeremias, *Unknown Sayings of Jesus* (London: SPCK, 1958), p. 83.
[29] Hennecke-Schneemelcher, *op. cit.,* vol. 2, p. 647.
[30] *Ibid.,* p. 648.

saw no (more) the men who were standing before him: his eyes were open, but his mouth was silent and the consciousness in his body was taken from him; but his breath was still in him, for he saw a vision.[31]

Isaiah is then led on a tour of the heavens by an angel; when he reaches the sixth heaven, he relates the following experience:
And (power) was given to me and I sang praise with them, and that angel also, and our praise was like theirs [the other angels]. And there they all named the primal Father and his Beloved Christ and the Holy Spirit, all with one voice, but it was not like the voice of the angels in the fifth heaven, nor like their speech, but another voice resounded there, and there was much light there.[32]

When they reach the seventh heaven, Isaiah sees the Lord, but he also sees a second angel standing to the left of the Lord. He asks who that angel is, and his angelic tourguide replies:
"Worship him, for this is the angel of the Holy Spirit who speaks through thee and the rest of the righteous." *Isaiah continues:* And I beheld the great glory, for the eyes of my spirit were open and I was not thereafter able to see, nor the angel who was with me, nor all the angels whom I had seen worshipping my Lord. But I saw the righteous beholding with great power the glory of that One. So my Lord drew near to me, and the angel of the Spirit, and said: "Behold, now it is granted to thee to behold God." . . . And I saw how my Lord worshipped, and the angel of the Holy Spirit, and how both together praised God. Thereupon all the righteous drew near and worshipped, and the angels approached and worshipped, and all the angels sang praise.[33]

During Isaiah's martyrdom, the Holy Spirit stood by him:
But while he was being sawn asunder Isaiah neither cried out nor wept, but his mouth conversed with the Holy Spirit until he had been sawn apart.[34]

Infancy Story According to Thomas

"The Account of Thomas the Israelite Philosopher concerning the Childhood of the Lord," or The Infancy Story according to Thomas *is one of those second-century romances on the childhood of Jesus, filling in the hidden years between Jesus' birth and the beginning of*

[31] *Ibid.,* p. 652.
[32] *Ibid.,* p. 656.
[33] *Ibid.,* pp. 658-659.
[34] *Ibid.,* p. 651.

*his ministry with fanciful tales of his powers while yet a child, similar
to the one such story contained in a canonical Gospel (Luke 2:41-52).
It is noteworthy that there exist parallels in the legends of India to the
stories told in this infancy narrative by Thomas, who is traditionally
called the Apostle of India. In this particular story, Jesus is described
as filled with the charisma of teaching and already under the
charismation of the Holy Spirit as a child:*

A good friend of Joseph's said to him: "Bring the child to me to the
school. Perhaps I by persuasion can teach him the letters [of the
alphabet]." And Joseph said to him: "If you have the courage,
brother, take him with you." [In the previous story, the youth Jesus
cursed another teacher, who had struck him on the head for being
impertinent during a session on the alphabet. The teacher died.
Joseph was moved to say to Mary: "Do not let him go outside the
door, for all those who provoke him die."] And he took him with fear
and anxiety, but the child went gladly. And he went boldly into the
school and found a book lying on the reading-desk and took it, but
did not read the letters in it, but opened his mouth and spoke by the
Holy Spirit and taught the law to those that stood by. And a large
crowd assembled and stood there listening to him, wondering at the
grace of his teaching and the readiness of his *words,* that although an
infant he made such utterances. But when Joseph heard it, he was
afraid and ran to the school, wondering whether this teacher also was
without skill (maimed). But the teacher said to Joseph: "Know,
brother, that I took the child as a disciple; but he is full of great grace
and wisdom; and now I beg you, brother, take him to your house."
And when the child heard this, he at once smiled on him and said:
"Since you have spoken well and have testified rightly, for your sake
shall he also that was smitten be healed." And immediately the other
teacher was healed. And Joseph took the child and went away to his
house.[35]

*The next story attributes power to Jesus' breath (spirit) and links
this charisma of the Spirit with the power over serpents promised to
the disciples (cf. Luke 10:19; Mark 15:18).*

Joseph sent his son James to bind wood and take it into his house, and
the child Jesus followed him. And while James was gathering the
sticks, a viper bit the hand of James [cf. Acts 28:3-61]. And as he lay
stretched out and about to die, Jesus came near and breathed upon

[35] *Ibid.,* vol. 1, pp. 397-398.

the bite, and immediately the pain ceased, and the creature burst, and at once James became well.[36]

Gospel/Questions of Bartholomew

In the fifth-century Questions of Bartholomew, *probably the later edition of an earlier* Gospel *of Bartholomew, the Apostles are gathered together and Bartholomew asks Mary to explain the mystery of the incarnation of Christ in her womb. To this query she replies that if she were to answer that, fire would issue forth out of her mouth and consume the world; and indeed, after she begins her speech, fire does come out of her mouth and is about to destroy creation, except that Jesus appears, puts his hand over her mouth, forbids her to divulge the mystery, and saves the world by quenching the fire (II 5,22).*

Before Mary begins her discourse, however, she prays to God, speaking in tongues several words which are then given a much longer interpretation by the author of the Gospel:

Then Mary stood up before them and spread out her hands toward the heaven and began to speak thus: Elphue Zarethra Charboum Nemioth Melitho Thraboutha Mephnounos Chemiath Aroura Maridōn Elison Marmiadōn Section Hesaboutha Ennouna Saktinos Athoor Belelam Ōpheōth Abō Chrasar, which is in the Greek tongue: O God the exceeding great and all-wise and king of the worlds, that art not to be described, the ineffable, that didst establish the greatness of the heavens and all things by a word, that out of darkness didst constitute and fasten together the poles of heaven in harmony, didst bring into shape the matter that was in confusion, didst bring into order the things that were without order, didst part the misty darkness from the light, didst establish in one place the foundations of the waters, thou that makest the beings of the air to tremble, and art the fear of them that are on the earth, that didst settle the earth and not suffer it to perish, and filledst it, which is the nourisher of all things, with showers of blessing: (Son of) the Father, thou whom the seven heavens hardly contained, but who wast well-pleased to be contained without pain in me, thou that art thyself the full word of the Father, in whom all things came to be: give glory to thine exceeding great name, and bid me to speak before thy holy apostles.[37]

[36] *Ibid.*, p. 398.
[37] James, *op. cit.*, p. 171.

James comments that in the Syriac versions, the tongue differs from the wording in the Greek; he also gives the tongue as it appears in the Latin version: "Helfoith Alaritha arbar Neniotho Melitho Tarasunt Chanebonos Umia Theirura Marado Seliso Heliphomar Mabon Saruth Gefutha Enunnas Sacinos Thatis Etelelam Tetheo abocia Rusar."[38]

In the same Questions of Bartholomew, *in answer to one of Bartholomew's questions, Jesus gives a short discourse on the unforgivable sin against the Holy Spirit:*
And Bartholomew saith unto him: What is the sin against the Holy Ghost? Jesus saith unto him: Whosoever shall decree against any man who has served my holy Father hath blasphemed against the Holy Ghost. For every man that serveth God worshipfully is worthy of the Holy Ghost, and he that speaketh anything evil against him shall not be forgiven.[39]

The Discourse of St. John the Divine Concerning the Falling Asleep of Mary

As late as the fifth century, the habit of writing biblical books having become so prevalent among Christians, a "new" theological idea such as the assumption into heaven of the Blessed Virgin Mary or the definition of her as the God-bearer ("theotokos"), which had been promulgated at the Ecumenical Council of Ephesus in 431, could best be gotten across by issuing a "forgery" in the name of some biblical writer or apostle. The Discourse of St. John *dates from the time when Christians with a particularly strong devotion to Mary were expanding Christian eschatology to include her prophetic assumption into heaven, thus giving all the rest of us mere humans the hope that we, too, like her will take our bodies on high. The power, inspiration, and, indeed, the organization of this momentous event is ascribed by "St. John" to the Holy Spirit.*

I, John, said unto her [the holy mother of God]. . . . : Your holy and precious body shall not see corruption. And she answered and said to me: Bring a censer and put incense in it and pray. And there came a voice from heaven and said the Amen.

---

[38] *Ibid.* See also Hennecke-Schneemelcher, *op. cit.,* vol. 1, p. 493, where the translator, who seems not to have appreciated the import of the "other tongue," comments, "I have omitted the supposedly original Hebrew at the beginning" (footnote 2).

[39] James, *op. cit.,* pp. 180-181.

And I, John, listened unto that voice, and the Holy Ghost said unto me: John, heardest thou this voice which was uttered in heaven after the ending of the prayer? And I answered and said: Yea, I heard it. And the Holy Ghost said unto me: This voice which thou heardest signifieth the coming of thy brethren the apostles and of the holy powers which is to be: for today they are coming hither.

And thereupon I, John, fell to prayer. And the Holy Ghost said unto the apostles: All of you together mount up upon clouds from the ends of the world and gather yourselves together at Bethlehem the holy because of the mother of our Lord Jesus Christ, in a moment of time: Peter from Rome, Paul from Tiberia, Thomas out of the inmost Indies, James from Jerusalem, Andrew the brother of Peter, and Philip, Luke and Simon the Canaanite, and Thaddaeus, which were fallen asleep, were raised up by the Holy Ghost out of their sepulchres; unto whom said the Holy Ghost: Think not that the resurrection is now; but for this cause are ye risen up out of your graves, that you may go to salute for an honour and a wonderful sign for the mother of your Lord and Saviour Jesus Christ; for the day is come near of her departure and going to abide in heaven. And Mark, who was yet alive, came also from Alexandria with the rest, as hath been said, from their several countries.

But Peter when he was lifted up by the cloud stood between the heaven and the earth, for the Holy Ghost sustained him, and beheld while the rest of the apostles also were caught up in the clouds to be present with Peter. And so all came together by the means of the Holy Ghost.

After this, each of the apostles takes his turn recounting how the Holy Spirit found him at his work, or in his grave, and summoned him to become a witness of the Assumption.[40]

---

[40] *Ibid.*, pp. 201-209.

THE PRIMITIVE CHURCH

3

Ignatius of Antioch

(c. 110)

Ignatius was the bishop of the church in Antioch who became a martyr for his faith during the reign of Trajan (98–117). As he was being taken to Rome to be fed to the lions, he wrote seven letters, six to churches and one to Polycarp in Smyrna, which reveal in brilliant colors the person of a devout bishop, martyr, charismatic, and theologian of the end of the first Christian century. Ignatius was deeply involved in the evolution of the form of church government known as the "monarchical episcopate"—the rule of a single bishop over a church or over a number of churches in a given area. Ignatius's urging that his understanding of church organization was a matter of charismatic revelation shows the way in which early Christians understood the Holy Spirit to reveal a "word of knowledge" or a "word of understanding" for the building up of the church.

. . . you are as stones of the temple of the Father, made ready for the building of God our Father, carried up to the heights by the engine of Jesus Christ, that is the cross, and using as a rope the Holy Spirit. Your faith is your windlass and love is the road which leads up to God.[1]

[1] "To the Ephesians" 9, in Kirsopp Lake, trans., *The Apostolic Fathers* (2 volumes), Loeb Classical Library (Cambridge: Harvard University Press, 1912, 1954), vol. 1, p. 183.

Ignatius conceives the organizational structure of the church in trinitarian terms, although, for some reason, he hesitates specifically to identify a given church order with the Holy Spirit.

Be zealous to do all things in harmony with God, with the bishop presiding in the place of God, and the presbyters in the place of the Council of the Apostles, and the deacons. . . .[2]

Be diligent therefore to be confirmed in . . . the Son and the Father and the Spirit, at the beginning and at the end, together with your revered bishop and with your presbytery, that aptly woven spiritual crown, and with the godly deacons.[3]

Likewise let all respect the deacons as Jesus Christ, even as the bishop is also a type of the Father, and the presbyters as the council of God and the college of Apostles. Without these the name of "Church" is not given.[4]

Ignatius, who is also called Theophorus [God-bearer], to the Church of God the Father and of the Lord Jesus Christ, which is in Philadelphia in Asia . . . with the bishop and with the presbyters and deacons, who together with him have been appointed according to the mind of Jesus Christ, and he established them in security according to his own will by his Holy Spirit.[5]

For even if some desired to deceive me after the flesh, the spirit is not deceived, for it is from God. For it "knoweth whence it comes and whither it goes" and tests secret things. I cried out while I was with you, I spoke with a great voice,—with God's own voice,—"Give heed to the bishop and to the presbytery and deacons." But some suspected me of saying this because I had previous knowledge of the division of some persons: but he in whom I am bound is my witness that I had no knowledge of this from any human being, but the Spirit was preaching, and saying this, "Do nothing without the bishop; keep your flesh as the temple of God, love unity, flee from divisions, be imitators of Jesus Christ, as was he also of his Father.[6]

[2]"To the Magnesians" 6:1, in *ibid.,* pp. 201 and 203. Lake notes that the Apostolic Constitutions 2:26 say: "Let the Deacon be honoured as a type of Holy Spirit."
[3]"To the Magnesians," 13:1, in *ibid.,* p. 209.
[4]"To the Trallians," 3:1, in *ibid.,* p. 215.
[5]"To the Philadelphians," Preface in *ibid.,* p. 239.
[6]"To the Philadelphians," 7:1-2, in *ibid.,* pp. 245 and 247.

4

The Epistle of Barnabas

(after 132)

*The letter was not written by Paul's fellow-missionary Barnabas;
we do not know where or when or by whom, though perhaps this
early Christian treatise on the allegorical interpretation of the Old
Testament was written in Alexandria, where it was read as scripture
well into the third century.*

*Concerning how the Lord foretold the water of baptism and the
cross:* Mark how he described the water and the cross together. . . .
another Prophet says: "And the land of Jacob was praised above
every land." He means to say that he is glorifying the vessel of his
Spirit. What does he say next? "And there was a river flowing on the
right hand, and beautiful trees grew out of it, and whoever shall eat of
them shall live for ever." He means to say that we go down into the
water full of sins and foulness, and we come up bearing the fruit of
fear in our hearts, and having hope on Jesus in the Spirit.[1]

When we received the remission of sins, and put our hope on the
Name, we became new, being created again from the beginning;
wherefore God truly dwells in us, in the habitation which we are.

[1] Kirsopp Lake, trans., *The Apostolic Fathers,* Loeb Classical Library (Cambridge:
Harvard University Press, 1912, 1954), vol. 1, pp. 381 and 383.

How? His word of faith, the calling of his promise, the wisdom of the ordinances, the commands of the teaching, himself prophesying in us, himself dwelling in us, by opening the door of the temple (that is the mouth) to us, giving repentance to us, and thus he leads us, who have been enslaved to death into the incorruptible temple. For he who desires to be saved looks not at the man, but at him who dwells and speaks in him, and is amazed at him, for he has never either heard him speak such words with his mouth, nor has he himself ever desired to hear them. This is a spiritual temple being built for the Lord.[2]

Thou shalt not command in bitterness thy slave or handmaid who hope on the same God, lest they cease to fear the God who is over you both; for he came not to call men with respect of persons, but those whom the Spirit has prepared.[3]

[2] *Ibid.*, p. 399.
[3] *Ibid.*, p. 405.

5

The Didache

(c. 150)

The Didache, *or* Teaching of the Twelve Apostles, *contains the most ancient church order we now possess, dating back perhaps before* A.D. *100. It is evidence of church life, perhaps in Syria, during the period when charismatic prophets and traveling apostles were still commonplace. Its concern with the persistent problem of how to distinguish a true from a false prophet is formulated in a way that lets us know we are looking directly into the heart and daily life of an early Christian community. The Didache was read as scripture in some early churches.*

Concerning baptism, baptise thus: Having first rehearsed all these things, "baptise, in the Name of the Father and of the Son and of the Holy Spirit," in running water; but if thou hast no running water, baptise in other water, and if thou canst not in cold, then in warm. But if thou hast neither, pour water three times on the head "in the name of the Father, Son and Holy Spirit." [1]

And concerning the Eucharist. . . . But suffer the prophets to hold Eucharist as they will. [2]

And concerning the Apostles and Prophets, act thus according to

[1] Kirsopp Lake, trans., *The Apostolic Fathers,* Loeb Classical Library (Cambridge: Harvard University Press, 1912, 1954), vol. 1, pp. 319 and 321.

[2] *Ibid.,* pp. 323, 325.

the ordinance of the Gospel. Let every Apostle who comes to you be received as the Lord, but let him not stay more than one day, or if need be a second as well; but if he stay three days, he is a false prophet. And when an Apostle goes forth let him accept nothing but bread till he reach his night's lodging; but if he ask for money, he is a false prophet.

Do not test or examine any prophet who is speaking in a spirit, "for every sin shall be forgiven, but this sin shall not be forgiven" [Matthew 12:31]. But not everyone who speaks in a spirit is a prophet, except he have the behaviour of the Lord. From his behaviour, then, the false prophet and the true prophet shall be known. And no prophet who orders a meal in a spirit shall eat of it; otherwise he is a false prophet. And every prophet who teaches the truth, if he do not what he teaches, is a false prophet. But no prophet who has been tried and is genuine, though he enact a worldly mystery of the Church, if he teach not others to do what he does himself, shall be judged by you: for he has his judgment with God, for so also did the prophets of old. But whosoever shall say in a spirit "Give me money, or something else," you shall not listen to him; but if he tell you to give on behalf of others in want, let none judge him.

Let everyone who "comes in the Name of the Lord" be received; but when you have tested him you shall know him, for you shall have understanding of true and false.

But every true prophet who wishes to settle among you is "worthy of his food." Likewise a true teacher is himself worthy, like the workman, of his food. Therefore thou shalt take the firstfruit of the produce of the winepress and of the threshing-floor and of oxen and sheep, and shalt give them as the firstfruits to the prophets, for they are your high priests. But if you have not a prophet, give to the poor. If thou makest bread, take the firstfruits, and give it according to the commandment. Likewise, when thou openest a jar of wine or oil, give the firstfruits to the prophets. Of money also and clothes, and of all your possessions, take the firstfruits, as it seem best to you, and give according to the commandment.[3]

Appoint therefore for yourselves bishops and deacons worthy of the Lord, meek men, and not lovers of money, and truthful and approved, for they also minister to you the ministry of the prophets and teachers.[4]

[3] *Ibid.,* pp. 327 and 329.
[4] *Ibid.,* p. 331.

6

The Shepherd of Hermas

(c. 140–155)

The apocalypse of Hermas of Rome is one of the books most widely accepted and read as scripture by the early churches which is no longer considered canonical. It ought, in an anthology of texts about the Holy Spirit, to be quoted in toto, since it claims to be a series of prophetic visions, inspired by heavenly messengers and given to the church of Rome for her instruction. The activities of Hermas indicate the mechanics of receiving revelations as he experienced them in the Roman church toward the middle of the second century. His theology of the Holy Spirit, by later standards, is quite eccentric. The Holy Spirit is alternately identified with the Angel of Repentance or with the Son of God. Sometimes it is practically identified with the human spirit when it is inspired to religious greatness; other times, there seem to be several spirits, all of whom could be called "holy." The most outstanding aspect of Hermas's understanding of the Spirit is his teaching in the parable of the vineyard, according to which the Holy Spirit is the natural Son of God, whereas Jesus, a mere man, is adopted to co-sonship and co-heirship with the Spirit on the basis of his good works. Hermas, who was neither Gnostic nor Ebionite, presents the most flawless statement of one of the earliest christologies—adoptionism: the idea that Jesus, the son of Mary,

*from his birth until his baptism or perhaps his resurrection, was only
a man, not a God; but, when the Holy Spirit descended on him or
raised him from the dead, he was adopted into the divine family and
thus became the Son of God.*

And a spirit seized me and took me away through a certain pathless
district, through which a man could not walk, but the ground was
precipitous and broken up by the streams of water.[1]

I heard great and wonderful things which I cannot remember; for all
the words were frightful, such as a man cannot bear.[2]

The Ancient Lady [the messenger of the revelation] said: . . . the
revelation was not for you alone, but for you to explain it to them all.
. . . But I charge you first, Hermas . . . to speak [these words] into the
ears of the saints, that they may hear them and do them and be
cleansed from their wickedness, and you with them.[3]

The Angel of Repentance says to Hermas: . . . For if you are
courageous, the Holy Spirit which dwells in you will be pure, not
obscured by another evil spirit, but will dwell at large and rejoice and
be glad with the body in which it dwells, and will serve God in great
cheerfulness, having well-being in itself. But if any ill temper enter, at
once the Holy Spirit, which is delicate, is oppressed, finding the place
impure, and seeks to depart out of the place, for it is choked by the
evil spirit, having no room to serve the Lord as it will, but is
contaminated by the bitterness. For the Lord dwells in long-suffering
and the devil dwells in ill temper. If therefore, both spirits dwell in the
same place it is unprofitable and evil for that man in whom they
dwell. For if you take a little wormwood, and pour it into a jar of
honey, is not the whole honey spoilt? And a great quantity of honey is
ruined by a very little wormwood, and it spoils the sweetness of the
honey, and it has no longer the same favour with the master, because
it has been mixed and he has lost its use. . . . Keep from [ill-temper],
for I am with you . . . for all have been made righteous by the most
revered angel.[4]

[1] Kirsopp Lake, trans., *The Apostolic Fathers,* Loeb Classical Library (Cambridge:
Harvard University Press, 1912, 1954), vol. 2, Vision 1:1, p. 7.
[2] *Ibid.,* Vision 1:3, p. 15.
[3] *Ibid.,* Vision 3:9, p. 49.
[4] *Ibid.,* Mandate 5:1, pp. 87-91.

When [evil spirits] dwell in one vessel, where also the Holy Spirit dwells, there is no room in that vessel, but it is overcrowded. Therefore the delicate Spirit which is unaccustomed to dwell with an evil spirit, or with hardness, departs from such a man, and seeks to dwell with gentleness and quietness. Then, when it departs from that man where it was dwelling, that man becomes empty of the righteous spirit, and for the future is filled with evil spirits, and is disorderly in all his actions, being dragged here and there by the evil spirits and is wholly blinded from goodness of thought.[5]

There are two angels with man, one of righteousness and one of wickedness. . . . The angel of righteousness is delicate and modest and meek and gentle. When, then, he comes into your heart he at once speaks with you of righteousness, of purity, of reverence, of self-control, of every righteous deed, and of all glorious virtue. When all these things come into your heart, know that the angel of righteousness is with you. These things, then, are the deeds of the angel of righteousness. Therefore believe him and his works. . . . Though a man or woman be very evil, if there rise in his heart the deeds of the angel of righteousness, it must needs be that he do some good act. You see, therefore . . . that it is good to follow the angel of righteousness but to keep away from the angel of wickedness. This commandment makes plain the things of the faith, that you may believe the works of the angel of righteousness and by doing them live to God.[6]

. . . grief is more evil than all the spirits, and is most terrible to the servants of God, and corrupts man beyond all the spirits, and wears out the Holy Spirit—and again saves us.[7]

Hear . . . now, foolish man, how grief wears out the Holy Spirit and again brings salvation. . . . Both . . . are grievous to the Spirit; double-mindedness and ill temper. Put therefore away from yourself, grief, and do not oppress the Holy Spirit which dwells in you, lest it beseech God, and it depart from you. For the Spirit of God which is given to this flesh endures neither grief nor oppression . . . just as vinegar mixed with wine has not the same agreeableness, so also grief

[5] *Ibid.,* Mandate 5:2, p. 93.
[6] *Ibid.,* Mandate 10, pp. 97-99.
[7] *Ibid.,* Mandate 10, pp. 111-113.

mixed with the Holy Spirit, has not the same power of intercession.[8] "He who is sitting on the chair is a false prophet. . . . Therefore he corrupts the understanding of the double-minded, not of the faithful. Therefore these double-minded men come to him as to a wizard, and ask him concerning their future; and that false prophet, having no power of the Divine Spirit in himself, speaks with them according to their requests. . . . for he is empty and makes empty answers to empty men. . . . But he also speaks some true words, for the devil fills him with his spirit, to see if he can break any of the righteous. . . . For every spirit which is given from God is not asked questions, but has the power of the Godhead and speaks all things of itself, because it is from above, from the power of the Divine Spirit. . . ."

[Hermas asks:] "How, then, sir, shall a man know which of them is a true prophet and which a false prophet?" . . .

"Test the man who has the Divine Spirit by his life. In the first place, he who has the spirit which is from above, is meek and gentle, and lowly-minded, and refrains from all wickedness and evil desire of this world, and makes himself poorer than all men and gives no answers to anyone when he is consulted, nor does he speak by himself (for the Holy Spirit does not speak when a man wishes to speak), but he speaks at that time when God wishes him to speak. Therefore, when the man who has the Divine Spirit comes into a meeting of righteous men who have the faith of the Divine Spirit, and intercession is made to God from the assembly of those men, then the angel of the prophetic spirit rests on him and fills the man, and the man, being filled with the Holy Spirit, speaks to the congregation as the Lord wills. . . . Such, then, is the power of the Lord concerning the Spirit of the Godhead. . . .

"[The false prophet] exalts himself and wishes to have the first place, and he is instantly impudent and shameless and talkative, and lives in great luxury and in many other deceits, and accepts rewards for his prophecy, and if he does not receive them, he does not prophesy. Is it then possible for a Divine Spirit to accept rewards and prophesy? It is not possible for a prophet of God to do this, but the spirit of such prophets is of the earth. Next, on no account does he come near to an assembly of righteous men, but shuns them. But he cleaves to the double-minded and empty, and prophesies to them in a corner. . . .

[8] *Ibid.,* Mandate 10, pp. 115-117.

But when he comes into a meeting full of righteous men, who have a spirit of the Godhead, and intercession is made by them, that man is made empty and the earthly spirit flees from him in fear, and that man is made dumb and is altogether broken up, being able to say nothing. For if you stack wine or oil in a cellar, and put among them an empty jar, and again wish to unstack the cellar, the jar which you put in empty you will find still empty. So also the prophets who are empty, when they come to the spirits of just men, are found out to be such as when they came. You have the life of both the prophets. Test, then, from his life and deeds, the man who says that he is inspired. . . . Take a stone and throw it up to Heaven and see if you can touch it; or take a syringe and squirt it towards the sky, and see if you can make a hole in the Heavens." "How, sir," [says Hermas,] "can these things be? For both these things . . . are impossible." "Even," said he, "as these are impossible, so also are the earthly spirits without power and feeble. Take now the power which comes from above. The hail is a very little grain, and when it falls on a man's head, how it hurts! Or, again, take a drop which falls on the ground from the roof, and makes a hole in the stone. You see, then, that the smallest things which come from above and fall on the earth have great power; so also the Divine Spirit which comes from above is powerful. Have faith, then, in this Spirit, but refrain from the other."[9]

[A parable:] A certain man had a field, and many servants, and on part of the field he planted a vineyard. And he chose out a certain servant, who was faithful, in good esteem and honour with him, and he called him and said to him: "Take this vineyard which I have planted, and fence it until I come, and do nothing more to the vineyard. Follow this order of mine and you shall have your freedom from me. And the master of the servant went abroad. Now when he had gone, the servant took and fenced the vineyard, and when he had finished the fencing of the vineyard he saw that the vineyard was full of weeds. Therefore he reasoned in himself, saying: I have finished this order of the Lord; I will next dig this vineyard, and it will be better when it is dug, and having no weeds will yield more fruit, not being choked by the weeds. He took and dug the vineyard, and pulled out all the weeds which were in the vineyard. And that vineyard became very beautiful and fertile with no weeds to choke it. After a time the master of the servant and the field came, and entered into the

[9] *Ibid.*, Mandate 11, pp. 117-125.

vineyard, and seeing the vineyard beautifully fenced, and moreover dug, and all the weeds pulled up and vines fertile, he was greatly pleased at the acts of the servant. So he called his beloved son, whom he had as heir, and his friends whom he had as counsellors, and told them what he had ordered his servant, and what he had found accomplished. . . . And he said to them: I promised this servant his freedom if he kept the orders which I gave him. Now he has kept my orders, and has added good work in the vineyard and greatly pleased me. So in reward for this work which he has done, I wish to make him joint heir with my son. . . . After a few days he made a feast and sent to him much food from the feast. But the servant took the food which was sent to him by the master, kept what was sufficient for himself, and distributed the rest to his fellow-servants. And his fellow-servants were glad when they received the food, and began to pray for him, that he might find greater favour with his master, because he had treated them thus. His master heard all these events, and again rejoiced greatly at this conduct. The master again assembled his friends and his son and reported to them what he had done with the food which he had received, and they were still more pleased that the servant should be made joint heir with his son." [10]

[The understanding of the parable:] "The field is this world," and the Lord of the field is "He who created everything" and perfected it and gave it strength. And the servant is the Son of God, and the vines are this people which he planted. And the fences are the holy Angels of the Lord who support his people. And the weeds which are pulled up out of the vineyard are iniquities of the servants of God. And the food which he sent to him from the supper is the commandments which he gave to his people through his Son, and the friends and counsellors are the holy Angels who were first created. And the absence of the Master is the time which remains before his coming. . . . [Hermas asks:] "Why, sir, is the Son of God in the parable given the form of a servant?" . . . The Holy Spirit which preexists, which created all creation, did God make to dwell in the flesh which he willed. Therefore this flesh, in which the Holy Spirit dwelled, served the Spirit well, walking in holiness and purity, and did not in any way defile the Spirit. When, therefore, it had lived nobly and purely, and had laboured with the Spirit, and worked with in every deed, behaving with power and bravery, [God] chose it as companion with

[10] *Ibid.,* Similitude 5, pp. 155-159.

the Holy Spirit; for the conduct of this flesh pleased him, because it was not defiled while it was bearing the Holy Spirit on earth. Therefore [God] took the Son and the glorious angels as counsellors, that this flesh also, having served the Spirit blamelessly, should have some place of sojourn, and not seem to have lost the reward of its service. For all flesh in which the Holy Spirit has dwelt shall receive a reward if it be found undefiled and spotless. . . . For if you defile your flesh you defile also the Holy Spirit; and if you defile the flesh you shall not live. . . . If, for the future, you defile neither the flesh nor the Spirit; for both are in communion, and neither can be defiled without the other, and therefore keep both pure, you shall live to God. [11]

"I wish to show you what the Holy Spirit which spoke with you in the form of the Church showed you, for that Spirit is the Son of God." [12]
This tower is the Church. [And these maidens] are holy spirits. A man cannot be found in the kingdom of God in any other way, except they clothe him with their clothing. For if you receive the name alone but do not receive the clothing from them, you will benefit nothing, for these maidens are the powers of the Son of God. If you bear the name, but do not bear his power you will be bearing his name in vain. . . . Their names themselves are their raiment. Whoever bears the name of the Son of God must also bear their names; for even the Son himself bears the names of these maidens. . . . So also those who believe on the Lord through his Son, and put on these spirits will become "one spirit and one body," and the colour of their raiment will be one. And the dwelling of such as bear the names of the maidens is in the tower. . . . [Their names are] Faith . . . Temperance . . . Power . . . Long-suffering . . . Simplicity, Guilelessness, Holiness, Joyfulness, Truth, Understanding, Concord, Love. He who bears these names and the name of the Son of God "shall be able to enter into the Kingdom of God." [13]

. . . All the nations which dwell under heaven, when they heard and believed were called after the name of the Son of God. So then when they received the seal they had one understanding and one mind, and their faith became one, and their love one, and they bore the spirits of the maidens together with the name. [14]

[11] *Ibid.,* Similitude 5, pp. 165-171.
[12] *Ibid.,* Similitude 9, p. 217.
[13] *Ibid.,* Similitude 9, pp. 253-259.
[14] *Ibid.,* Similitude 9, pp. 265-267.

7

Montanus, Priscilla, and Maximilla

(c. 156 or 172)

Montanus was a native of Phrygia in Asia Minor and perhaps before his conversion to Christ had been a priest of Cybele, the cult of the Great Mother. With his two prophetess friends, Priscilla and Maximilla, he prophesied the imminent coming to earth of the New Jerusalem, but at Pepuza, a city in Phrygia. Montanus identified himself as the medium through which the Paraclete was speaking the ongoing will of God to the churches. The Montanist movement spread far fast; in its North African phase, where Tertullian, the first Latin father of the church was its brighest light, it took on rigorously ascetical qualities (see 12 in this book). Montanism was not so much a "new prophecy" as it was the continuation of an earlier, original impulse in Christianity which had now been bypassed by the larger church. As the church grew more lax and less expectant of an immediate return of Christ, she staunchly opposed the more excitable Montanists; repressive laws against the Montanists are to be found in the imperial Codes of Theodosian and Justinian. Montanism stands more or less in continuity with the style of Christianity which produced the Revelation of John *with its vigorous eschatology, prophetism, chiliasm or millennialism, and moral hardiness. It may not be too much to suggest, considering not only these similarities but also the geographical proximity of Phrygia to Ephesus, in Asia Minor from which both movements came, that* Revelation *may have received its final editing at the hand of a proto-Montanist. Montanus, Priscilla, and Maximilla are all three reported to have composed several writings, none of which, thanks to the censorship of the church, is now extant. These few remnant sayings have been gathered from the writings of Epiphanius, Tertullian, and elsewhere.*

1. (Montanus says:) I am the Father and I am the Son and I am the Paraclete.
   (Dialogue of a Montanist with an Orthodox; cf. Didymus the Blind, *On the Trinity* III 41 i)

2. (Montanus says:) I the Lord, the Almighty God, remain among men.
   (Epiphanius, *Heresies* 48:11:1)

3. (Montanus says:) Neither angel nor ambassador, but I, the Lord God the Father, am come.
   (Epiphanius, *Heresies* 48:11:9)

4. (Montanus says:) Behold, man is like a lyre and I rush thereon like a plectrum. Man sleeps and I awake. Behold, the Lord is he who arouses the hearts of men (throws them into ecstasy) and gives to men a new heart.
   (Epiphanius, *Heresies* 48:4:1)

5. (Montanus says:) Why dost thou call the super-man (?) saved? For the righteous man, he says, will shine a hundred times more strongly than the sun, but the little ones who are saved among you will shine a hundred times stronger than the moon.
   (Epiphanius, *Heresies* 48:10:3)

6. (The Paraclete in the "new prophets" says:) The Church can forgive sins, but I will not do it, lest they sin yet again.
   (Tertullian, *On Modesty* 21:7)

7. (The Spirit says:) Thou wilt be publicly displayed: that is good for thee; for whosoever is not publicly displayed before men will be publicly displayed before God. Let it not perplex thee! Righteousness brings thee into the midst (of men). What perplexes thee about winning glory? Opportunity is given when thou art seen by men.
   (Tertullian, *On Flight under Persecution* 9:4)

8. (The Spirit speaks:) Do not desire to die in bed, nor in delivery of children, nor by enervating fevers, but in martyrdom, that He may be glorified who has suffered for you.
   (Tertullian, *On Flight* 9:4; cf. his *On the Soul* 55:5)

9. (The Paraclete says through the prophetess Prisca:) They are flesh and (yet) they hate the flesh.
   (Tertullian, *On the Resurrection of the Dead* 11:2)

10. (The holy prophetess Prisca proclaims:) A holy minister must understand how to minister holiness. For if the heart gives purification (?), says she, they will also see visions, and if they lower their faces, then they will perceive saving voices, as clear as they were obscure.
    (Tertullian, *On Exhortation to Chastity* 10:5)

11. (Quintilla or Priscilla says:) In the form of a woman, says she, arrayed in shining garments, came Christ to me and set wisdom upon me and revealed to me that this place (= Pepuza) is holy and that Jerusalem will come down hither from heaven.
    (Epiphanius, *Heresies* 49:1:2-3)

12. (Maximilla says:) After me there will be no more prophets, but (only) the consummation.
    (Epiphanius, *Heresies* 48:2:4)

13. (Maximilla says:) Listen not to me, but to Christ.
    (Epiphanius, *Heresies* 48:12:4)

14. (Maximilla says:) The Lord has sent me as adherent, preacher and interpreter of this affliction and this covenant and this promise; he has compelled me, willingly or unwillingly, to learn the knowledge of God.
    (Epiphanius, *Heresies* 48:13:1)

15. (The Spirit says through Maximilla:) I am chased like a wolf from (the flock of) sheep; I am not a wolf; I am word and spirit and power.
    (Eusebius, *Church History* 5:16:17)[1]

---

[1] E. Hennecke, *New Testament Apocrypha,* ed. W. Schneemelcher (Philadelphia: The Westminster Press, 1959, 1963, 1964), vol. 2, pp. 686-687.

8

Justin the Martyr

(c. 100–c. 165)

Justin was a convert to Christ after a long search for truth through philosophy. He had by turns been a Stoic, an Aristotelian, a Pythagorean and a Platonist until he was moved by Old Testament prophecies to see that Christianity is the truly rational belief. First at Ephesus, where he was the teacher of Tatian, and later at Rome, he continued to wear his philosopher's gown and defend the Christian faith with the best of his philosophical reason. Denounced by the Cynic philosopher Crescens, he was finally scourged and beheaded for refusing to sacrifice to the gods of Rome. Justin's main concern was to explain the faith, whether to his Jewish debate partner, Trypho, or to his pagan audience, including the Senate and Emperor Marcus Aurelius.

Hence we are called atheists. And we confess that we are atheists, so far as gods of this [pagan] sort are concerned, but not with respect to the most true God, the Father of righteousness.... Both him and the Son (who came forth from him and taught us these things, and the host of the other good angels who follow and are made like to Him), and the prophetic Spirit, we worship and adore.[1]

[1] *First Apology* 6 in *Ante-Nicene Fathers,* ed. J. Donaldson, rev. American edition, A. C. Coxe (Oxford, 1885; republished in Grand Rapids: William B. Eerdmans Company), vol. 1, p. 164.

[Christ Jesus is our teacher] . . . we reasonably worship Him, having learned that he is the Son of the true God himself, and holding him in the second place, and the prophetic Spirit in the third place.[2]

For Justin, the Holy Spirit is foremost the "Holy Spirit of prophecy," whom he sometimes identifies with the Logos or Son, seeing them both as messengers or angels of God the Father. The Spirit can thus speak "from" the Father or the Son, depending on the point of view being taken.

Justin, like the Montanists and other Christians of Justin's time and place, believed in a prophetic vision of Messianic peace on earth. This hope was kept alive for them especially through the words of the prophets whom they considered to be inspired with the same "Holy Spirit of prophecy" who had inspired the Old Testament prophets.
For the prophetical gifts remain with us, even to the present time. And hence you ought to understand that (the gifts) formerly among your nation [Trypho's Jewish nation] have been transferred to us. And just as there were false prophets contemporaneous with your holy prophets, so are there now many false teachers among us. . . .[3]

The scripture says that these enumerated powers of the Spirit have come on Him [Jesus], not because he stood in need of them, but because they would rest in Him, i.e., would find their accomplishment in Him, so that there would be no more prophets in your nation after the ancient custom: and this fact you plainly perceive. For after Him no prophet has arisen among you. Now (you may know that) your prophets, each receiving some one or two powers from God, did and spoke the things which we have learned from the Scriptures. . . . Solomon possessed the spirit of wisdom, Daniel that of understanding and counsel, Moses that of might and piety, Elijah that of fear, Isaiah that of knowledge, and so with the others. . . . Accordingly, the [Spirit] rested, i.e., ceased, when [Christ] came, after whom, in the times of this dispensation wrought out by him amongst men it was requisite that such gifts should cease from you; and having received their rest in Him, should again, as had been predicted, become gifts which, from the grace of his Spirit's power, He imparts to those who believe in Him according as he deems each man worthy thereof. . . . it had been prophesied that this would be done by Him after His ascension to heaven. It is accordingly said: "He ascended on high, He led captivity captive, He gave gifts to the sons of men." And again in

---

[2] *First Apology* 13, in *ibid.,* p. 166.
[3] *Dialogue with Trypho the Jew* 82, in *ibid.,* p. 240.

another prophesy it is said: "And it shall come to pass after this, I will pour out My Spirit on all flesh, and on My servants and on my Handmaids and they shall prophesy. Now, it is possible to see among us women and men who possess gifts of the Spirit of God; so that it was prophesied that the powers enumerated by Isaiah [cf. Isaiah 11:2] would come upon Him, not because He needed power, but because these would not continue [in Israel] after Him.[4]

When you hear the utterances of the prophets spoken as it were personally, you must not suppose that they are spoken by the inspired themselves, but by the Divine Word who moves them. For sometimes He declares things that are to come to pass, in the manner of one who foretells the future; sometimes He speaks as from the person of God the Lord and Father of all; sometimes as from the person of Christ; sometimes as from the person of the people answering the Lord or His Father, just as you can see even in your own [pagan] writers, one man being the writer of the whole, but introducing the persons who converse.[5]

After this, Justin gives examples of the Spirit speaking "from the person of the Father," "from the person of Christ," *and* "as predicting things that are to come to pass."

But the angels transgressed this appointment, and were captivated by love of women and begat children who are those that are called demons; and besides, they afterwards subdued the human race to themselves, partly by magical writings and partly by fears and punishments. . . . But Jesus . . . was made man . . . for the sake of believing men, and for the destruction of the demons. And now you can learn this from what is under your own observation. For numberless demoniacs throughout the whole world and in your city, many of our Christian men exorcising them in the name of Jesus Christ, who was crucified under Pontius Pilate, have healed and do heal, rendering helpless and driving the possessing devils out of the men, though they could not be cured by all the other exorcists and those who use incantations and drugs.[6]

Pseudo-Justin, a late second- or early third-century follower of Justin the Martyr, built on Justin's understanding of the Spirit,

[4] *Dialogue* 87, 88, in *ibid.*, p. 243.
[5] *First Apology* 36, in *ibid.*, p. 175.
[6] *Second Apology* 5, in *ibid.*, p. 190.

especially as it is expressed in Justin's Dialogue with Trypho the Jew, *#7. Pseudo-Justin identifies the "virtue," or prophetic strength, which was in the philosopher Plato with the Holy Spirit. Thus the most spiritual Greeks were considered "Christians before Christ."* If any one will attentively consider the gift that descends from God on the holy men—which gift the sacred prophets call the Holy Ghost— he shall find that this was announced under another name by Plato in the dialogue with Meno. For, fearing to name the gift of God "the Holy Ghost," lest he should seem, by following the teaching of the prophets, to be an enemy to the Greeks, he acknowledges, indeed, that it comes down from God, yet does not think fit to name it the Holy Spirit, but virtue. . . . For as the sacred prophets say that one and the same spirit is divided into seven spirits, so he also, naming it one and the same virtue, says this is divided into four virtues, wishing by all means to avoid mention of the Holy Spirit, but clearly declaring in a kind of allegory what the prophets had said of the Holy Spirit. For to this effect he spoke in the dialogue with Meno towards the close: "From this reasoning, Meno, it appears that virtue comes to those to whom it does come by a divine destiny." . . . You see how he calls only by the name of virtue the gift that descends from above.[7]

---

[7] *Exhortation to the Greeks* 32, in *ibid.,* pp. 286-287.

9

The Plea of Athenagoras

(176/177)

Athenagoras was a Christian apologist, a student of Justin the Martyr, and a Platonist philosopher. His Plea, a defense of the Faith to the Emperor Marcus Aurelius and his son Lucius Aurelius Commodus, is one of the finest literary statements of what early Christianity in the Roman Empire was all about. His trinitarian theology is remarkably well-balanced; his understanding of inspiration as the musical technology of the Holy Spirit was not to be challenged until modern times; and his denunciation of the pagan gods as fallen demons became commonplace in Christian polemic with retreating paganism.

If, then, Plato is not an atheist when he considers the one uncreated maker of the universe to be God, neither are we atheists when we recognize and affirm him to be God by whose Word all things were created and by whose Spirit they are held together. (6)[1]

. . . we should be acting unreasonably were we to abandon our belief

[1] Cyril C. Richardson, *Early Christian Fathers,* Volume 1, The Library of Christian Classics (Philadelphia: The Westminster Press, 1970), p. 306. Used by permission.

in God's Spirit, which moved the mouths of the prophets like instruments. . . . (7)[2]

Under the impulse of the divine Spirit and raised above their own thoughts, the prophets proclaimed the things with which they were inspired. For the Spirit used them just as a flute player blows on a flute. (9)[3]

And since the Son is in the Father and the Father in the Son by the unity and power of the Spirit, the Son of God is the Mind and Word of the Father. . . . Indeed we say that the Holy Spirit himself, who inspires those who utter prophecies, is an effluence from God, flowing from him and returning like a ray of the sun. Who, then, would not be astonished to hear those called atheists who admit God the Father, God the Son, and the Holy Spirit, and who teach their unity in power and their distinction in rank? (10)[4]

We speak of God, of the Son, his Word, and of the Holy Spirit; and we say that the Father, the Son, and the Spirit are united in power. For the Son is the intelligence, reason and wisdom of the Father, and the Spirit is an effluence, as light from fire. (24)[5]

Athenagoras names the gods, admitting their power and even the power of their idols, calling them the demonic hosts of the fallen angel who is now "Prince of Matter."

It is, however, the demonic movements and operations, coming from the opposing spirit, which produce chaotic onslaughts. They affect men, some in one way, some in another. They influence them within and without, individually and by nations, separately and in common, both according to the principle of matter and to the principle of harmony with the divine. (25)[6]

The irrational powers of the soul, which produce fantasies, bring forth all kinds of images. Some they derive from matter. Others they form and project by themselves. The soul experiences this especially when it partakes of the spirit of matter and is mingled with it. . . . Hence the demons which haunt matter, eager for the smell and blood of sacrifices, and ready to lead men astray, avail themselves of these

[2] *Ibid.,* p. 307.
[3] *Ibid.,* p. 308.
[4] *Ibid.,* p. 309.
[5] *Ibid.,* p. 326.
[6] *Ibid.,* p. 328.

capacities for fantasy in the souls of the multitude. Occupying their minds, they pour visions into them, making it seem as if these came from the idols and statues. Moreover, in whatever ways the soul, because of its immortality, is moved by reason to foretell the future or to heal the present, the demons reap the glory of them all. (27)[7]

[7] *Ibid.,* p. 330.

10

Second Clement

(c. 170)

Second Clement *is not, as its traditional title suggests, the second
letter of Clement of Rome which was sent subsequent to his first letter
to the Corinthians. It is, rather, an anonymous sermon under
Clement's name dating from the middle to late second century,
produced most likely in Egypt. It is the earliest example of Christian
homiletics which has come down to us. Written in a context where
Gnostic ideas were usual for the Christians,* Second Clement's
*adaptation of the Gnostic idea of the church as a preexistent spiritual
entity which took visible form in the flesh of Christ and, as an
extension of the incarnation, in the flesh of Christians is a well-
moderated expansion on notions that arose under the teaching of the
apostle Paul. But the effect of then identifying the Spirit in the church
with Christ effectively makes of* Second Clement *a binitarian, once
again in continuity with the teaching of the apostle Paul (cf. 1
Corinthians 15:45).*

Thus, brethren, if we do the will of our Father, God, we shall belong
to the first Church, the spiritual one which was created before the sun
and moon. . . . let us choose to belong to the Church of life, that we
may win salvation. Now I imagine that you are not ignorant that the

living "Church is the body of Christ." For the scripture says, "God made man male and female"; the male is Christ, the female is the Church. And moreover the books and the Apostles declare that the Church belongs not to the present, but has existed from the beginning; for she was spiritual, as was also our Jesus, but he was made manifest in the last days that he might save us; and the Church, which is spiritual, was made manifest in the flesh of Christ, showing us that if any of us guard her in the flesh without corruption, he shall receive her back again in the Holy Spirit. For this flesh is an anti-type of the Spirit; no one therefore who has corrupted the anti-type shall receive the reality. So, then, he means this, brethren: Guard the flesh, that you may receive the Spirit. Now if we say that the flesh is the Church, and the Spirit is Christ, of course he who has abused the flesh, has abused the Church. Such a one therefore will not receive the Spirit, which is Christ. So great a gift of life and immortality has this flesh the power to receive, if the Holy Spirit be joined to it, nor can any man express or speak of the things "which the Lord hath prepared" for his elect.[1]

[1] Kirsopp Lake, trans., *The Apostolic Fathers,* Loeb Classical Library (Cambridge: Harvard University Press, 1912, 1954), vol. 1, pp. 151-153.

THE GROWTH
OF ORTHODOXY

11

Irenaeus of Lyon

(140/160–c. 200)

Irenaeus was a disciple of Polycarp of Smyrna who had been a disciple of the apostle John. Irenaeus thus inherited the "viva vox" of the living apostolic tradition, which he felt particularly responsible to defend against the various forms of Christian Gnosticism which he considered heretical. In response to the theology of the Spirit and the spiritual exercises of the Gnostics, Irenaeus was moved to considerable reflection on the work of the Holy Spirit: He upheld the Spirit's inspiration of the Old Testament prophets, against a depreciation of the Old Testament like that of Marcion's or the suggestion that the Old Testament was inspired by angels or an inferior deity. He upheld the continuing activity of the Spirit in the charismas given to Christians, while criticizing the misuse of the charismas of the Spirit as urged by the Gnostics in their spiritual manipulations. He describes the scheme of redemption from creation at the "two hands of God" (i. e., the Son and the Spirit), through the anointing of Jesus Christ at his baptism, to the deification of mankind by the indwelling of the Spirit fully sanctifying Christians without any intervention of the aeons of the Gnostic pleroma. Irenaeus made a careful and lasting distinction between two easily confused but quite different moments within the divine life: the incarnation of the Word of God in the flesh of Jesus, which took place before and apart from the Spirit's anointing of the God-become-the-God/Man, and then, the descent of the Spirit upon the already incarnate Word at his baptism. Irenaeus thus provided the deathblow to christological Adoptionism. Despite Irenaeus's own awareness of the ongoing activity of the Spirit in the church, his identification of the "spiritual man" as one who possesses the breath of the Spirit in the church by rightly believing and holding to the apostolic tradition as handed down by the succession of catholic bishops (as opposed to the novelties of the Gnostics) tended to move subsequent interest away from the presence of the charismating power of the Spirit to a more manageable understanding of the Spirit as enshrined in the official teaching of the church.

Irenaeus describes a Gnostic baptism, including a trinitarian (quadritarian?) formula according to which the Holy Spirit is mother, followed by speaking in tongues:

Others . . . baptize them, with the utterance of these words: "Into the name of the unknown Father of the universe—into Truth, the Mother of all things—into Him [the Christ] who descended on Jesus—into union, and redemption, and communion with the powers." Still others repeat certain Hebrew words in order the more thoroughly to bewilder those who are being initiated, as follows: "Basema, Chamosse, Baoenaora, Mistadia, Ruada, Kousta, Babaphor, Kalachthei." The interpretation of these terms runs thus: "I invoke that which is above every power of the Father, which is called light, and good Spirit, and life, because Thou hast reigned in the body."[1]

Describing the magical chicanery of a certain Gnostic, Marcus, and how he inducts especially wealthy women into his sect, Irenaeus gives evidence of the age-old techniques of suggestion used by a well-known style of charismatic practitioner:

It appears probable enough that this man possesses a demon as his familiar spirit, by means of whom he seems able to prophesy, and also enables as many as he counts worthy to be partakers of his Charis [grace] themselves to prophesy. He devotes himself especially to women and those such as are well-bred and elegantly attired and of

---

[1] Irenaeus, *Against Heresies* I 21 iii, in *Ante-Nicene Fathers*, ed. J. Donaldson, rev. American edition, A. C. Coxe (Oxford, 1885; republished in Grand Rapids: William B. Eerdmans Company), vol. 1, p. 346.

great wealth . . . addressing them in such seductive words as these: "I am eager to make thee a partaker of my Charis, since the Father of all doth continually behold thy angel before His face. Now the place of thy angel is among us: it behoves us to become one. Receive first from me and by me (the gift of) Charis. Adorn thyself as a bride who is expecting her bridegroom, that thou mayest be what I am, and I what thou art. Establish the germ of light in thy nuptial chamber. Receive from me a spouse, and become receptive of him, while thou art received by him. Behold Charis has descended upon thee; open thy mouth and prophesy;" On the woman replying, "I have never at any time prophesied, nor do I know how to prophesy;" then engaging, for the second time, in certain invocations, so as to astound his deluded victim, he says to her, "Open thy mouth, speak whatsoever occurs to thee, and thou shalt prophesy." She then, vainly puffed up and elated by these words, and greatly excited in soul by the expectation that it is herself who is to prophesy, her heart beating violently (from emotion), reaches the requisite pitch of audacity, and idly as well as impudently utters some nonsense as it happens to occur to her. . . . Henceforth she reckons herself a prophetess, and expresses her thanks to Marcus . . . not only by the gift of her possessions, but also by yielding up to him her person.[2]

On the other hand, Irenaeus also knew the true exercise of the charismas in the church of his time:

Those who are in truth His [Christ's] disciples, receiving grace from Him, do in His name perform (miracles), so as to promote the welfare of other men, according to the gift which each one has received from Him. For some do certainly and truly drive out devils, so that those who have thus been cleansed from evil spirits frequently both believe (in Christ) and join themselves to the church. Others have foreknowledge of things to come: they see visions and utter prophetic expressions. Others, still, heal the sick by laying their hands upon them, and they are made whole. Yea, moreover, as I have said, even the dead have been raised up and remained among us for many years. And what more shall I say? It is not possible to name the number of the gifts which the Church (scattered), throughout the whole world, has received from God. . . . Nor does she perform anything by means of angelic invocations, nor by incantations, or by any other wicked curious art; but, directing her prayers to the Lord, who made all things, in a pure, sincere and straightforward spirit, and calling upon

[2] I 13 iii, in *ibid.,* pp. 334-335.

the name of our Lord Jesus Christ, she has been accustomed to work miracles for the advantage of mankind, and not to lead them into error. If, therefore, the name of our Lord Jesus Christ even now confers benefits (upon men) and cures thoroughly and effectively all who anywhere believe on Him, but not that of Simon or Menander or Carpocrates or of any other man whatever, it is manifest that, when He was made man, He held fellowship with His own creation.[3]

Irenaeus quotes Matthew's version concerning the baptism of Jesus and adds:

For Christ did not at that time descend upon Jesus, neither was Christ one and Jesus another: but the Word of God . . . who did also take upon him flesh was anointed by the Spirit from the Father. . . .[4]

For (God) promised that in the last times He would pour Him (the Spirit) upon (His) servants and handmaids, that they might prophesy; wherefore He did also descend upon the Son of God, made the Son of man, becoming accustomed in fellowship with Him to dwell in the human race, to rest with human beings, and to dwell in the workmanship of God, working the will of the Father in them, and renewing them from their old habits into the newness of Christ. . . . [The Spirit also] descended at the day of Pentecost upon the disciples after the Lord's ascension, having power to admit all nations to the entrance of life and to the opening of the new covenant; from whence also with one accord in all languages, they uttered praise to God, the Spirit bringing distant tribes to unity and offering to the Father the firstfruits of all nations. . . . For as a compacted lump of dough cannot be formed of dry wheat without fluid matter, nor can a loaf possess unity, so, in like manner, neither could we, being many, be made one in Christ Jesus without the water from heaven. And as dry earth does not bring forth unless it receive moisture, in like manner we also, being originally a dry tree, could never have brought forth fruit unto life without the voluntary rain from above. For our bodies have received unity among themselves by means of the laver which leads to incorruption [baptism]; but our souls, by means of the Spirit. Wherefore both are necessary, since both contribute towards the life of God. . . . The Lord, receiving this as a gift from His Father, does Himself then confer it upon those who are partakers of Himself, sending the Holy Spirit upon all the earth. Gideon . . . forseeing this

---

[3] II 32 iv-v, in *ibid.,* p. 409.
[4] III 9 iii, in *ibid.,* p. 423.

gracious gift, changed his request and prophesied that there would be dryness upon the fleece of wool (a type of the people), on which alone at first there had been dew, thus indicating that they alone should no longer have the Holy Spirit from God, . . . but that the dew, which is the Spirit of God, who descended upon the Lord, should be diffused throughout all the earth. . . . Wherefore we have need of the dew of God, that we be not consumed by fire . . . so that where we have an accuser there we may also have an Advocate. So also, the Lord [the Good Samaritan] commended to the Holy Spirit [the inn keeper] His own man [the human race], who had fallen among thieves, whom He Himself had compassionated and bound up his wounds, giving two royal [coins], so that we, receiving by the Spirit the image and superscription of the Father and the Son, might cause the [coin] entrusted to us to be fruitful, counting out the increase (thereof) to the Lord [cf. Matthew 25:14-30].[5]

Now man is a mixed organization of soul and flesh, who was formed after the likeness of God, and moulded by His hands, that is, by the Son and Holy Spirit, to whom also he said, "Let us make man." [Genesis 1:26]. . . .[6]

For by means of the very same hands through which they [Enoch and Elijah] were moulded at the beginning did they receive this translation and assumption. For in Adam the hands of God had become accustomed to set in order, to rule, and to sustain His own workmanship. . . .[7]

. . . that the Word, namely the Son, was always with the Father; and that Wisdom also, which is the Spirit, was present with Him, anterior to all creation, He declares by Solomon: [cf. Proverbs 3:19; 8:22]. . . . There is therefore one God, who by the Word and Wisdom created and arranged all things. . . .[8]

In another writing of Irenaeus, the Demonstration of the Gospel, *chapter 10, he describes the Son and Holy Spirit in terms that link him with the angel-pneumatology/ Christology of the Jewish Christians:*

[5] III 17i-iii, in *ibid.,* pp. 444-445.
[6] IV Preface, in *ibid.,* p. 463.
[7] V 6 i, in *ibid.,* p. 531.
[8] IV 20 iii and iv, in *ibid.,* p. 488.

Now this God is glorified by his Word, who is his eternal Son, and by the Holy Spirit, who is Wisdom and the Father of all; and their power, that of the Word and Wisdom, who are called Cherubim and Seraphim, glorified God with unceasing voice.[9]

In Against Heresies, *Irenaeus continues his discussion of the role of the Holy Spirit:*

For man does not see God by his own powers; but when He pleases He is seen by men. . . . [He was seen] at that time indeed, prophetically through the Spirit, and seen too, adoptively through the Son; and He shall also be seen paternally in the kingdom of heaven, the Spirit truly preparing man in the Son of God, and the Son leading him to the Father, while the Father, too, confers (upon him) incorruption for eternal life.[10]

The "spiritual man" or the "perfect man" is, then, the one who is being brought to God along this path:

Now God shall be glorified in His handiwork. . . . For by the hands of the Father, that is, by the Son and the Holy Spirit, man, and not (merely) a part of man, was made in the likeness of God . . . for the perfect man consists in the commingling and the union of the soul receiving the spirit of the Father, and the admixture of that fleshly nature which was moulded after the image of God. For this reason does the apostle declare, "We speak wisdom among them that are perfect," terming those persons "perfect" who have received the Spirit of God, and who through the Spirit of God do speak in all languages, as he used Himself also to speak. In like manner we do also hear many brethren in the Church, who possess prophetic gifts, and who through the Spirit speak all kinds of languages, and bring to light for the general benefit the hidden things of men, and declare the mysteries of God, whom also the apostle terms "spiritual," they being spiritual because they partake of the Spirit, and not because their flesh has been stripped off and taken away, and because they have become purely spiritual. For if any one take away the substance of flesh, that is, of the handiwork (of God), and understand that which is purely spiritual, such then would not be a spiritual man, but would be the spirit of a man, or the Spirit of God. But when the spirit here blended with the soul is united to (God's) handiwork, the man is rendered spiritual and perfect because of the outpouring of the Spirit,

---

[9] Jean Danielou, *The Theology of Jewish Christianity* (Chicago: Henry Regnery Company, 1964), p. 138.

[10] *Against Heresies* IF 20 v, *Ante-Nicene Fathers,* p. 489.

and this is he who was made in the image and likeness of God.[11]

The preaching of the Church is everywhere consistent and continues in an even course and receives testimony from the prophets, the apostles and all the disciples . . . that well-grounded system which tends to man's salvation, namely, our faith; which we have received from the Church we do preserve and which always, by the Spirit of God, renewing its youth, as if it were some precious deposit in an excellent vessel, causes the vessel itself containing it to renew its youth also. For this gift of God has been entrusted to the Church, as breath was to the first created man, for the purpose that all the members receiving it may be made vivified, and the (means of) communion with Christ has been distributed throughout [the Church], that is, the Holy Spirit, the earnest of incorruption, the means of confirming our faith and the ladder of ascent to God. "For in the Church," it is said, "God has placed apostles, prophets, teachers," and all the other means through which the Spirit works, of which all those are not partakers who do not join themselves to the Church. . . . For where the church is, there is the Spirit of God; and where the Spirit of God is, there is the Church, and every kind of grace; but the Spirit is truth. Those, therefore, who do not partake of Him are neither nourished into life from the mother's breasts nor do they enjoy that most limpid fountain which issues from the body of Christ. . . .[12]

The final result of the presence of the Spirit, working through all his gifts and means including the eucharist, is the immortalization and deification of mortal humanity.

In (the times of the) end, the Word of the Father and the Spirit of God, having become united with the ancient substance of Adam's formation, rendered man living and perfect.[13]

Just as a cutting from a vine planted in the ground fructifies in its season, or as a corn of wheat falling into the earth and becoming decomposed rises with manifold increase by the Spirit of God, who contains all things, and them, through the Wisdom of God, serves for the use of men, and having received the Word of God, becomes the Eucharist, which is the body and blood of Christ, so also our bodies, being nourished by it and deposited in the earth, suffering

[11] V 6 i, in *ibid.,* pp. 531-532.
[12] III 24 1, in *ibid.,* p. 458.
[13] V 1 3, in *ibid.,* p. 527.

decomposition there, shall rise at their appointed time. . . .[14]

But we do now receive a certain portion of His Spirit, tending towards perfection, and preparing us for incorruption, being little by little accustomed to receive and bear God. . . . This "earnest" [Ephesians 1:13-14], therefore, indwelling us renders us spiritual even now, and the mortal is swallowed up by immortality. . . . This, however, does not take place by a casting away of the flesh but by the impartation of the Spirit. . . . If, therefore, at the present time, having the earnest, we do cry: "Abba, Father," what shall it be when, on rising again, we behold him face to face; when all the members shall burst out into a continuous hymn of triumph, glorifying Him who raised them from the dead, and gave the gift of eternal life? For if the earnest, gathering man into itself, does even now cause him to cry "Abba, Father," what shall the complete grace of the Spirit effect, which shall be given to men by God? It will render us like unto Him and accomplish the will of the Father, for it shall make man after the image and likeness of God.

Those persons, then, who possess the earnest of the Spirit and who are not enslaved by the lusts of the flesh but are subject to the Spirit and who in all things walk according to the light of reason, does the apostle properly term "spiritual" because the Spirit of God dwells in them. . . .[15]

The flesh is capable of corruption; so is it also capable of incorruption, . . . For the breath of life which also rendered man an animated being is one thing and the vivifying Spirit another, which caused him to become spiritual.[16]

. . . Now the final result of the work of the Spirit is the salvation of the flesh. For what other visible fruit is there of the invisible Spirit than the rendering of the flesh mature and capable of incorruption?[17]

. . . [The saved thus] ascend through the Spirit to the Son and through the Son to the Father; and that in due time the Son will yield up His work to the Father . . . free from the bondage of corruption . . . passing beyond the angels, and be made after the image and likeness of God.[18]

[14] V 2 3, in *ibid.,* p. 528.
[15] V 8 i-ii, in *ibid.,* pp. 533-534.
[16] V 12 i, in *ibid.,* p. 537.
[17] V 12 iv, in *ibid.,* p. 538.
[18] V 36, ii-iii, in *ibid.,* p. 567.

12

Tertullian

(c. 160–after 220)

The cantankerous lawyer from Carthage, Tertullian, was famous in the Roman Christian world for his extremes. He began as a licentious, adulterous pagan, then converted to Roman Christianity but finally became as far out in his rigorous excesses as the church's first great pentecostal theologian and convert to Montanism as he had been when he was a sinner. His path of changes is reflected in his writings: around 200, in a treatise To His Wife, *Tertullian advised a Christian widow to remain unmarried the second time around, although admitting that second marriage is no sin. Between 204 and 212, now under the influence of Montanist teaching, his former advice became a rigid command in his* Exhortation to Chastity. *By 217, second marriage is called adultery and listed as one of the sins unforgiveable by the church—a "discipline" which, he says in his writing* On Monogamy, *the Paraclete, the Holy Spirit, forewarned though deferred in Scripture but now, through the New Prophecy of the Montanist "Church of the Spirit," is definitively appointing and exacting.*[1]

[1] Tertullian, *On Monogamy* 3, in *Ante-Nicene Fathers*, ed. J. Donaldson, rev. American edition, A. C. Coxe (Oxford, 1885; republished in Grand Rapids: William B. Eerdmans Company), vol. 4, pp. 59-61.

Heretic and schismatic though he was, Tertullian was also a fervent Christian and one of the most creative and inventive theological minds of the ancient church. As the first writer of theological Latin, he bequeathed the church its language of "trinity" and "persons" and a host of memorable and pithy quotables and concepts which have not lost their effectiveness even now. In the face of the ambiguity of the doctrinal situation regarding the nature of the Trinity in a century when Gnosticism, Sabellianism, Patripassianism, and some other alternatives were the working matrix out of which the orthodox teaching would not evolve until a hundred years later, Tertullian, the Montanist doctor of the church, according to his charismatic experience of the fully individual action of the Third Person of the Godhead, was able to distinguish three persons distinct from one another yet united in their Godhood. It is no exaggeration to suggest that Tertullian's Montanist experience of the Holy Spirit enabled him to distinguish the personhood of the Paraclete from that of the Father and the Son and thus to provide the experiential-theological ground for the orthodox teaching on the Trinity.

Tertullian's sectarian church was one of the places where the ancient practice of tongue-speaking, prophesying, and receiving revelatory dreams and visions continued, albeit under the name of the "New Prophecy" in polemic against the larger church, which was conceived to have fallen away from true spirituality to a condition of being what Tertullian called "psychic." Between the bishops (Victor) and the heretics (Praxeas), Tertullian argues that the Roman church had denied the Spirit and confused the persons of the Trinity as a result of banishing the New Prophecy:

After the Bishop of Rome (Victor) had acknowledged the prophetic gifts of Montanus, Prisca, and Maximilla, and, in consequence of the acknowledgment, had bestowed his peace on the churches of Asia and Phrygia [Praxeas] by importunately urging false accusations against the prophets themselves and their churches and insisting on the authority of the bishop's predecessors in the see, compelled him to recall the pacific letter which he had issued as well as to desist from his purpose of acknowledging the *said* gifts. By this, Praxeas did a twofold service for the devil at Rome: he drove away prophecy and he brought in heresy, he put to flight the Paraclete and he crucified the Father.[2]

[2] *Against Praxeas* 1, in *ibid.*, vol. 3, p. 597.

Throughout his writing Tertullian gives an occasional brief description of the New Prophecy, although he never wrote systematically on the subject.

For example, on the text Luke 9:33, that Peter, on the Mount of Transfiguration, did not know what he said, Tertullian wrote:
How knew not? Was his ignorance the result of simple error? Or was it on the principle which we maintain in the cause of the new prophecy, that to grace ecstacy or rapture is incident. For when a man is rapt in the Spirit, especially when he beholds the glory of God, or when God speaks through him, he necessarily loses his sensation, because he is overshadowed with the power of God—a point concerning which there is a debate between us and the carnally minded.[3]

Concerning how the Holy Spirit now illuminates scripture so as to do away with the former misinterpretations of the resurrection of the flesh by the heretics:
It was fit and proper, therefore, that the Holy Ghost should no longer withhold the effusions of His gracious light upon these inspired writings, in order that they might be able to disseminate the seeds *of truth* with no admixture of heretical subtleties, and pluck out from it their tares. He has now accordingly dispersed all the perplexities of the past, and their self-chosen allegories and parables, by the open and perspicuous explanation of the entire mystery through the new prophecy which descends in copious streams from the Paraclete. If you will only draw water from His fountains, you will never thirst for other doctrine: no feverish craving after subtle questions will again consume you; *but* by drinking in evermore the resurrection of the flesh, you will be satisfied with the refreshing draughts.[4]

On the nature of the gifts of the Spirit and Tertullian's confidence that their presence in his church is evidence of spiritual superiority over Marcion's church:
Now, on the subject of spiritual gifts, I have to remark that these also were promised by the Creator through Christ. . . . In this Christ the whole *substantia* of the Spirit would have to rest, not meaning that it would be as it were some subsequent acquisition accruing to him who was always, even before His incarnation, the Spirit of God. . . . There would have to rest upon Him the entire operation of the Spirit of

---

[3] *Against Marcion,* 22 in *ibid.,* p. 383.
[4] *On the Resurrection of the Flesh* 63, in *ibid.,* p. 594.

grace, which, so far as the Jews were concerned, would cease and come to an end. . . .[5]

When enjoining silence on women in the church, that they not speak merely for the sake of learning (although they do have the right of prophesying, as he has already shown, when he covers the woman that prophesies with a veil [1 Corinthians 11:5, 6]) Paul goes to the law for his sanction that woman should be under obedience. Now this law, let me say once for all, he ought to have referred to only to destroy it. But that we may now leave the subject of spiritual gifts, facts themselves will be enough to prove which of us acts rashly in claiming them for his God, and whether it is possible that they are opposed to our side, even if [as Marcion teaches] the Creator promised them for His Christ who is not yet revealed, as being destined only for the Jews, to have their operations in His time, in His Christ, and among His [Jewish] people. Let Marcion then exhibit, as gifts of his god, some prophets who have not spoken by human sense but with the Spirit of God and have both predicted things to come and have made manifest the secrets of the heart; let him [Marcion] produce a psalm, a vision, a prayer—only let it be by the Spirit, in an ecstasy, that is, in a rapture, whenever an interpretation of tongues has occurred to him. Let him show to me also that any woman of boastful tongue in his community has ever prophesied from among those specially holy sisters of his. Now all of these signs (of spiritual gifts) are forthcoming from my side without any difficulty, and they agree, too, with the rules and the dispensations and the instructions of the Creator therefore, without doubt the Christ, and the Spirit, and the apostle [Paul] belong, severally to my God. Here, then, is my frank avowal for anyone who cares to require it.[6]

As for ourselves, indeed, we ascribe on the soul the lineaments of corporeity, not simply from the assurance which reasoning has taught us of its corporeal nature but also from the firm conviction which divine grace impresses on us by revelation. For, seeing that we acknowledge spiritual *charismata* or gifts, we too have merited the attainment of the prophetic gift, although coming after John (the Baptist). We have now amongst us a sister whose lot it has been to be favoured with various gifts of revelation, which she experiences in the

[5] *Against Marcion* 8, in *ibid.,* p. 445.
[6] *Ibid.,* pp. 446-447.

Spirit by ecstatic vision amidst the sacred rites of the Lord's Day in the church. She converses with angels, and sometimes with the Lord. She both sees and hears mysterious communications; some men's hearts she understands, and to them who are in need she distributes remedies. Whether it be in the reading of Scriptures, or in the chanting of psalms, or in the preaching of sermons, or in the offering up of prayers, in all these religious services, matter and opportunity are afforded to her of seeing visions. It may possibly have happened to us whilst this sister of ours was rapt in the Spirit that we had discoursed in some ineffable way about the soul. After the people are dismissed at the conclusion of the sacred services, she is in the regular habit of reporting to us whatever things she may have seen in visions (for all her communications are examined with the most scrupulous care, in order that their truth may be probed). "Amongst other things," says she, "there has been shown to me a soul in bodily shape, and a spirit has been in the habit of appearing to me; not, however, a void and empty illusion, but such as would offer itself to be even grasped by the hand, soft and transparent and of an etherial color, and in form resembling that of a human being in every respect." This was her vision, and for her witness there was God; and the apostle most assuredly foretold that there were to be "spiritual gifts" in the church.[7]

Concerning the recompense of departed souls for their sin in Hades (purgatory), Tertullian also claims the teaching of the Holy Spirit: This point the Paraclete has also pressed home on our attention in most frequent admonitions, whenever any of us has admitted the force of His words from a knowledge of His promised spiritual disclosures.[8]

On the subject of the forgiveness of sins after baptism, the Spirit in the church is both the source of this forgiveness and of Tertullian's hesitance to make forgiving use of the power of the keys: ... power is the Spirit, but the Spirit is God . . . Who, moreover, was able to forgive sins? This is His alone prerogative, for who remitteth sins but God alone? . . . But, you say, "The Church has the power of forgiving sins." This I acknowledge and adjudge more (than you, I) who have the Paraclete Himself in the persons of the new prophets, saying, "The Church has the power to forgive sins; but I [the Paraclete] will not do it [forgive] lest they commit others withal." . . .

[7] *On the Soul* 9, in *ibid.,* p. 188.
[8] *On the Soul* 58, in *ibid.,* p. 235.

For the very Church itself is, properly and principally, the Spirit Himself, in whom is the Trinity of the One Divinity—Father, Son and Holy Spirit. (The Spirit) combines that Church which the Lord has made to consist in "three" . . . And accordingly the Church, it is true, will forgive sins: but (it will be) the Church of the Spirit, by means of a spiritual man; not the Church which consists of a number of bishops. For the right and arbitrament belongs to the Lord, not to the servant; God's Himself, not the priest's.[9]

The Paraclete, according to Tertullian, is operative across the spectrum of piety, faith, and experience for those who have received the New Prophecy. The Spirit is foremost the "Determiner of discipline," [10] *that is, the source of new revelations which lead to the rigorous religion of the Montanists—fasting, martyrdom, and the veiling of women, as well as dreams, visions, ecstasies, and prophecy (the latter of which seems, by definition, to include tongue-speaking):* granting that upon the centurion Cornelius, even *before baptism,* the honourable gift of the Holy Spirit, together with the gift of prophecy besides, had hastened to descend, we see that *his fasts* had been heard [cf. Acts 10:44-48].[11]

For what kind of (supposition) is it, that, while the devil is always operating and adding daily to the ingenuities of iniquity, the work of God should either have ceased, or else have desisted from advancing? whereas the reason why the Lord sent the Paraclete was, that, since human mediocrity was unable to take in all things at once, discipline should, little by little, be directed, and ordained, and carried on to perfection by that Vicar of the Lord, the Holy Spirit. . . . What, then, is the Paraclete's administrative office but this: the direction of discipline, the revelation of the scriptures, the re-formation of the intellect, the advancement toward the "better things"? Nothing is without stages of growth: all things await their season. . . . So, too, righteousness—for the God of righteousness and of creation is the same. . . . now, through the Paraclete, it [righteousness] is settling into maturity. He will be, after Christ, the only one to be called and revered as Master. . . . He is the only prelate, because He alone succeeds Christ. They who have received Him set truth before custom. They who have heard Him prophesying even to the present

---

[9] *On Modesty,* 21, in *ibid.,* vol. 4, pp. 98-100.
[10] *On Modesty* 11, in *ibid.,* p. 85.
[11] *On Fasting* 8, in *ibid.,* p. 107.

time, not of old, bid virgins be wholly covered.[12]

Tertullian's theory of dreaming and ecstasy is extensive, according to which the Holy Spirit is the source of all those visions "emanating, which may be compared to the actual grace of God, as being honest, holy, prophetic, inspired, instructive, inviting to virtue, the bountiful nature of which causes them to overflow even to the profane, since God, with grand impartiality, 'sends His showers and sunshine on the just and on the unjust.'"[13]

He also recognizes the demons and the natural soul as other sources of dreaming. Examples of these different kinds of spiritual possession are the cases of Adam and Saul. God breathed the natural soul of the breath of life into Adam at his creation, but thereafter, when he prophesied about Christ and the church (cf. Genesis 2:24-25, Ephesians 5:31-32), "he experienced the influence of the Spirit. For there fell upon him that ecstasy which is the Holy Ghost's operative virtue of prophecy. And even the evil spirit too is an influence which comes upon a man. Indeed, the Spirit of God no more really 'turned Saul into another man,' that is to say, into a prophet, when 'people said to one another: . . . Is Saul also among the prophets?' than did the evil spirit afterwards turn him into another man, that is to say, into an apostate [1 Samuel 10:6, 11]."[14]

To the martyrs-designate, Tertullian wrote: "O blessed, grieve not the Holy Spirit who has entered the prison with you; for if he had not gone with you there, you would not have been there this day. Strive with all endeavor, therefore, to retain him; so let him lead you thence to your Lord."[15]

If you ask counsel of the Spirit, what does He approve more than that utterance of the Spirit? For [the Spirit] incites all, almost, to go and offer themselves in martyrdom, not to flee from it; so that we also make mention of it. If you are exposed to public infamy, says he, it is for your good; for he who is not exposed to dishonour among men is sure to be so before the Lord.[16]

If anyone recognizes the Spirit also, he will hear him branding the runaways [from martyrdom]. . . .[17]

[12] *On the Veiling of Virgins* 1, in *ibid.,* pp. 27-28.
[13] *Treatise on the Soul* 47, in *ibid.,* vol. 3, pp. 225-226.
[14] *Treatise on the Soul* 11, in *ibid.,* p. 191.
[15] *To the Martyrs* 1, in *ibid.,* p. 693.
[16] *Concerning Flight during Persecution* 9, in *ibid.,* vol. 4, p. 121.
[17] *Concerning Flight* 11, in *ibid.,* p. 122.

And therefore the Comforter is requisite, who guides into all truth and animates to all endurance. And they who have received Him will neither stoop to flee from persecution nor to buy it off, for they have the Lord Himself, One who will stand by us to aid us in suffering as well as to be our mouth when we are put to the question [cf. Matthew 10:19-20].[18]

Tertullian's opponents argue that the Montanists' Paraclete has revealed a novelty that goes beyond the teachings of Christ in the burdensome assertion of no remarriage; to which Tertullian replies: Now concerning each point the Lord Himself has pronounced. For in saying "I still have many things to say to you, but you are not yet able to bear them; when the Holy Spirit shall come, He will lead you into all truth" [John 16:12, 13], He sufficiently, of course, sets before us that he will bring such (teachings) as may be esteemed alike *novel,* as having never before been published, and finally *burdensome,* as if that were the reason why they were not published. "It follows," you say, "that by this line of argument, anything you please which is novel and burdensome may be ascribed to the Paraclete, even if it have come from the adversary spirit." No, of course. . . . The Paraclete, having many things to teach fully which the Lord deferred till He [the Paraclete] came (according to the pre-definition) will begin by bearing emphatic witness to Christ. . . . And when He has thus been recognised (as the promised Comforter), on the ground of the cardinal rule, He will reveal those "many things" which appertain to disciplines; while the integrity of His preaching commands credit for these revelations, albeit they be "novel," inasmuch as they are now in course of revelation, albeit they be "burdensome," inasmuch as not even *now* are they found bearable: (revelations) however, of none other Christ than (the One) who said that He had withal "many other things" which were to be fully taught by the Paraclete, no less burdensome to men of our own day than to them by whom they were then "not yet able to be borne."[19]

"Hardness of heart" reigned till Christ's time [cf. Mark 10:5]; let "infirmity of the flesh" (be content to) have reigned till the time of the Paraclete. The New Law abrogated divorce—it has (somewhat) to abrogate; the New Prophecy (abrogates) second marriage, (which is) no less a divorce of the former (marriage).[20]

[18] *Concerning Flight* 14, in *ibid.,* p. 125.
[19] *On Monogamy* 2, in *ibid.,* p. 60.
[20] *On Monogamy* 14, in *ibid.,* p. 71.

The wrangling of the opposite party is silenced, while they say: "It is either a pseudo-prophecy, if it is a spiritual voice which institutes these solemnities; or else a heresy, if it is a human presumption which devises them." . . . But you again set up boundary-posts to God, as with regard to grace, so with regard to discipline; as with regard to gifts, so, too, with regard to solemnities [namely, fasting in this case]: so that our observances are supposed to have ceased in like manner as His benefits; just as you; and you thus deny that He still continues to impose duties, because in this case again, "The Law and the prophets (were) until John." It remains for you to banish Him wholly, as far as He is, at least as far as lies in you, so otiose. . . . Grant that from the time of John the Paraclete had grown mute, we ourselves would have arisen as prophets to ourselves, for this cause chiefly: not, I say, now to bring by our prayers down God's anger nor to obtain his protection or grace; but to secure by premonition the moral position of the "latest times" [by forarming ourself through every kind of lowliness of mind in preparation for martyrdom].[21]

Tertullian teaches that the Spirit is the active agent at every step of becoming a Christian through baptism:
The Spirit of God, who hovered over (the waters) from the beginning [Genesis 1:2], would continue to linger over the waters of the baptized. . . . Thus the nature of the waters, sanctified by the Holy One, itself conceived withal the power of sanctifying. . . . It makes no difference whether a man be washed in a sea or a pool, a stream or a fount, a lake or a trough. . . . All waters, therefore, in virtue of the pristine privilege of their origin do, after an invocation of God, attain the sacramental power of sanctification; for the Spirit immediately supervenes from the heavens and rests over the waters, sanctifying them from Himself; and being thus sanctified, they imbibe at the same time the power of sanctifying. . . . Therefore, after the waters have been in a manner endued with medicinal virtue through the intervention of the Angel [cf. John 5:4], the spirit is corporally washed in the waters and the flesh is in the same spiritually cleansed.[22]

Not that *in* the waters we obtain the Holy Spirit, but in the water, under (the witness) of the angel, we are cleansed and prepared for the Holy Spirit. . . . After this, when we have issued from the font, we are thoroughly anointed with a blessed unction. . . . In the next place, the

---

[21] *On Fasting* 11, 12, in *ibid.,* p. 110.
[22] *On Baptism* 4, in *ibid.,* vol. 3, p. 671.

hand is laid on us, invoking and inviting the Spirit through benediction. . . .[23]

Then over our cleansed and blessed bodies willingly descends from the Father that Holiest Spirit. Over the waters of baptism, recognising it as His primeval seat He reposes. . . . For just as, after the waters of the deluge, by which the old iniquity was purged—after the baptism, so to say, of the world—a *dove* was the herald which announced to the earth the assuagement of celestial wrath, . . . so by the self-same law of heavenly effect, to earth—that is, to our flesh—as it emerges from the font after its old sins, flies the dove of the Holy Spirit, bringing us the peace of God, sent out from the heavens.[24]

For all his stress on New Prophecy, Tertullian's constant assertion was that the revelations of the Paraclete were perfectly conformable to the tradition of the church as it had been faithfully handed down. When Praxeas brought his heresy to Rome, Tertullian says he separated himself from the carnally minded in order to preserve the better teachings of the Paraclete: Then he substantially quotes the contents of "the Apostles' Creed"—the traditional statement of faith of the ancient church:

Now the Spirit indeed is third from God and the Son, just as the fruit of the tree is third from the root, or as the stream out of the river is third from the fountain, or as the apex of the ray is third from the sun. Nothing, however, is alien from that original source whence it derives its own properties. In like manner the Trinity, flowing down from the Father through intertwined and connected steps, does not at all disturb the *Monarchy* [the unity of Godhead] while at the same time guarding the state of the *Economy* [the distinction of three persons].[25]

For we who by the grace of God possess an insight into both the times and the occasions of the Sacred Writings, especially we who are followers of the Paraclete, not of human *teachers,* do indeed definitively declare that *Two* Beings are God, the Father and the Son, and, with the addition of the Holy Spirit, even *Three,* according to the principle of the *divine* economy.[26]

---

[23] *On Baptism* 6, 7, 8, in *ibid.,* p. 672.
[24] *On Baptism* 8, in *ibid.,* p. 673.
[25] *Against Praxeas* 8, in *ibid.,* p. 603.
[26] *Against Praxeas* 13, in *ibid.,* p. 608.

13

The Martyrdom of Perpetua and Felicitas

(202)

On March 7, 202, five saints testified to their faith by giving up their lives in the arena at Carthage. Saturninus and Revocatus were slain by a leopard and a bear. Saturus died after one bite by the leopard. Perpetua, a nobly born and well-educated matron, and her handmaid Felicitas, who had only a few days previous given birth, were finally taken away by the gladiator's sword when a fierce cow was unable to gore them to death. The account of their spirituality, their visions, and their death was redacted by the unmistakable hand of an adherent of the Montanist "New Prophecy," very likely Tertullian himself.

If ancient illustrations of faith which both testify to God's grace and tend to man's edification are collected in writing, so that by perusal of them, as if by the reproduction of the facts, as well God may be honoured and man may be strengthened, why should not new instances also be collected? . . . But let men look to it if they judge the power of the Holy Spirit to be one, according to the times and seasons; since some things of later date must be esteemed of more account as being nearer to the very last times, in accordance with the exuberance of grace manifested to the final periods determined for the world [He quotes Joel 2:28, 29]. And thus we—who both acknowledge and reverence, even as we do the prophecies, modern visions as equally promised to us, and consider the other powers of the Holy Spirit to be an agency of the Church for which also He was sent, administering all gifts in all, even as the Lord distributed to everyone [1 Corinthians 12:11] as well needfully collect them in writing just as we commemorate them in reading to God's glory so that no weakness or despondency of faith may suppose that the divine grace abode only among the ancients, whether in respect of the condescension that raised up martyrs or that gave revelations; since God always carries into effect what He has promised, for a testimony to unbelievers, to believers for a benefit.[1]

At the time of her arrest, Perpetua was still a catechumen, having not yet been baptized. At the time, then, of her baptism, the Spirit indicated that she should understand her baptism as a preparation for martyrdom:

In that same interval of a few days we were baptized, and to me the Spirit prescribed that in the water *of baptism* nothing else was to be sought for than bodily endurance. After a few days, we were taken into the dungeon. . . . Then my brother said to me: "My dear sister, you are already in a position of great dignity, and are such that you may ask for a vision, and that it may be made known to you whether this is to result in a passion or an escape." And I, who knew that I was privileged to converse with the Lord, whose kindnesses I had found to be so great, boldly promised him: "Tomorrow I will tell you." And I asked, and this is what was shown me: I saw a golden ladder of marvellous height, reaching up even to heaven, and very narrow, so that persons could only ascend it one by one, and on the sides of the ladder were fixed every kind of iron weapon. There were swords, lances, hooks, daggers; so that if any one went up carelessly, or not looking upwards, he would be torn to pieces and his flesh would cleave to the iron weapons. . . .

(The martyrs go up the ladder one by one, treading on the head of a fierce dragon who tries to impede their journey. . . .)

And I went up, and I saw an immense extent of garden, and in the midst of the garden a white-haired man sitting in the dress of a

---

[1] *The Passion of the Holy Martyrs Perpetua and Felicitas,* in *Ante-Nicene Fathers,* ed. J. Donaldson, rev. American edition, A. C. Coxe (Oxford, 1885; republished in Grand Rapids: William B. Eerdmans Company), vol. 3, p. 699.

shepherd [the "Shepherd" of Hermas], of large stature, milking sheep; and standing around were many thousand white-robed ones. He raised his head and looked upon me and said to me: "Thou art welcome, daughter." . . . And we understood that it was to be a passion, and we ceased henceforth to have any hope in this world.[2]

This vision is followed by some others, including one regarding Perpetua's younger brother Dinocrates, who is released from purgatory as a result of her prayers. One vision reassures Perpetua that in her martyrdom she will triumph over the devil. Another, received by Saturus, pictures their reception into heaven as the angels shout: "Here they are! Here they are!" *and* "Come, first enter, and greet your Lord!"[3] *On the day of her "victory," the eyewitness account of Perpetua's death describes her modesty when the enraged cow rips away her clothing, and her state of rapture:*

. . . and she, as if aroused from sleep, so deeply had she been in the Spirit and in an ecstasy, began to look round her, and to say to the amazement of all: "I cannot tell when we are to be led out to that cow." And when she heard what had already happened, she did not believe it until she noted certain signs of injury in her body and in her dress. . . . "Stand fast in the faith" [she cried], "and love one another, all of you, and be not offended at my sufferings!"

O most brave and blessed martyrs! O truly called and chosen unto the glory of our Lord Jesus Christ! Whom whoever magnifies, and honours, and adores assuredly ought to read these examples for the edification of the Church, not less than the ancient ones, so that new virtues also may testify that one and the same Holy Spirit is always operating even until now.[4]

[2] *Ibid.*, p. 700.
[3] *Ibid.*, p. 703.
[4] *Ibid.*, pp. 705-706.

14

Origen

(c. 185–c. 254)

Origen of Alexandria was the greatest scholar of the ancient church. A student both of Clement of Alexandria and the pagan philosopher Ammonius Saccas, and as well an heir to the riches of Egyptian Christian Gnoticism, Origen combined in himself the right elements to produce systematic theology. His De Principiis *(On First Principles) is the first inclusive attempt to set forth a balanced presentation of the whole of Christian doctrine and is a clear indication of the stage to which Christian reflection on the Holy Spirit had come at that time. A creative and independent mind, Origen was capable of coming up with ideas which left him in bad repute among more traditional thinkers: his hesitance to ascribe coeternality and consubstantiality to the Spirit made of him a subordinationist, ranking the Spirit beneath the Son beneath the Father. This point of view was held by Origen's heirs, the Arians, a hundred years later. Origen describes the steps of salvation in such a way as to indicate an intimate and necessary part played by the Holy Spirit, preparing men to receive God. Origen's all-important allegorical interpretation of Scripture, a method of reading the Bible devised by Philo the Jew of Alexandria and passed on to the church as perhaps Origen's most influential single contribution, is also ascribed to the working of the Holy Spirit. Apart from systematic theological speculations, Origen, like others in the early church, was also aware of the ongoing and living reality of the charismating Spirit.*

"All things were made through him" [John 1:3]. . . . If all things were made . . . through the Logos, then they were not made "by" the Logos, but by a stronger and greater than he. And who else could this be but the Father? Now if, as we have seen, all things were made through Him, we have to inquire if the Holy Spirit also was made through Him. It appears to me that those who hold the Holy Spirit to be created, and who also admit that "all things were made through him," must necessarily assume that the Holy Spirit was made through the Logos, the Logos accordingly being older than he.
And he who shrinks from allowing the Holy Spirit to have been made through Christ must, if he admits the truth of the statements of this Gospel, assume the Spirit to be uncreated. There is a third resource besides these two (that of allowing the Spirit to have been made by the Word, and that of regarding it as uncreated), namely, to assert that the Holy Spirit has no essence of His own beyond the Father and the Son. But on further thought one may perhaps see reason to consider that the Son is second beside the Father, He being the same as the Father, while manifestly a distinction is drawn between the Spirit and the Son. . . . We consider, therefore, that there are three hypostases, the Father and the Son and the Holy Spirit; and at the same time we believe nothing to be uncreated but the Father. We therefore as the more pious and the truer course, admit that all things were made by the Logos, and that the Holy Spirit is the most excellent and the first in order of all that was made by the Father through Christ. And this, perhaps, is the reason why the Spirit is not said to be God's own Son. The Only-begotten only is by nature and from the beginning a Son; and the Holy Spirit seems to have need of the Son, to minister His essence to Him, so as to enable Him not only to exist but to be wise and reasonable and just and all that we must think of him as being. All this he has by participation of the character of Christ.[1]

And I consider that the Holy Spirit supplies to those who, through Him and through participation in Him, are called saints, the material

[1] Origen, *Commentary on John,* II 6, in *Ante-Nicene Fathers,* ed. J. Donaldson, rev. American edition, A. C. Coxe (Oxford, 1885; revised and republished in Grand Rapids: William B. Eerdmans Company), vol. 10, p. 328.

of the gifts, which come from God; so that the said material of the gifts is made powerful by God, is ministered by Christ and owes its actual existence in men to the Holy Spirit. I am led to this view of the charisms by the words of Paul. . . .
For example, the Gospel saying that sin against the Son will be forgiven, but sin against the Spirit will not be forgiven.
There are some passages in which the Spirit is placed above Christ.
. . . What is the reason for this? Is it because the Holy Spirit is of more value than Christ that the sin against Him cannot be forgiven? May it not rather be that all rational beings have part in Christ, and that forgiveness is extended to them when they repent of their sins, while only those have part in the Holy Spirit who have been found worthy of it, and that there cannot well be any forgiveness for those who fall away to evil in spite of such great and powerful cooperation, and who defeat the counsels of the Spirit who is in them. When we find the Lord saying, as he does in Isaiah [48:16], that he is sent by the Father and by his Spirit, we have to point out here also that the Spirit is not originally superior to the Saviour, but that the Saviour takes a lower place than He in order to carry out the plan which has been made that the Son of God should become man. . . . The Father, therefore, the principal, sends the Son, but the Holy Spirit also sends Him and directs Him to go before, promising to descend, when the time comes, to the Son of God, and to work with Him for the salvation of men. This He did, when, in a bodily shape like a dove, He flew to Him after the baptism. He remained on Him and did not pass Him by, as He might have done with men not able continuously to bear his glory.

If any one should lend credence to the Gospel according to the Hebrews, where the Saviour Himself says: "My mother, the Holy Spirit, took me just now by one of my hairs and carried me off to the great mount Tabor," he will have to face the difficulty of explaining how the Holy Spirit can be the mother of Christ when it was itself brought into existence through the Word. But neither the passage nor this difficulty is hard to explain. For if he who does the will of the Father in heaven is Christ's brother and sister and mother, and if the name of brother of Christ may be applied, not only to the race of men, but to beings of diviner rank than they, then there is nothing absurd in the Holy Spirit's being His mother, every one being His mother who does the will of the Father in heaven.[2]

2 *Ibid.,* pp. 329-330.

The Holy Spirit is, for Origen, supremely the inspirer of holy scripture. He is also of such authority and dignity that baptism apart from his name is not complete. But with reference to his origin, since according to scripture, including Enoch and the Shepherd of Hermas, which Origen quotes at this point, "all things were created by God," it should follow that the Holy Spirit was also created by God. Nevertheless in De Principiis *Origen argues:*

To the present time we have been able to find no statement in holy Scripture in which the Holy Spirit could be said to be made or created, not even in the way in which we have shown above that the divine Wisdom is spoken of by Solomon, or in which those expressions which we have discussed are to be understood of the Life or the Word or the other appellations of the Son of God.[3]

Next Origen makes the distinction that whenever the word "Spirit" occurs in scripture without qualifying adjectives, still the Holy Spirit is meant; therefore, Origen argues:

For without doubt, every one who walks upon the earth . . . is a partaker also of the Holy Spirit, receiving it from God. My Hebrew master also used to say that those two seraphim in Isaiah [6:3], which are described as having each six wings and calling to one another and saying: "Holy, holy, holy is the Lord God of hosts," were to be understood of the only-begotten Son of God and of the Holy Spirit. And we think that that expression also which occurs in the hymn of Habakkuk [3:2]: "In the midst of the two living beings wilt Thou be known," ought to be understood of Christ and the Holy Spirit. For all knowledge of the Father is obtained by revelation of the Son through the Holy Spirit, so that both of these beings which, according to the prophet, are called either "living things" or "lives," exist as the ground of the knowledge of God the Father. . . . We are not, however, to suppose that the Spirit derives His knowledge through revelation from the Son. For if the Holy Spirit knows the Father through the Son's revelation, He passes from a state of ignorance into one of knowledge; but it is alike impious and foolish to confess the Holy Spirit, and yet to ascribe to Him ignorance. For even though something else existed before the Holy Spirit, it was not by progressive advancement that He came to be the Holy Spirit; as if any one should venture to say that at the time when He was not yet the Holy Spirit He was ignorant of the Father, but that after He had received knowledge He was made the Holy Spirit. For if this were the

[3] Origen, *De Principiis* I 3 iii, in *ibid.,* vol. 4, p. 252.

case, the Holy Spirit would never be reckoned in the Unity of the Trinity.

[One] who is regenerated by God unto salvation has to do with Father and Son and Holy Spirit, and does not obtain salvation unless with the co-operation of the entire Trinity; it is impossible to become a partaker of the Father or the Son without the Holy Spirit. . . . I am of the opinion that the working of the Father and of the Son takes place as well in saints as in sinners, in rational beings and in dumb animals; nay, even in those things which are without life, and in all things universally which exist; but that the operation of the Holy Spirit does not take place at all in those things which are without life, or in those which, although living, are yet dumb; nay, is not found even in those who are endued indeed with reason but are engaged in evil courses and not at all converted to a better life. In those persons alone do I think that the operation of the Holy Spirit takes place who are already turning to a better life, and walking along the way which leads to Jesus Christ, i. e., who are engaged in the performance of good actions and who abide in God. . . . All who are rational beings are partakers of the Word, i. e., of reason, and by this means bear certain seeds, implanted within them, of wisdom and justice, which is Christ. Now, in Him who truly exists, and who said by Moses: "I am who I am," all things, whatever they are, participate. . . . the Spirit of God is taken away from all who are unworthy. . . . He will take up His dwelling, not in all men, nor in those who are flesh, but in those whose land has been renewed. Lastly, for this reason the grace and revelation of the Holy Spirit was bestowed by the imposition of the apostles' hands after baptism. Our Saviour after the resurrection, when old things had already passed away and all things had become new . . . says: "Receive the Holy Spirit." This is doubtless what the Lord the Saviour meant to convey in the Gospel when He said that new wine cannot be put into old bottles, but commanded that the bottles should be made new, i. e., that men should walk in newness of life, that they might receive the new wine, i. e., that newness of grace of the Holy Spirit. In this manner, then, is the working of the power of God the Father and of the Son extended without distinction to every creature; but a share in the Holy Spirit we find possessed only by the saints. . . . The grace of the Holy Ghost [is] present that those beings which are not holy in their essence may be rendered holy by participating in it. Seeing, then, that firstly, they derive their existence from God the Father; secondly, their rational nature from the Word;

thirdly, their holiness from the Holy Spirit—those who have been previously sanctified by the Holy Spirit are again made capable of receiving Christ in respect that He is the righteousness of God, and those who have earned advancement to this grade by the sanctification of the Holy Spirit will then obtain the gift of wisdom according to the power and working of the Spirit of God.... That this may be the case and that those whom He has created may be unceasingly and inseparably present with HIM WHO IS, it is the business of wisdom to instruct and train them and to bring them to perfection by confirmation of his Holy Spirit and unceasing sanctification, by which alone they are capable of receiving God. In this way, then, by the renewal of the ceaseless working of Father, Son, and Holy Spirit in us, in its various stages of progress, we shall be able at some future time perhaps, although with difficulty, to behold the holy and the blessed life.[4]

The chief advent of the Holy Spirit is declared to men after the ascension of Christ to heaven rather than before His coming into the world. For, before that, it was upon the prophets alone and upon a few individuals—if there happened to be any among the people who deserved it—that the gift of the Holy Spirit was conferred.... By the grace, then, of the Holy Spirit, along with numerous other results, this most glorious consequence is clearly demonstrated, that with regard to those things which were written in the prophets or in the law of Moses, it was only a few persons at that time ... who were able to look beyond the mere corporeal meaning and discover something greater, i. e., something spiritual; ... but now there are countless multitudes of believers who, although unable to unfold methodically and clearly the results of their spiritual understanding, are nevertheless most firmly persuaded that neither ought circumcision to be understood literally, nor the rest of the Sabbath, nor the pouring out of the blood of an animal, nor that answers were given by God to Moses on these points. And this method of apprehension is undoubtedly suggested to the minds of all by the power of the Holy Spirit.

And as there are many ways of apprehending Christ ... so also I think it is with the Holy Spirit, in whom is contained every kind of gifts. For on some is bestowed by the Spirit the word of wisdom, on others the word of knowledge, on others faith; and so to each

[4] *De Principiis* I 3 iv-viii, in *ibid.,* pp. 253-255.

individual of those who are capable of receiving Him, the Spirit Himself is made to be that quality, or understood to be that which is needed by the individual who has deserved to participate.[5]

I think the wonders wrought by Jesus are a proof of the Holy Spirit's having then appeared in the form of a dove, although Celsus, from a desire to cast discredit upon them, alleges that He performed only what He had learned among the Egyptians. . . . And there are still preserved among Christians traces of that Holy Spirit which appeared in the form of a dove. They expel evil spirits and perform many cures and foresee certain events according to the will of the Logos. And although Celsus . . . may treat with mockery what I am going to say, I shall say it nevertheless: that many have been converted to Christianity as if against their will, some sort of spirit having suddenly transformed their minds from a hatred of the doctrine to a readiness to die in its defence, and having appeared to them either in a waking vision or a dream of the night. Many such instances have we known, which, if we were to commit to writing, although they were seen and witnessed by ourselves, we should afford great occasion for ridicule to unbelievers, who would imagine that we . . . [had] invented such things. But God is witness of our conscientious desire, not by false statements, but by testimonies of different kinds, to establish the divinity of the doctrine of Jesus.[6]

Moreover, the Holy Spirit gave signs of His presence at the beginning of Christ's ministry, and after His ascension He gave still more; but since that time these signs have diminished, although there are still traces of His presence in a few who have had their souls purified by the Gospel, and their actions regulated by its influence.[7]

---

[5] *De Principiis* II 7 i-iii, in *ibid.*, pp. 284-285.
[6] *Against Celsus* I 46, in *ibid.*, pp. 415-416.
[7] *Against Celsus* VII 8, in *ibid.*, p. 614.

15

Novatian

(c. 200–258)

The first Latin writer of the Roman Church, Novatian was also a
rigorist and opponent of the laxness which he felt to be creeping into
the church during the pontificate of Pope Cornelius. Novatian's
thinking was that of an earlier stage of the church's life; he had not yet
conceived the idea of the divine personhood of the Holy Spirit. But he
is a trustworthy witness to the experience of the Spirit, at least among
the "conservatives" of his time.

He is therefore one and the same Spirit who was in the prophets and
apostles, except that in the former He was occasional, in the latter
always. But in the former not as being always in them, in the latter as
abiding always in them; in the former distributed with reserve, in the
latter all poured out; in the former given sparingly, in the latter
liberally bestowed. . . . This is He who strengthened their hearts and
minds, who marked out the Gospel sacraments, who was in them the
enlightener of divine things; and they being strengthened, feared, for
the sake of the Lord's name, neither dungeons nor chains, nay, even
trod under foot the very powers of the world and its tortures, since
they were henceforth armed and strengthened by the same Spirit,
having in themselves the gifts which this same Spirit distributes and

appropriates to the Church, the spouse of Christ, as he ornaments her. This is He who places prophets in the Church, instructs teachers, directs tongues, gives powers and healings, does wonderful works, offers discrimination of spirits, affords powers of government, suggests counsels, and orders and arranges whatever other gifts there are of *charismata;* and thus makes the Lord's Church everywhere, and in all, perfected and completed.

. . . An inhabitant given for our bodies and an effector of their holiness, Who, working in us for eternity, can also produce our bodies at the resurrection of immortality, accustoming them to be associated in Himself with heavenly power, and to be allied with the divine eternity of the Holy Spirit. For our bodies are both trained in Him and by Him to advance to immortality, by learning to govern themselves with moderation according to His decrees. . . . This is He who restrains insatiable desires, controls immoderate lusts, quenches unlawful fires, conquers reckless impulses, repels drunkenness, checks avarice, drives away luxurious revellings, links love, binds together affections, keeps down sects, orders the rule of truth, overcomes heretics, turns out the wicked, guards the Gospel. . . . This is he who in the apostles gives testimony to Christ; in the martyrs shows forth the constant faithfulness of their religion; in virgins restrains the admirable continency of their sealed chastity; in others guards the laws of the Lord's doctrine incorrupt and uncontaminated; destroys heretics, corrects the perverse, condemns infidels, makes known pretenders; moreover, rebukes the wicked, keeps the Church uncorrupt and inviolate in the sanctity of a perpetual virginity and truth.[1]

---

[1] Novatian, *Treatise Concerning the Trinity* 29, in *Ante-Nicene Fathers,* ed. J. Donaldson, rev. American edition, A. C. Coxe (Oxford, 1885; republished in Grand Rapids: William B. Eerdmans Company), vol. 5, pp. 640-641.

16

Eusebius of Caesarea

(c. 260–c. 340)

Eusebius was the "court theologian" of the first Christian emperor, Constantine, and the chief proponent of Roman civil religion. The fact that Eusebius was among the moderate Arian party at the Council of Nicaea, which Emperor Constantine himself convoked in 325, and thus on the losing side in the theological debate did not diminish Eusebius's faithfulness to his emperor, whom he considered God's agent for the salvation of the persecuted churches. Eusebius rode the crest of his religious and political association with Constantine as high as it would carry him and repaid the emperor, after his death in 337, with the writing of the Life of Constantine, *a book after the style of the Old Testament Chronicler in which Constantine's victories are described as victories of and for God. In line with this official theology of the Empire, Eusebius's portrayal of the Council of Nicaea (325) as a second and better Pentecost shows how he conceived of the Spirit's ability to work through political powers and structures, even though Eusebius himself did not particularly agree with the dogmatic conclusion of the Council.*

Resolved, therefore, to bring as it were a divine array against this enemy, [Constantine] convoked a general council, and invited the speedy attendance of bishops from all quarters, in letters expressive of the honourable estimation in which he held them. . . . Now when they were all assembled, it appeared evident that the proceeding was the work of God, inasmuch as men who had been most widely separated, not merely in sentiment, but also personally, and by difference of country, place and nation, were here brought together and comprised within the walls of a single city, forming as it were a vast garland of priests, composed of a variety of the choicest flowers.

In effect, the most distinguished of God's ministers from all the churches which abounded in Europe, Africa, and Asia were here assembled. And a single house of prayer, as though divinely enlarged, sufficed to contain at once Syrians and Cilicians, Phoenicians and Arabians, delegates from Palestine, and others from Egypt; Thebans and Libyans, with those who came from Mesopotamia. A Persian bishop too was present at this conference, nor was even a Scythian found wanting to the number. Pontus, Galatia and Pamphylia, Cappadocia, Asia, and Phrygia [cf. Acts 2:9-10] furnished their most distinguished prelates; while those who dwelt in the remotest districts of Thrace and Macedonia, of Achaia and Epirus were notwithstanding in attendance. Even from Spain itself, one whose fame was widely spread [Hosius of Cordoba] took his seat as an individual in the great assembly. The prelate of the Imperial City was prevented from attending by extreme old age; but his presbyters were present and supplied his place. Constantine is the first prince of any age who bound together such a garland as this with the bond of peace and presented it to Christ his Saviour as a thank-offering for the victories he had obtained over every foe, thus exhibiting in our own times a similitude of the apostolic company.

For it is said that in the Apostles' age, devout men were gathered from every nation under heaven; among whom were Parthians and Medes and Elamites and the dwellers in Mesopotamia and in Judea and Cappadocia, in Pontus and Asia, Phrygia and Pamphylia, in Egypt, and the parts of Libya about Cyrene; and strangers of Rome, Jews and proselytes, Cretes and Arabians [Acts 2:9-10]. Now the defect of that assembly was that not all who composed it were ministers of God: but in the present company, the number of bishops exceeded two hundred and fifty, while that of the presbyters and deacons in their train and the crowd of acolytes and other attendants was altogether beyond computation.

Of these ministers of God, some were distinguished by wisdom and eloquence, others by the gravity of their lives and by patient fortitude of character, while others against united in themselves all these grace. . . .[1]

After the decision of the Council was heard, Constantine promulgated its definition as law:

Receive, then, with all willingness this truly divine injunction and regard it as the gift of God. For whatever is determined in the holy assemblies of the bishops is to be regarded as indicative of the Divine will.[2]

---

[1] Eusebius Pamphilus, *The Life of the Blessed Emperor Constantine* (London: Samuel Bagster and Sons, 1845), bk. III, chapters 6-9, pp. 119-121.

[2] *Ibid.,* chapter 20, p. 132.

17

Athanasius of Alexandria

(296–373)

Athanasius was the theologian at the Council of Nicaea in 325 whose understanding of the Trinity, that the Son is of the same substance (homoousios) *with the Father, became the official teaching of the church. Later, as bishop of Alexandria, Athanasius in 367 was the first to list the twenty-seven book canon of the New Testament as we now receive it. His theological opponents, the Arians, who taught that the Son is lesser in nature than the Father and therefore a creature rather than God himself, also extended their understanding to the Holy Spirit. Athanasius, writing to Sarapion (359/360), a fellow bishop in exile, opposes the teaching of the Tropici, a group of theological thinkers of whom nothing else is known except what may be gathered concerning them from these four letters of Athanasius. They are, however, to be classed along with the Semiarians or Pneumatomachi ("those who fight against the Spirit") or Macedonians who were anathematized in 381 at the First Council of Constantinople for refusing to confess that the Holy Spirit, like the Son, is "homoousios" with the Father. These letters of Athanasius represent an important stage in the development of Christian thought about the Holy Spirit between the Council of Nicaea (325), when belief in the Holy Spirit was merely affirmed, and the First Council of*

Constantinople (381), when the view of Athanasius and others such as Didymus the Blind of Alexandria and the Cappadocian Fathers, was officially promulgated. Athanasius wrote these letters during his third exile, under persecution for his faith that the Son and the Holy Spirit, with the Father, are God.

Certain persons, having forsaken the Arians on account of their blasphemy against the Son of God, yet oppose the Holy Spirit, saying that He is not only a creature, but actually one of the ministering spirits, and differs from the angels only in degree . . . as the Arians in denying the Son deny also the Father, so also these men in speaking evil of the Holy Spirit speak evil also of the Son.[1]

What doctrine of God is this, which compounds him out of creator and creature? Either he is not a Triad, but a dyad with the creature left over, or, if he be Triad—as indeed he is!—then how do they class the Spirit who belongs to the Triad with the creatures which come after the Triad? . . . If they thought correctly of the Word, they would think soundly of the Spirit also, who proceeds from the Father, and, belonging to the Son, is given from him to the disciples and all who believe in him.[2]

Moses too knew that the angels are creatures and that the Holy Spirit is united with the Son and the Father. For when God said to him: "Depart . . . out of the land of Egypt . . . and I will send my angel before thy face . . . ," he refused him, saying: "If thou goest not with us thyself, carry me not up hence." [Exodus 33:15] For he did not desire a creature to lead the people, lest they should learn to worship the creature beyond God who created all things. So, of course, he refused the angel, and besought God himself to lead them. . . . When God promised to lead them, lo! he promises no longer to send an angel, but the Spirit who is above the angels, and he leads the people. He shows that the Spirit does not belong to the creature nor is he an angel, but is above the creation, united to the Godhead of the Father. For it was God himself who, through the Word, in the Spirit, led the people.[3]

It is madness to call him a creature. If he were a creature, he would not

[1] C. R. B. Shapland, *The Letters of Saint Athanasius Concerning the Holy Spirit* (London: The Epworth Press, 1951), pp. 59-60.

[2] *Ibid.,* pp. 63-65.

[3] *Ibid.,* pp. 89-90.

be ranked with the Triad. For the whole Triad is one God. It is enough to know that the Spirit is not a creature, nor is he numbered with the things that are made. For nothing foreign is mixed with the Triad; it is indivisible and consistent. These things are sufficient for the faithful. Thus far human knowledge goes.[4]

But [the Tropici] proclaiming out of the abundance of their own heart: "If he is not a creature nor one of the angels, but proceeds from the Father, then he is himself also a son, and he and the Word are two brothers. And if he is a brother, how is the Word only-begotten? How is it then that they are not equal, but the one is named after the Father and the other after the Son? How, if he is from the Father, is he not also said to be begotten or called son, but just Holy Spirit? But if the Spirit is of the Son, then the Father is the Spirit's grandfather." Thus the wretches make mock, like busybodies desiring to "search the deep things of God" which "no one knows but the Spirit of God," against whom they speak evil.[5]

Just as we cannot ascribe a father to the Father, so neither can we ascribe a brother to the Son. Other than the Father, as we have written already, there is no God; there is no other Son than the Son, for he is only begotten. Hence the Father, being One and Only, is Father of a Son who is One and Only.... For the Spirit is not given the name of son in the scriptures, lest he be taken for a brother; nor son of the Son, lest the Father be thought to be a grandfather. But the Son is called Son of the Father, and the Spirit of the Father is called Spirit of the Son. Thus the Godhead of the holy Triad and faith therein is one.[6]

The Father is always Father, and the Son always Son, and the Holy Spirit is and is called always Holy Spirit. In human relations it is not so, despite the Arians' delusions, ... For in the case of men the father is not always a father nor the son always a son. The same man becomes father of a son who was himself another's son; and the son, being his father's son, becomes another's father. Abraham, for example, being son of Nahor, became father of Isaac; and Isaac, being son of Abraham, became father of Jacob. ... But with the

---

[4] *Ibid.*, pp. 103-104.
[5] *Ibid.*, pp. 95-98.
[6] *Ibid.*, pp. 99-101, 103.

Godhead it is not so. . . . Thus the Father is not from a father; wherefore he begets not one who should become another's father. Nor is the Son a part of the Father; wherefore he is not a thing begotten to beget a son.[7]

As then the Father is light and the Son is his radiance . . . we may see in the Son the Spirit also by whom we are enlightened. . . . But when we are enlightened by the Spirit, it is Christ who in him enlightens us. . . . Again, as the Father is fountain and the Son is called river, we are said to drink of the Spirit. . . . But when we are made to drink of the Spirit, we drink of Christ. . . . Again, as Christ is true Son, so we, when we receive the Spirit, are made sons. . . . But if by the Spirit we are made sons, it is clear that it is in Christ we are called children of God . . . as the Son is Wisdom, so we, receiving the Spirit of Wisdom, have the Son and are made wise in him.[8]

But if there is such coordination and unity within the holy Triad, who can separate either the Son from the Father, or the Spirit from the Son or from the Father himself? Who would be so audacious as to say that the Triad is unlike itself and diverse in nature, or that the Son is in essence foreign from the Father, or the Spirit alien from the Son? But how are these things? . . . How, when the Spirit is in us, the Son is said to be in us? How, when the Son is in us, the Father is said to be in us? Or how, when it is truly a Triad, the Triad is described as one? Or why, when the One is in us, the Triad is said to be in us? . . . first divide the radiance from the light, or wisdom from the wise.[9]

Again the Son is the Power of God and Lord of Glory, and the Spirit is called Spirit of Power and Glory. . . . In [the Spirit] the Word makes glorious the creation, and, by bestowing upon it divine life and sonship, draws it to the Father. But that which joins creation to the Word cannot belong to the creatures; and that which bestows sonship upon the creation could not be alien from the Son . . . he in whom creation is made divine cannot be outside the Godhead of the Father.[10]

The Father creates all things through the Word in the Spirit; for

[7] *Ibid.*, pp. 187-188.
[8] *Ibid.*, pp. 110-112.
[9] *Ibid.*, pp. 113-114.
[10] *Ibid.*, pp. 127 and 129.

where the Word is, there is the Spirit also, and the things which are created through the Word have their vital strength out of the Spirit from the Word.[11]

Thus the Spirit is not a creature but proper to the essence of the Word and proper to God in whom he is said to be.[12]

The creatures came from nothing, having a beginning from which they came into being. . . . The Holy Spirit is said to be from God. . . . That which is from God could not be from that which is not, nor could it be a creature. . . . Would it not be evil speech to call the Spirit, who is in God, a creature, him who searches even the deep things of God? For from this, the speaker will learn to say that the spirit of man is outside the man himself, and that the Word of God, who is in the Father, is a creature[13]

It is through the Spirit that we are all said to be partakers of God. . . . If he makes men divine, it is not to be doubted that his nature is of God.[14]

But beyond these sayings, let us look at the very tradition, teaching and faith of the Catholic Church from the beginning, which the Lord gave, the Apostles preached, and the Fathers kept. . . . There is, then, a triad, holy and complete, confessed to be God in Father, Son, and Holy Spirit, having nothing foreign or external mixed with it, not composed of one that creates and one that is created, but all creative. . . . The Father does all things through the Word in the Holy Spirit. Thus the unity of the holy Triad is preserved . . . this to be the faith of the Church: . . . the Lord when sending forth the Apostles, he ordered them to lay this foundation for the Church. . . . "baptizing them in the name of the Father and of the Son and of the Holy Spirit." The Apostles went, and thus they taught; and this is the preaching that extends to the whole Church which is under heaven. . . .[15]

He who takes away anything from the Triad, and is baptized in the name of the Father alone, or in the name of the Son alone, or in the Father and the Son without the Holy Spirit, receives nothing, but remains ineffective and uninitiated. . . . he who divides the Son from

[11] *Ibid.,* p. 174.
[12] *Ibid.,* p. 184.
[13] *Ibid.,* p. 121.
[14] *Ibid.,* pp. 125 and 127.
[15] *Ibid.,* pp. 133-136.

the Father or who reduces the Spirit to the level of the creatures has neither the Son nor the Father but is without God, worse than an unbeliever and anything but a Christian.[16]

In these terms the catholic faith is expressed. But as for those who speak evil of the Spirit and call him a creature, if what we have said does not make them repent, then may what we are about to say overwhelm them with shame. If there is a Triad, and if the faith is faith in a Triad, let them tell us whether it was always a Triad, or whether there was once when it was not a Triad. If the Triad is eternal, the Spirit is not a creature, for he coexists eternally with the Word and is in him. As for the creatures, there was a time when they were not. If he is a creature, and the creatures are from nothing, it is clear that there was once when the Triad was not a Triad but a dyad. What greater impiety can man utter? They are saying that the Triad owes its existence to alteration and progress; that it was a dyad, and waited for the birth of a creature which should be ranked with the Father and the Son, and with them become the Triad. God forbid that such a notion should so much as enter the minds of Christian people! As the Son, because he always exists, is not a creature, so, because the Triad always exists, there is no creature in it: Therefore the Spirit is not a creature. As it always was, so it now is; as it now is, so it always was. It is the Triad, and therein Father, Son and Holy Spirit. And God is one, the Father, who is "over all and through all and in all," who is "blessed for ever. Amen."[17]

---

[16] *Ibid.,* pp. 139-140.
[17] *Ibid.,* p. 177.

18

Hilary of Poitiers

(c. 315–c. 367)

When Hilary was exiled from France to Phrygia by the Arian Emperor, Constantius II, he came in contact with the Eastern theologians and their writings. He thus became a connecting link between East and West and a source in Western Christian thought of Eastern ideas. He was a defender of Nicene Orthodoxy and of Athanasius. This excerpt shows his grasp of the connection between dogmatic theology and spiritual experience.

The Lord said [to the woman of Samaria] that the time had come when God should be worshipped neither on mountain nor in temple. For Spirit cannot be cabined or confined; it is omnipresent in space and time, and under all conditions present in its fulness. . . . The words, *God is Spirit,* do not alter the fact that the Holy Spirit has a Name of His own, and that He is the Gift to us.

For the Holy Ghost is everywhere One, enlightening all patriarchs and prophets and the whole company of the Law, inspiring John even in his mother's womb, given in due time to the Apostles and other believers, that they might recognize the truth vouchsafed them. . . .

[The Paraclete-sayings in *John*] were spoken to show how multitudes should enter the kingdom of heaven; they contain an assurance of the goodwill of the Giver, and of the mode and terms of the Gift. They tell how, because our feeble minds cannot comprehend the Father or the Son, our faith, which finds God's incarnation hard of credence, shall be illumined by the gift of the Holy Ghost, the Bond of union and the Source of light.

The next step naturally is to listen to the Apostle's account of the powers and functions of this Gift. [Romans 8:14, 15; 1 Corinthians 12:3-11] Here we have a statement of the purpose and results of the Gift; and I cannot conceive what doubt can remain, after so clear a definition of His Origin, His action, and His power.

Let us therefore make use of this great benefit, and seek for personal experience of this most needful Gift. . . . We receive Him, then, that we máy know. Faculties of the human body, if denied their exercise, will lie dormant. The eye without light, natural or artificial, cannot fulfil its office; the ear will be ignorant of its function unless some voice or sound be heard; the nostrils, unconscious of their purpose, unless some scent be breathed. Not that the faculty will be absent, because it is never called into use, but that there will be no experience of its existence. So, too, the soul of man unless through faith it have appropriated the gift of the Spirit, will have the innate faculty of apprehending God, but be destitute of the light of knowledge. That Gift, which is in Christ, is One, yet offered and offered fully, to all; denied to none, and given to each according to the measure of his willingness to receive; its stores the richer, the more earnest the desire to earn them. This gift is with us unto the end of the world; the solace of our waiting; the assurance, by the favors which He bestows, of the hope that shall be ours; the light of our minds; the sun of our souls. This Holy Spirit we must seek and must earn, and then hold fast by faith and obedience to the commands of God.[1]

[1] Hilary, *On the Trinity* II, 31, 32, 33, 34, 35 in *Nicene and Post-Nicene Fathers,* second series, P. Schaff and H. Wace, editors (Edinburgh: T. and T. Clark, 1887; republished in Grand Rapids: William B. Eerdmans Company), vol. 9, pp. 60-61.

19

Basil of Caesarea

(c. 329–379)

A man of outstanding qualifications, Basil of Caesarea was the aristocratic doctor of the ancient church whose defense of Nicene orthodoxy against his former teacher, the Pneumatomachian Eustathius of Sebaste, epitomizes orthodoxy on the Holy Spirit for the fourth century. He is called the "doctor of the Spirit." Traces of the philosophy of Plotinus are evident in the work as is the conscious acknowledgment that the tradition of the church is to be seen as definitive along with scripture of the articles of Christian faith.

Let us now investigate what are our common conceptions concerning the Spirit, as well those which have been gathered by us from Holy Scripture concerning It as those which we have received from the unwritten tradition of the Fathers. First of all we ask, who on hearing the titles of the Spirit is not lifted up in soul, who does not raise his conception to the supreme nature? . . . Its proper and peculiar title is "Holy Spirit," which is a name specially appropriate to everything incorporeal, purely immaterial and indivisible. So our Lord, when teaching the woman who thought God to be an object of local worship that the incorporeal is incomprehensible, said: "God is a spirit" [John 4:24]. On our hearing, then, of a spirit, it is impossible to form the idea of a nature circumscribed, subject to change and variation, or at all like the creature. We are compelled to advance in our conceptions to the highest, and to think of an intelligent essence, in power infinite, in magnitude unlimited, unmeasured by times or ages, generous of It's [sic] good gifts, to whom turn all things needing sanctification, after whom reach all things that live in virtue, as being watered by It's [sic] inspiration and helped on toward their natural and proper end; perfecting all other things, but Itself in nothing lacking; living not as needing restoration, but as Supplier of life; not growing by additions, but straightway full, self-established, omnipresent, origin of sanctification, light perceptible to the mind, supplying, as it were, through Itself, illumination to every faculty in the search for truth; by nature unapproachable, apprehended by reason of goodness, filling all things with Its power, but communicated only to the worthy; not shared in one measure, but distributing Its energy according to "the proportion of faith"; in essence simple, in powers various, wholly present in each and being wholly everywhere; impassively divided, shared without loss of ceasing to be entire, after the likeness of the sunbeam, whose kindly light falls on him who enjoys it as though it shone for him alone, yet illumines land and sea and mingles with the air. So, too, is the Spirit to every one who receives It, as though given to him alone, and yet It sends forth grace sufficient and full for all mankind, and is enjoyed by all who share It, according to the capacity, not of Its power, but of their nature. . . .

Shining upon those that are cleansed from every spot, He makes them spiritual by fellowship with Himself. Just as when a sunbeam falls on bright and transparent bodies, they themselves become brilliant too, and shed forth a fresh brightness from themselves, so souls wherein the Spirit dwells, illuminated by the Spirit, themselves become spiritual, and send forth their grace to others. Hence comes foreknowledge of the future, understanding of mysteries, apprehension of what is hidden, distribution of good gifts, the heavenly citizenship, a place in the chorus of angels, joy without end, abiding in God, the being made like to God, and, highest of all, the being made God.[1]

Whence is it that we are Christians? Through our faith, would be the

---

[1] Basil, *On the Holy Spirit* 9, in *Nicene and Post-Nicene Fathers,* second series, P. Schaff and H. Wace, editors (Edinburgh: T. and T. Clark, 1887; republished in Grand Rapids: William B. Eerdmans Company), vol. 8, pp. 15-16.

universal answer. And in what way are we saved? Plainly because we were regenerate through the grace given in our baptism.[2] Baptism then symbolically signifies the putting off of the works of the flesh. . . . And there is, as it were, a cleansing of the soul from filth. . . . For this cause the Lord, who is the Dispenser of our life, gave us the covenant of baptism, containing a type of life and death, for the water fulfils the image of death and the Spirit gives us the earnest of life. Hence follows the answer to our question why the water was associated with the Spirit: the reason is because in baptism two ends were proposed. On the one hand, the destroying of the body of sin, that it may never bear fruit unto death; on the other hand, our living unto the Spirit and having our fruit in holiness; the water receiving the body as in a tomb figures death, while the Spirit pours in the quickening power, renewing our souls from the deadness of sin unto their original life. . . . It follows that if there is any grace in the water, it is not of the nature of the water but of the presence of the Spirit. . . .

Through the Holy Spirit comes our restoration to paradise, our ascension into the kingdom of heaven, our return to the adoption of sons, our liberty to call God our Father, our being made partakers of the grace of Christ, our being called children of light, our sharing in eternal glory, and, in a word, our being brought into a state of all "fulness of blessing," both in this world and in the world to come, of all the good gifts that are in store for us, by promise whereof, through faith, beholding the reflection of their grace as though they were already present, we await the full enjoyment. If such is the down-payment, what the perfection? If such the first fruits, what the complete fulfilment?[3]

What reason is there for robbing of [the Spirit's] share of glory Him Who is everywhere associated with the Godhead; in the confession of the Faith, in the baptism of redemption, in the working of miracles, in the indwelling of the saints, in the graces bestowed on obedience? There is not even one single gift which reaches creation without the Holy Ghost; when not even a single word can be spoken in defence of Christ except by them that are aided by the Spirit. . . .[4]

[2] *On the Holy Spirit* 10, in *ibid.,* p. 17.
[3] *On the Holy Spirit* 15, in *ibid.,* pp. 21-22.
[4] *On the Holy Spirit* 24, in *ibid.,* p. 35.

20

John Chrysostom

(c. 349–407)

The most famous preacher of the ancient church, Chrysostom, was a man of upright moral life, reformer's zeal, and a student and interpreter of scripture in the Antiochene tradition. His sermons almost always reflect his concern for encouraging his hearers to more loving, more heroic, more moral Christian living. Though Chrysostom had himself lived as a hermit monk, he gives little evidence of awareness of extraordinary spiritual charismation. As bishop of Constantinople, he spent the latter years of his life struggling with the Empress Eudoxia and conniving bishops; imperial and episcopal intrigues were a context in which the gifts of the Spirit were unwelcome.

On I Cor. 12:1-2:
This whole place is very obscure; but the obscurity is produced by our ignorance of the facts referred to, and by their cessation, being such as then used to occur, but now no longer take place. And why do they not happen now? Why look now, the cause, too, of the obscurity hath produced us again another question; namely, why did they happen then, and now do so no more? . . . Well, what did happen then? Whoever was baptized he straightway spoke with tongues and not

with tongues only, but many also prophesied, and some also performed many other wonderful works. For since on their coming over from idols, without any clear knowledge, or training in the ancient Scriptures, they at once on their baptism received the Spirit, yet the Spirit they saw not, for It is invisible; therefore God's grace bestowed some sensible proof of that energy. And one straightway spoke in the Persian, another in the Roman, another in the Indian, another in some other such tongue; and this made manifest to them that were without that it is the Spirit in the very person speaking.[1]

But the miracles, perhaps, are what ye seek after, such as they wrought when they entered in; the lepers cleansed, the devils driven out, and the dead raised? Nay, but this is the great indication of your high birth, and of your love, that ye should believe God without pledges. And in fact this, and one other thing, were the reasons why God made miracles to cease. I mean, that if when miracles are not performed, they that plume themselves on other advantages,—for instance, either on the word of wisdom, or on show of piety,—grow vainglorious, are puffed up, are separated from one another; did miracles also take place, how could there but be violent rendings? And that what I say is not mere conjecture, the Corinthians bear witness, who from this cause were divided into many parties.

Do not thou therefore see signs, but the soul's health. Seek not to see one dead man raised; nay, for thou hast learnt that the whole world is arising. Seek not to see a blind man healed, but behold all now restored unto that better and more profitable sight; and do thou too learn to look chastely, and amend thine eye.

For in truth, if we all lived as we ought, workers of miracles would not be admired so much as we by the children of the heathen. For as to the signs, they often carry with them either a notion of mere fancy, or another evil suspicion, although ours be not such. But a pure life cannot admit of any such reproach; yea, all men's mouths are stopped by the acquisition of virtue. . . .

But if thou wouldest work miracles also, be rid of transgressions, and thou hast quite accomplished it. Yea, for sin is a great demon, beloved; and if thou exterminate this, thou hast wrought a greater thing than they who drive out ten thousand demons. . . . as to

---

[1] *The Homilies of St. John Chrysostom on I Corinthians,* Homily # 29, in *Nicene and Post-Nicene Fathers,* series 1, P. Schaff and H. Wace, editors (Edinburgh: T. and T. Clark, 1887; republished in Grand Rapids: William B. Eerdmans Company), vol. 12, p. 168.

miracles, they oftentimes, while they profited another, have injured him who had the power, by lifting him up to pride and vainglory, or haply in some other way. . . .

These then let us perform with much diligence. For if thou change from inhumanity to almsgiving, thou hast stretched forth the hand that was withered. If thou withdraw from theatres and go to the church, thou hast cured the lame foot. If thou draw back thine eyes from an harlot, and from beauty not thine own, thou hast opened them when they were blind. If instead of satanical songs, thou hast learned spiritual psalms, being dumb, thou hast spoken.

These are the greatest miracles, these the wonderful signs.[2]

[2] Homily # 32, in *ibid.,* vol. 10, pp. 218-219.

21

Augustine of Hippo

(354–430)

Augustine is the greatest theologian and teacher of the ancient church. His was the dominant theological point of view throughout the Middle Ages and into the Reformation period. He continues to hold fascination for modern Christians. In his reflections on the Trinity, while accepting the conclusions of Niceno-Constantinopolitan orthodoxy and the theological results of the Greek. church, Augustine changes the topic of conversation from a discussion of the Trinity understood in terms of its ontological unity to a discussion of the Trinity as a relationship between three equal persons. In so doing, he makes place for the first extensive development of the special activity of the Holy Spirit within the life of God as the communion of mutual love between the Father and the Son. Augustine's moral preoccupation contributes to his elaboration of the work of the Holy Spirit since, in terms of his understanding of the memory, intellect, and will in the human psyche as vestiges of God's trinitarian being in whose image and likeness the person is created, the Holy Spirit is likened to the faculty of the will. Because the will is the source of a person's obedience to and love of God and the neighbor, the Holy Spirit is seen to be the person of the Trinity operative in renewing the human person's moral faculty so that the person can become obedient to God's law by the Spirit's pouring out the love of God in the human heart. This grasp of God's immediate activity in the life of the believer through the Holy Spirit in connection with his understanding of justification by grace according to God's eternal decree of election is the point at which the Protestant Reformation made the greatest use of Augustine's thought.

Augustine was also aware of the charismating activity of the Spirit in his time, although for him as for other medieval Christians, the miraculous and wonderful activity of God came to be related to the actions of the saints themselves rather than to the Source of their charismatic powers. In his stress on the proper work of the Spirit as pouring out love into our hearts (Romans 5:5), Augustine all but identifies the Holy Spirit with love (charity) itself, thus loosing somewhat his grasp of the unique personhood of the Spirit. Augustine specifically denies the continuity in the church of the charisma of tongues (although he admits of other miraculous activities), supporting his argument with the evidence that infants do not speak in tongues when they are baptized. Augustine gives an allegorical interpretation of the first-century gift of tongues which indicates that he did not understand that particular charisma of the Spirit.

The Holy Spirit is a certain unutterable communion of the Father and the Son. . . . He Himself is called specially that which they are called in common; because both the Father is a spirit and the Son is a spirit, both the Father is holy and the Son is holy. In order, therefore, that the communion of both may be signified from a name which is suitable to both, the Holy Spirit is called the gift of both.[1] . . .

The Spirit is both the Spirit of God who gave Him and ours who have received Him. . . . The Father and the Son are a Beginning of the Holy Spirit, not two Beginnings; but as the Father and Son are one God and one Creator and one Lord relative to the creature, so are they one Beginning relative to the Holy Spirit. But the Father, the Son, and the Holy Spirit is one Beginning in respect to the creature, as also one Creator and one God.[2]

Therefore, the Holy Spirit, whatever it is, is something common both

---

[1] Augustine, *On the Trinity* V 11 xii, in *Nicene and Post-Nicene Fathers*, series 1, P. Schaff and H. Wace, editors (Edinburgh: T & T Clark; 1887; republished in Grand Rapids: William B. Eerdmans Company), vol. 3, p. 93.

[2] *On the Trinity* V. 14 xv, in *ibid.*, p. 95.

to the Father and Son. But that communion itself is consubstantial and co-eternal; and if it may fitly be called friendship, let it be so called; but it is more aptly called love. And this is also a substance, since God is a substance, and "God is love," as it is written.[3]. . . The Holy Spirit, according to the Holy Scriptures, is neither of the Father alone, nor of the Son alone, but of both; and so intimates to us a mutual love wherewith the Father and the Son reciprocally love one another. . . . As then we call the only Word of God specially by the name of Wisdom, although universally both the Holy Spirit and the Father Himself is wisdom, so the Holy Spirit is specially called by the name of Love, although universally both the Father and the Son are love.[4]

God the Holy Spirit, who proceedeth from the Father, when He has been given to man, inflames him to the love of God and of his neighbor, and is Himself love. For man has not whence to love God unless from God; and therefore he says a little after: "Let us love him because he first loved us."[1 John 4:19] The Apostle Paul, too, says: "The love of God is shed abroad in our hearts by the Holy Spirit, which is given to us." [Romans 5:5]

There is no gift of God more excellent than this. It alone distinguishes the sons of the eternal kingdom and the sons of eternal perdition. Other gifts, too, are given by the Holy Spirit, but without love they profit nothing. . . . Love, therefore, which is of God and is God, is specially the Holy Spirit, by whom the love of God is shed abroad in our hearts, by which love the whole Trinity dwells in us. And therefore most rightly is the Holy Spirit, although He is God, called also the gift of God. And by that gift what else can properly be understood except love, which brings to God, and without which any other gift of God whatsoever does not bring to God?[5]

The human will is divinely assisted to do the right in such manner that, besides man's creation with the endowment of freedom to choose, and besides the teaching by which he is instructed how he ought to live, he receives the Holy Spirit, whereby there arises in his

---

[3] *On the Trinity* VI 5 vii, in *ibid.,* p. 100.

[4] *On the Trinity* XV 17 xxvii, in *ibid.,* pp. 215-216.

[5] *On the Trinity* V 17-8 xxxi-xxxii, in *ibid.,* pp. 216-217. Augustine explains why the Holy Spirit is not a son of God in IX 12 xvii and why it is not the mother of the Son in XII 5 v.

soul the delight in and the love of God, the supreme and changeless God. This gift is his here and now, while he walks by faith, not yet by sight: that having this as earnest of God's free bounty, he may be fired in heart to cleave to his creator, kindled in mind to come within the shining of the true light; and thus receive from the source of his being the only real well-being. Free choice alone, if the way of truth is hidden, avails for nothing but sin; and when the right action and the true aim has begun to appear clearly, there is still no doing, no devotion, no good life, unless it be also delighted in and loved. And that it may be loved, the love of God is shed abroad in our hearts, not by the free choice whose spring is in ourselves, but through the Holy Spirit which is given us.

The good life is a divine gift: not only because God has given man the power of free choice, without which moral life were impossible; not only because he has given the commandment to teach us how to live; but because through the Holy Spirit he sheds abroad charity in the hearts of those whom he foreknew that he might predestinate, predestinated that he might call, called that he might justify, and justified that he might glorify. . . . The divine aid for the working of righteousness consists not in God's gift of the law, full as it is of good and holy commands, but in that our will itself, without which we cannot do the good, is aided and uplifted by the imparting of the Spirit of grace. Without that aid, the teaching is a letter that kills, since it rather holds men in the guilt of transgression than justifies the ungodly.

This is the Spirit of God by whose gift we are justified. Hereby it comes to pass in us that we find our delight in not sinning—which means liberty, whereas apart from the Spirit we find delight in sinning—which means servitude, from the works of which we are to abstain, that is, keep Sabbath in the spirit. That Holy Spirit, through whom charity which is the fulness of the law is shed abroad in our hearts, is also called in the Gospel the finger of God. That those tables of the law were written by the finger of God, and that the finger of God is God's Spirit through whom we are sanctified, so that living by faith we may do good works through love—how striking here is at once the agreement and the difference! . . .

In the Old Testament, the people is held back by a fearful dread from approaching the place where the law was given; whereas in the New the Holy Spirit comes upon those who were assembled together waiting for his promised coming. There the finger of God worked upon tables of stone: here upon the hearts of men. So there the law was set outside men to be a terror to the unjust: here it was given within them to be their justification. . . . Apart from the Spirit's aid, it is indubitably the letter that killeth: only when the life-giving Spirit is present does he cause to be written within, and loved, that which when it was written externally the law caused to be feared. . . .

It follows that the laws of God, written by God himself upon the heart, are nothing but the very presence of the Holy Spirit who is the finger of God; the presence by which charity, the fulness of the law and the end of the commandment, is shed abroad in our hearts.

As the apostle says: "Whether there be prophecies, they shall be brought to naught, whether there be tongues, they shall cease; whether there be knowledge, it shall be brought to nought." [1 Corinthians 13:8-10] He speaks of that knowledge of children in which our life here passes, a knowledge "in part, through a mirror darkly." For because of it prophecy is needed, while past still gives place to future; because of it there is use for tongues, the variety of meanings whereby one thing is conveyed by another in allegory to the mind that cannot yet contemplate in purity the eternal light of transparent truth. But "when that which is perfect has come," and all that is in part has been done away, then the Word, which took flesh to appear to flesh, shall show himself to his lovers; then it will be life eternal for us to know the one true God. . . .[6]

"And ye have no need that any man should teach you because his anointing teacheth you concerning all things.". . . You must not think that anyone learns from a man. The noise of our voice can be no more than a prompting; if there be no teacher within, that noise of ours is useless. Brethren, do you need that I should explain further? Have you not all heard this sermon? Yet how many will leave this place untaught! For my part, I have spoken to all; but those who hear not

[6] *On the Spirit and the Letter,* trans. and edited by Cyril C. Richardson in *Augustine: Later Works,* Vol. 8, The Library of Christian Classics (Philadelphia: The Westminster Press, 1953), pp. 197, 198. 199, 212, 216, 217, 219, 221, 225. Used by permission.

the inward speech of that same anointing, those whom the Holy Spirit teaches not inwardly, go home untaught. Outward teachings are but a kind of helps and promptings: the teacher of hearts has his chair in heaven. . . . Let him then speak to you within, when no man is there; indeed there may be no man in your heart, though a man be at your side. . . . Where that inspiration and that anointing are lacking, the noise of words from without is vain.[7]

At the Church's beginning the Holy Spirit fell upon the believers, and they spoke with tongues unlearnt, as the Spirit gave them utterance. It was a sign, fitted to the time: all the world's tongues were a fitting signification of the Holy Spirit, because the gospel of God was to have its course through every tongue in all parts of the earth. The sign was given, and then passed away. We no longer expect that those upon whom the hand is laid, that they may receive the Holy Spirit, will speak with tongues. When we laid our hand upon these "infants," the Church's new-born members, none of you (I think) looked to see if they would speak with tongues, or, seeing that they did not, had the perversity to argue that they had not received the Holy Spirit, for if they had received, they would have spoken with tongues as happened at the first. If then the Holy Spirit's presence is no longer testified by such marvels, on what is anyone to ground assurance that he has received the Holy Spirit? Let him enquire of his own heart: if he loves his brother, the Spirit of God abides in him . . . let him see if there is in him the love of peace and unity, love of the Church that is spread throughout all the world.[8]

Now put the question to every heretic: "Did Christ come in the flesh?" "He did: so I believe and confess." "Nay, but you deny it." "How so" . . . "You have not charity because you break up unity to do yourself honor."—Hence, then, you may know the Spirit that is of God. Tap with your finger on the earthenware vessel and see whether the sound it gives be cracked or false. See if it sounds true and whole: see if charity is there.[9]

For all who love not God are strangers, Antichrists. Though they enter our churches, they cannot be counted among the sons of God: that fountain of life belongs not to them. The evil man as well as the good can possess baptism; the evil man as well as the good can possess

---

[7] Augustine, *Homilies on I John,* in *ibid.,* p. 285.
[8] *Ibid.,* p. 308.
[9] *Ibid.,* p. 311.

the gift of prophecy; . . . The evil man as well as the good can receive the sacrament of the Body and Blood of the Lord; . . . The evil man as well as the good can have the name of Christ, can be called a Christian. . . . All these sacraments may be possessed by the evil man; but to have charity and be an evil man is not possible. This therefore is the peculiar gift of the Spirit: he is the one and only fountain. God's Spirit calls you to drink of it; God's Spirit calls you to drink of himself.[10]

Why, it is asked, do no miracles occur nowadays, such as occurred in former times? I could reply that they were necessary then, before the world came to believe, in order to win the world's belief. . . . In fact, many miracles have occurred, as we cannot deny, to testify to that one supreme miracle of salvation, the miracle of Christ's ascension into heaven in the flesh in which he rose from the dead. Those miracles are all recorded, as we know, in the Scriptures, which never lie. . . . And in fact, even now miracles are being performed in Christ's name either by his sacrament or by the prayers or the memorials of his saints, but they do not enjoy the blaze of publicity which would spread their fame with a glory to equal that of those earlier marvels.

The canon of holy Scripture, which had to be defined, ensured that those earlier miracles should be read everywhere, and should stick in the memory of the people everywhere, whereas the more recent examples, wherever they occur, are scarcely known to the whole community there, or even throughout the particular neighborhood. Even there only a very few know about them in most instances, and all the rest are quite unaware, especially if it is a city of any great size; and when the story comes to other places and other people it is not confirmed by sufficient authority to ensure ready or even hesitating acceptance, although faithful Christians pass the news on to others of the faithful.

A miracle that happened at Milan while I was there, when a blind man had his sight restored, succeeded in becoming more widely known because Milan is an important city, and because the emperor was there at the time. A great crowd had gathered to see the bodies of the martyrs Protasius and Gervasius, and the miracle took place before all those witnesses. Those bodies had been lost and nothing at all was known about them; but their hiding-place was revealed in a dream to Ambrose, bishop of Milan, and they were discovered. It was

[10] *Ibid.*, p. 315.

there that the darkness, in which the blind man had lived so long, was dispelled; and he saw the light of day.

Now what am I to do? I am constrained by my promise to complete this work, a promise which must be fulfilled; and that means that I cannot relate all the stories of miracles that I know. But I have no doubt that many of my Christian friends, on reading what I have written, will be grieved that I have omitted so much that is quite as familiar to them as to me. . . . If I decided to record merely the miracles of healing, to say nothing of other marvels, which were performed at Calama and at Hippo through this martyr, the glorious St. Stephen, the record would fill many books. . . . I have been concerned that such accounts should be published because I saw that signs of divine power like those older days were frequently occurring in modern times too, and I felt that they should not pass into oblivion, unnoticed by the people in general. It is not yet two years since the shrine we have been speaking of was established at Hippo and, to my certain knowledge, many miracles have occurred there which are not recorded in the published documents; and nearly seventy of these documents have been produced. . . .

Thus even at this present time the same God who effected the miracles we read of is at work in the performance of many miracles by what agents he chooses and by what means he chooses for their performance. But these modern miracles are not so widely known; nor have they been pounded into the memory by frequent reading, as gravel is pounded into a path, to make sure that they do not pass out of the mind. At Hippo we have started the practice of reading to the people the accounts of those who receive such blessings. . . .

There was one miracle performed in our city . . . so widely famed that I should imagine no one from Hippo failed to witness it or at least to hear about it. . . . [*He tells of the healing of a young man with severe palsy at the shrine of St. Stephen.*] He had been cured, and he was standing there, completely recovered, meeting the stares of the congregation.

Who could then refrain from giving praise to God? The whole church was filled in every corner with shouts of thanksgiving. They ran with the news to where I was sitting, ready for the procession. They came rushing one after another, each one telling me, as if it were fresh news, what I had been told by the one before. . . . The church was packed and it rang with the shouts of joy: "Thanks be to God! God be praised!" The cries came from all sides; not a mouth was silent. I greeted the people; they replied with shouts expressing even greater fervour. At last silence was restored and the appointed lessons from holy Scripture were read. . . .

They rejoiced in the praises of God with wordless cries, with such a noise that my ears could scarcely endure it. Now was there anything in their hearts as they rejoiced except the same faith in Christ for which Stephen shed his blood?[11]

---

[11] Augustine, *City of God,* trans. Henry Bettenson, ed. David Knowles (New York: Penguin Books, 1972; Copyright © Henry Bettenson, 1972), book xxii, chapter 8, pp. 1033-1035, 1043-1047. Reprinted by permission of Penguin Books, Ltd.

22

Thomas Aquinas

(1225–1274)

The *"doctor communis"* of the Roman Catholic Church, Thomas Aquinas, developed a creative synthesis of the Christian-Augustinian theological tradition with what was then thought to be the best of philosophical thought, the philosophy of Aristotle as interpreted by his Muslim commentator, Averroes. Thomas's theology of the Spirit, scattered throughout his vast writings, is a summation of that which had gone before, impressed with the stamp of his own genius as he reflects upon the Spirit as the Spirit relates to and affects the human psyche. The primitive awareness of the Spirit as an untameable charismating power-source has more or less been poured into sacramental shapes and allowed to solidify into ecclesiastical forms, for example, in the ordained ministry. Thomas's exegesis of 1 Corinthians 12-14 spiritualizes the meaning of the charismas away from anything extravagant. It was only toward the end of his career that Thomas himself became something of an eleventh-hour charismatic.

Bartholomew of Capua relates that on December 6, 1273, while Thomas was resident at Naples and was working on completing the third part of his Summa Theologiae in the midst of his treatment of the sacraments, during his celebration of the Mass in the chapel of St.

Nicholas, Thomas experienced a transport of heavenly grace. Finally, in the last year of his life, he was in an ecstatic state for almost three days. When Reginald, his associate, prompted him to speak, he said, "Reginald, my son, I will tell you a secret which you must not repeat to anyone while I remain alive. All my writing is now at an end; for such things have been revealed to me that all I have taught and written seems quite trivial to me now."[1] Thomas died less than six months later.

Thomas's main concerns in reference to the Holy Spirit were to refine Augustine's basic concept of the Spirit as the mutual love of the Father and Son, appropriate of the faculty of the will in the human psyche; to defend the procession of the Spirit from both the Father and the Son; and to establish the full deity of the Spirit consubstantial with the Father and the Son.[2]

Thomas also discusses prophecy at length,[3] under which he understood all the knowledge-charismas to be included (faith, wisdom, discernment, knowledge). While his interest in prophecy indicates that he considered it something of a living reality, his much less satisfactory treatment of tongues shows that he considered that a matter relegated to the history of the church. At the same time, his appreciation of rapture, wisdom, and miracles indicates his awareness of the activities of the charismating Spirit.[4] His disregard for a person such as Joachim of Fiore was one root of his suspicion of actual, practicing prophetic spirits.[5]

Thomas's greatest contribution to the theology of the Spirit in the second part of the Summa Theologiae *is his detailed treatment and complex understanding of the virtues, fruits, gifts, and beatitudes of the Spirit at work in the human soul. The whole "Second Part" in and of itself is a comprehensive psychological examination of the effects*

[1] Bernard Gui, "The Life of St. Thomas" in Kenelm Foster, *The Life of Saint Thomas Aquinas* (London: Longmans, Green; Baltimore: Helicon, 1959), p. 46. See also Tocco, *Life of Thomas,* cap. 47.

[2] See *Commentary on the I Sentences* of Peter Lombard, dd. 10-18, 31-32; *Compendium Theologiae,* cap. 45-49, 58; *Contra Gentiles,* trans. Charles J. O'Neil (New York: Doubleday and Co., Inc., 1957), bk. 4, cap. 15-26, used by permission of Doubleday & Company, Inc.; *Summa Theologiae,* trans. Fathers of the English Dominican Province, revised by Daniel J. Sullivan (Chicago: Encyclopedia Britannica, Inc., 1952), *Great Books of the Western World,* vols. 19, 20, part I, qq. 36-38, 43.

[3] See *Quaestiones de veritate,* q. 12, and *Summa Theologiae* 2a 2ae qq. 171-174.

[4] *Summa Theologiae* 2a 2ae qq. 174-178.

[5] See Marjorie Reeves, *The Influence of Prophecy in the Later Middle Ages: A Study in Joachimism* (Oxford: Clarendon Press, 1969), pp. 67-69.

of the Spirit working the moral will of God in the heart and mind of persons whose human nature is being fulfilled by grace.

The appropriateness of [the name "Holy Ghost"] may be shown . . . from the proper signification of the name. For the name "spirit" in corporeal things seems to signify impulse and motion; for we call the breath and the wind by the term "spirit." Now it is a property of love to move and impel the will of the lover towards the thing loved. Further, holiness is attributed to whatever is ordered to God. Therefore because the divine person proceeds by way of the love whereby God is loved, that person is most properly named The Holy Ghost.[6]

The Son proceeds from God by way of the intellect as Word, and the Holy Ghost proceeds from God by way of the will as Love. Now love must proceed from a word. For we do not love anything unless we apprehend it by a mental conception. Hence also in this way it is manifest that the Holy Ghost proceeds from the Son. . . . The Word in God is not taken after the likeness of the vocal word, from which the breath (*spiritus*) does not proceed, for it would then be only metaphorical, but after the likeness of the mental word, from which proceeds love. . . . The Holy Spirit is himself Love . . . essentially and personally. When taken personally, it is the proper name of the Holy Spirit, just as Word is the proper name of the Son.[7]

In the comparison by the Apostle just given [1 Corinthians 2:10-11], the Holy Spirit is to God what the spirit of man is to man. Now, the spirit of man is intrinsic to man and is not extraneous to him in nature, but is of his nature. Therefore, the Holy Spirit as well is not by nature extraneous to God.[8]

We are not compelled to say that one must understand the Holy Spirit filling and dwelling in the minds of the saints in the same way that one understands the devil to be filling and dwelling in some minds. . . . For since the devil is a creature . . . he fills no one by a participation in himself, and he cannot dwell in a mind through his substance; rather, he is said to fill some men by the effect of his

---

[6] *Summa Theologiae*, part I, q. 36, art. 1, respondeo, p. 191.

[7] *Ibid.*, part I, q. 36, art. 2, respondeo; ad 5; q. 37, art. 1, respondeo, pp. 193-194.

[8] *Contra Gentiles*, bk. IV, cap. 17:8, p. 109.

wickedness. Hence Paul says to a certain one: "O full of all guile and of all deceit" (Acts 13:10). The Holy Spirit, of course, since He is God, dwells in a mind by His substance and makes men good by participation in Himself. For He is His own goodness, since He is God. And this can be true of no creature.[9]

Thomas's discussion of the Spirit in Contra Gentiles, *bk. IV, cap. 15-26, is a handbook of scriptural questions and answers concerning the pertinent issues relating to the Spirit. In the midst of this extensive catalogue of biblical texts, Thomas extemporizes on the friendship of the Spirit and how he makes humans to be friends with God.*

God manifestly loves in the greatest degree those whom He has made lovers of Himself through the Holy Spirit, for He would not confer so great a good save by loving us. . . . Therefore, by the Holy Spirit not only is God in us, but we are in God. . . . Of course, this is the proper mark of friendship: that one reveal his secrets to his friend. For, since charity unites affections and makes, as it were, one heart of two, one seems not to have dismissed from his heart that which he reveals to a friend; and so our Lord says to His disciples: "I will not now call you servants but friends: because all things whatsoever I have heard of My Father I have made known to you" (John 15:15). Therefore, since by the Holy Spirit we are established as friends of God, fittingly enough it is by the Holy Spirit that men are said to receive the revelation of the divine mysteries. . . . Now, it is not only proper to love that one reveal his secrets to a friend by reason of their unity in affection, but the same unity requires that what he has, he have in common with the friend. For, "since a man has a friend as another self" [Aristotle, *Nicomachean Ethics* 9:4 (1166a 32)], he must help the friend as he does himself, making his own possessions common with the friend, and so one takes this as the property of friendship, "to will and to do the good for a friend." [*Ibid.,* 1166a 3] . . . Therefore it is fitting that all the gifts of God are said to be gifts from the Holy Spirit (I Cor. 12:8, 11). . . . Of course, by the fact that a person is established as the friend of another, every offense is removed, because friendship and offense are contraries. Thus, we read in Proverbs (10:12): "Charity covereth all sins." Therefore, since we are established as friends of God by the Holy Spirit, it is by Him that God remits our sins, and so our Lord says to His disciples (John 20:22-23): "Receive ye the Holy Ghost. Whose sins you shall forgive, they are forgiven."

[9] *Ibid.,* bk. IV, cap. 18:9, pp. 115-116.

First, indeed, this appears to be especially proper to friendship: really to converse with the friend. Now, the conversation of man with God is by contemplation of Him. . . . Since, therefore, the Holy Spirit makes us lovers of God, we are in consequence established by the Holy Spirit as contemplators of God. . . . It is also a property of friendship that one take delight in a friend's presence, rejoice in his words and deeds, and find in him security against all anxieties; and so it is especially in our sorrows that we hasten to our friends for consolation. Since, then, the Holy Spirit constitutes us God's friends, and makes Him dwell in us and us dwell in Him . . . it follows that through the Holy Spirit we have joy in God and security against all the world's adversities and assaults.[10]

With regard to gratuitous graces (=charismas), it must be observed that some of them pertain to knowledge, some to speech, and some to action. Now all things pertaining to knowledge may be listed under prophecy, since prophetic revelation extends not only to future events relating to humans, but also to things relating to God, both as to those which are to be believed by all and are matters of faith, and as to yet higher mysteries, which concern the perfect and belong to wisdom. Again, prophetic revelation is about things pertaining to spiritual substances, by whom we are urged to good or evil; this pertains to the discernment of spirits. Moreover it extends to the direction of human acts, and this pertains to knowledge. . . .[11]

The prophetic light is in the prophet's soul by way of a passion or transitory impression. . . . Hence it is that even as the air is ever in need of a fresh enlightening, so too the prophet's mind is always in need of a fresh revelation. . . . Every gift of grace raises the person to something above human nature, and this may happen in two ways. First, as to the substance of the act; for instance, the working of miracles and the knowledge of the uncertain and hidden things of divine wisdom. For such acts as these, a person is not granted a habitual gift of grace. Secondly, a thing is above human nature as to the mode but not the substance of the act; for instance, to love God and to know Him in the mirror of His creatures. For this, a habitual gift of grace is given.[12]

[10] *Ibid.,* IV, cap. 21 and 22, pp. 122-126.

[11] *Summa Theologiae* 2a 2ae, q. 171, divisio textus, trans. Fathers of the English Dominican Province (London: Burns, Oates and Washburne, 1935), vol. 14, p. 2.

[12] *Ibid.,* 2a 2ae, q. 171, art. 2, respondeo, ad 3, in *ibid.,* pp. 7 and 8.

Is a natural disposition required for a person to prophesy? . . . On the contrary, Gregory says in a homily for Pentecost [xxx in Ev.]: "He [the Holy Spirit] fills the boy harpist and makes him a psalmist; he fills the herdsman plucking wild figs and makes him a prophet." Therefore prophecy requires no previous disposition but depends alone on the will of the Holy Spirit.[13]

Is a good life required for a person to prophesy? . . . On the contrary, . . . sanctifying grace is given chiefly in order that a person's soul may be united to God by love. . . . Hence whatever can be without love can be without sanctifying grace, and consequently without goodness of life. Now prophecy can be without love; and this is clear on two counts. First, on account of their respective acts; for prophecy pertains to the intellect, whose act precedes the act of the will, which power is perfected by love. For this reason the Apostle reckons prophecy with other things pertinent to the intellect that can be had without love. Secondly, on account of their respective ends; for prophecy like other gratuitous graces is given for the good of the church . . . and is not directly intended to unite man's affections to God, which is the purpose of love. Therefore prophecy can be without a good life. . . . God's gifts are not always bestowed on those who are simply the best, but sometimes are vouchsafed to those who are best as regards the receiving of this or that gift. Accordingly God grants the gift of prophecy to those whom He judges best to give it to.[14]

Prophetic revelation takes place in four ways: by the infusion of an intelligible light, by the infusion of intelligible thoughts, by impression or co-ordination of pictures in the imagination and by the outward presentation of sensible images. . . . The spirit of the prophets is said to be subject to the prophets as regards to the prophetic utterances (1 Cor. 14:32), because the prophets in declaring what they have seen speak their own mind and are not thrown off their mental balance, like persons who are possessed, as Priscilla and Montanus maintained.[15]

Christ's disciples were chosen by him in order that they might disperse throughout the whole world and preach his faith

---

[13] *Ibid.*, 2a 2ae, q. 172, art, 3, ad contra, in *ibid.*, p. 24.
[14] *Ibid.*, 2a 2ae, q. 172, art. 4, respondeo, ad. 4, in *ibid.*, pp. 27 and 28.
[15] *Ibid.*, 2a 2ae, q. 173, art. 3, respondeo, ad. 4, in *ibid.*, pp. 40 and 42.

everywhere. . . . Now it was not fitting that they who were being sent to teach others should need to be taught by others, either as to how they should speak to other people, or as to how they were to understand those who spoke to them. Since they that were sent were of one nation, that of Judea, . . . and were, moreover, poor and powerless, at the outset they would not have easily found someone to interpret their words faithfully to others, or to explain what others said to them, especially as they were sent to unbelievers. Consequently it was necessary that God provide them with the gift of tongues, in order that, as the diversity of tongues was brought upon the nations when they fell away into idolatry [Gen. 11], so when the nations were to be recalled to the worship of one God a remedy to this diversity might be applied by the gift of tongues.

Christ in his own person purposed preaching to only one nation, namely the Jews; consequently, although without any doubt he possessed most perfectly the knowledge of all languages, there was no need for him to speak in every tongue. And therefore, as Augustine says [Tract 32, *On John*], "Whereas even now the Holy Spirit is still being received, yet no one speaks in the tongues of all nations, because the church herself already speaks the languages of all nations; since whoever is not in the church does not receive the Holy Spirit." [16]

If we speak of gift and virtue with regard to the notion conveyed by the words themselves, there is no opposition between them; because the word virtue conveys the notion that it perfects man in relation to well-doing, . . . while the word "gift" refers to the cause from which it proceeds . . . some virtues are called gifts and some not, and . . . among the gifts there are some, fear for instance, which are not accounted virtues. . . . Accordingly, in order to differentiate the gifts from the virtues, we must be guided by the way in which scripture expresses itself. [*Thomas's list of the gifts is taken from Isaiah 11:2, 3.*]

Human virtues perfect man according as it is natural for him to be moved by his reason in his interior and exterior actions. Consequently man needs yet higher perfections by which he may be disposed to be moved by God. These perfections are called gifts, not only because they are infused by God, but also because by them man is disposed to become amenable to the Divine inspiration. . . . There is no need to

[16] *Ibid.,* 2a 2ae, q. 176, art. 1, respondeo, ad. 3., in *ibid.,* pp. 80-82.

take counsel according to human reason, but only to follow their inner promptings, since they are moved by a principle higher than human reason. . . . the gifts perfect man for acts which are higher than acts of virtue. . . . Wisdom is called an intellectual virtue in so far as it proceeds from the judgement of reason; but it is called a gift according as its work proceeds from the divine prompting. The same applies to the other virtues.[17]

A person's reason is perfected by God in two ways: first, with its natural perfection, that is, the natural light of reason; secondly, with a supernatural perfection, that is, the theological virtues [faith, hope, love] . . . the sun which possesses light perfectly can shine by itself, but the moon which has the nature of light imperfectly sheds only a borrowed light. . . .

Accordingly, in matters subject to human reason and directed to man's connatural end, man can work through the judgement of his reason. If, however, even in these things man receive help in the shape of special promptings from God, this will be out of God's superabundant goodness. . . . But in matters directed to the supernatural end, to which man's reason moves him . . . imperfectly informed by the theological virtues, the motion of reason does not suffice unless it receive in addition the prompting or motion of the Holy Ghost. . . . Now the Holy Ghost is not in a man without His gifts; therefore His gifts abide in man. Therefore they are not merely acts or passions but are lasting habits. . . . The gifts are perfections of man by which he follows well the promptings of the Holy Ghost. [As has been said elsewhere,] the moral virtues perfect the appetitive power as it partakes somewhat of the reason, in so far, that is, as it has a natural aptitude to be moved by the command of reason. Accordingly the gifts of the Holy Ghost are to man in relation to the Holy Ghost even as the moral virtues are to the appetitive power in relation to reason. Now the moral virtues are habits, by which the powers of appetite are disposed to obey reason promptly. Therefore the gifts of the Holy Ghost are habits by which man is perfected to obey readily the Holy Ghost. . . . The mind of a person is not moved by the Holy Spirit unless in some way it be united to Him, even as the instrument is not moved by the craftsman unless there be contact or some other kind of union between them. Now the primal union of humans with God is by faith, hope, and love, and hence these virtues are presupposed to the

[17] *Ibid.*, 1a 2ae, q. 68, art. 1, passim, in *Great Books*, pp. 88-89.

gifts, as being their roots. . . . The gifts are bestowed to assist the virtues to remedy certain defects. . . . Therefore, the gifts are more excellent than the virtues. . . . there are three kinds of virtues: for some are theological, some intellectual and some moral. The theological virtues are those by which man's mind is united to God; the intellectual virtues are those by which reason itself is perfected; and the moral virtues are those which perfect the powers of appetite in obedience to reason. On the other hand, the gifts of the Holy Spirit dispose all the powers of the soul to be subject to the divine motion.[18]

[The gifts] as to their essence . . . will be most perfectly in heaven. . . . The reason for this is that the gifts of the Holy Ghost perfect the human mind for following the motion of the Holy Ghost, which will be especially realized in heaven, where God will be *all in all* (1 Cor. 15:28), and man entirely subject unto Him. Secondly, they may be considered as regards the matter about which their operations are and thus in this present life they have an operation about a matter in respect of which they will have no operation in the state of glory. . . . Almost every gift includes something that passes away with the present state. . . . [As Gregory says,] "wisdom strengthens the mind with the hope and certainty of eternal things," of which two, hope passes and certainty remains. Of understanding, he says that "it penetrates the truths heard, refreshing the heart and enlightening its darkness," of which hearing passes away . . . but the enlightening of the mind remains.[19]

Certain things are included among the beatitudes that are neither virtues nor gifts, for example, poverty, mourning, and peace. Therefore the beatitudes differ from the virtues and gifts. . . . More is required for a beatitude than for a fruit. Because it is sufficient for a fruit to be something ultimate and delightful, while for a beatitude it must be something perfect and excellent. Hence all the beatitudes may be called fruits, but not vice versa. For the fruits are any virtuous deeds in which one delights, but the beatitudes are none but perfect works, and which, by reason of their perfection, are assigned to the gifts rather than to the virtues.[20]

---

[18] *Ibid.,* 1a 2ae, q. 68, pp. 90-92.
[19] *Ibid.,* 1a 2ae, q. 68, art. 6, respondeo, ad. 2, pp. 93-94.
[20] *Ibid.,* 1a 2ae, q. 69, art. 1, ad contra; q. 70, art. 2, respondeo, pp. 97 and 103.

The spiritual power from Christ, then flows into the ministers of the Church; the spiritual effects on us, of course, derived from Christ, are fulfilled under certain sensible signs [sacraments]; therefore, this spiritual power also had to be passed on to men under certain sensible signs. But fixed forms of words and determined acts are of this sort: the imposition of hands, for example, the anointing and the offering of the book or the chalice, or of something of this sort which belongs to the execution of the spiritual power. And whenever something spiritual is transferred under a bodily sign, we call it a sacrament. Clearly, then, in conferring the spiritual power, a certain sacrament is enacted which is called the sacrament of orders [the priesthood].[21]

---

[21] *Contra Gentiles*, bk. IV, 74:4, p. 287.

23

The Councils of the Church

The first ecumenical council, even before Nicaea, was held in Jerusalem, A.D. 48, under the presidency of James, the brother of the Lord. It promulgated a dogmatic constitution regarding the moral habits of Gentile Christians, beginning with this caption: "For it has seemed good to the Holy Spirit and to us to lay upon you no greater burden than these necessary things" (*Acts 15:28, RSV*).

A sense that the Holy Spirit has attended and inspired subsequent church councils, especially the ecumenical, or general, ones belongs to the orthodox understanding of the development of Christian doctrine. For example, the ecumenical Council of Ephesus decreed on 22 July 431 that it is unlawful "to bring forward, write, or compose a definition of the Faith other than the one of the holy fathers who were gathered together in Nicaea with the Holy Spirit."[1]

The III Council of Constantinople (680/681), in a letter called the "Prosphoneticus" to the Emperor Constantine Pogonatus, wrote:
Being inspired by the Holy Spirit, and all agreeing and consenting together and giving our approval to the doctrinal letter of our most blessed and exalted Pope, Agatho, which he sent to your mightiness,

[1] H. Denzinger and A. Schönmetzer, *Enchiridion Symbolorum,* Definitionum et Declarationum de Rebus Fidei et Morum (Herder, 1965), #265, author's translation.

as also agreeing to the suggestion of the holy Synod of the one hundred and twenty-five fathers held under him, we teach that One of the Holy Trinity, our Lord Jesus Christ, was incarnate, and must be celebrated in two perfect natures, without division and without confusion.[2]
  Cyril of Alexandria in a letter to John of Antioch concerning the Council fathers at Nicaea wrote: "It was not they who spoke, but the Spirit himself of God."[3]

Council of Nicaea (325)

    We believe in one God, the Father all-powerful,
      creator of all things visible and invisible;
    And in one Lord, Jesus Christ, the Son of God,
      the only-begotten Son of the Father,
      who is of the substance of the Father,
      God from God, Light from Light,
      true God of true God,
      begotten, not made,
      of the same substance with the Father,
      through whom all things were made,
        whether in heaven or on earth;
      who for us humans and our salvation
      descended, was incarnated and was made human
      and suffered and rose the third day
      and ascended into the heavens,
    who will come to judge the living and the dead;
    And in the Holy Spirit. Amen.[4]

Council of Constantinople (381)

  The usual creed of Nicaea was amplified by the Council of Constantinople in regard to the Holy Spirit to read:

        We believe in one God . . . .
        And in one Lord, Jesus Christ . . . .
        And in the Holy Spirit,
          the Lord and Giver of life,
          who proceeds from the Father

[2] J. E. C. Welldon, *The Revelation of the Holy Spirit* (London: Macmillan, 1902), p. 244.
[3] *Ibid.,* p. 245.
[4] Denzinger and Schönmetzer, *op. cit.,* #125, author's translation.

who together with the Father and the Son
is worshipped and glorified
who spoke through the prophets;
And in one, holy catholic and apostolic Church.
We confess one baptism for the remission of sins.
We expect the resurrection of the dead
and the life of the world to come. Amen.[5]

The phrase "and from the Son" (Latin: filioque) was added to the Creed by the Latin church in the seventh and eighth centuries. The Councils of Toledo, Spain, beginning with the third in 589, and the Council of Gentilly (767) in Gaul, introduced the addition in opposition to the Arian influences of the barbarian tribes which had invaded the Iberian peninsula. Defended especially by Charlemagne and his court theologian Alcuin, the filioque was fixed as a permanent part of the Western Creed over the opposition of the Greeks, led principally by Patriarch Photius of Constantinople (c. 820–891). A formal accord was reached between Greeks and Latins at the seventeenth ecumenical Council of Ferrara-Florence in 1439, but the addition to the Creed has never been accepted at a popular level in the East. The Roman Catholic Church now requires the Eastern Uniate churches to believe the doctrine of the filioque (that the Spirit proceeds also from the Son just as from the Father), though they are not required to recite the Creed with the addition. Eastern theology prefers the phrase "through the Son."

The "Quicumque-vult" or Athanasian Creed

The Athanasian Creed (middle of the fifth century) was not written by Athanasius, as the received tradition of the Middle Ages and Reformation taught. It does show the way in which dogmatic thinking about the person and nature of the Holy Spirit was worked out in extension of and in analogy to the creedal statements about the nature of the Trinity and about christology, formulated at the councils of Nicaea (325), Constantinople (381), Ephesus (431), and Chalcedon (451). Doctrinal development of the Holy Spirit proceeded not so much in terms of concerns which relate primarily to the uniqueness of the person and work of the Spirit but rather in terms designed to fill out in a logical fashion the "analogy of faith" regarding the Holy Spirit. "If such and such is true of the Father and the Son, then so and so must also be true of the Holy Spirit."

[5] *Ibid.,* #150, author's translation.

1. Whosoever will ("quicumque vult...") be saved, before all things it is necessary that he be told the catholic faith.

2. Which faith except every one do keep whole and inviolate, without doubt he shall perish in eternity.

3. This, then, is the catholic faith: That we worship one God in trinity, and trinity in unity;

4. Neither confounding the persons nor dividing the substance.

5. For there is one person of the Father, another of the Son, another of the Holy Spirit.

6. But the divinity of the Father and of the Son and of the Holy Spirit is one: the glory equal, the majesty coeternal.

7. In whatever way the Father is, such is the Son, so also the Holy Spirit:

8. The Father is uncreated, the Son is uncreated, the Holy Spirit is uncreated.

9. The Father is immeasurable, the Son is immeasurable, the Holy Spirit is immeasurable.

10. The Father is eternal, the Son is eternal, the Holy Spirit is eternal.

11. And yet, there are not three eternals, but one eternal.

12. So also are there not three uncreateds, nor three immeasurables; but one uncreated and one immeasurable.

13. Similarly, the Father is omnipotent, the Son omnipotent, the Holy Spirit omnipotent.

14. And yet there are not three omnipotents, but one omnipotent.

15. So, God Father, God Son, God Holy Spirit.

16. And yet there are not three Gods, but God is one.

17. So, Lord Father, Lord Son, Lord Holy Spirit.

18. And yet there are not three Lords, but the Lord is one.

19. For as we are compelled by Christian truth to confess that each person singularly is both God and Lord,

20. So are we prohibited by catholic religion from saying that there are three Gods or Lords.

21. The Father was made by no one, neither created nor begotten.

22. The Son is of the Father alone: not made nor created but begotten.

23. The Holy Spirit is of the Father and of the Son: not made nor created nor begotten, but proceeding.

24. Thus there is one Father, not three Fathers; one Son, not three Sons; one Holy Spirit, not three Holy Spirits.

25. And in this trinity none is before or after another, none is greater

or lesser than another.

26. But the whole three persons are coeternal with one another and coequal.

27. Thus, so that in all things as was said above, both the unity in trinity and the trinity in unity is to be worshipped.

28. He therefore who will be saved must think of the trinity in this way.

Sentences 29 through 42 are statements about the natures and person of Jesus Christ; they do not speak directly of the Holy Spirit.[6]

Council of Orange (529)

Augustine taught the irresistibility of grace, the totality and all-inclusiveness of Adamic original sin, predestination and reprobation, and necessity of the Holy Spirit's giving the grace by which the sinner may will and accomplish any good thing. Pelagius, a British monk, denied all this. After their debate had raged for a hundred years, the Council of Orange attempted to decide the issue, basically in Augustine's favor, though with some semi-Pelagian modifications:

Canon 4: If anyone maintains that God awaits our will to be cleansed from sin, but does not confess that even our will to be cleansed comes to us through the infusion and working of the Holy Spirit, he resists the Holy Spirit himself who says through Solomon, "The will is prepared by the Lord" (Prov. 8:35, LXX), and the salutary word of the Apostle, "It is God who works in you both to will and to accomplish" (Phil. 2:13).

Canon 5: If anyone says that not only the increase of faith but also its beginning and the very desire for faith, by which we believe in him who justifies the ungodly and come to regeneration of holy baptism— if anyone says that this belongs to us by nature and not by a gift of grace, that is, by the inspiration of the Holy Spirit amending our will and turning it from unbelief to faith and from godlessness to godliness, it is proof that he is opposed to the teaching of the Apostles. . . .

Canon 6: If anyone says that God has mercy upon us when, apart from his grace, we believe, will, desire, strive, labor, pray, watch, study, seek, ask, or knock, but does not confess that it is by the infusion and inspiration of the Holy Spirit within us that we have the faith, the will, or the strength to do all these things as we ought, . . . he contradicts the Apostle. . . .

[6] *Ibid.,* #75-76, author's translation.

Canon 7: If anyone affirms that we can form any right opinion or
make any right choice which relates to the salvation of eternal life, as
is expedient for us, or that we can be saved, that is, assent to the
preaching of the gospel through our natural powers without the
illumination and inspiration of the Holy Spirit, who makes all men
gladly assent to and believe in the truth, he is led astray by a heretical
spirit. . . .
Canon 17: The courage of the Gentiles is produced by simple greed,
but the courage of Christians by the love of God which "has been
poured into our hearts" not by freedom of the will from our own side
but "through the Holy Spirit which has been given to us" (Rom. 5:5).[7]

Eleventh Council of Toledo (675):

We believe . . . as well that the Holy Spirit,
who is the third Person in the trinity,
is one and the same God with God the Father
and the Son: of a single substance and also
of a single nature;
not that he was generated or created,
but that he proceeds from both of them,
is the Spirit of both.
Now the Holy Spirit is believed to be neither
ungenerated nor generated;
for, were we to say ungenerated, we would
speak of two Fathers; or if we were to
say generated, we would show ourselves
to be preaching two Sons.
He is thus not the Spirit of the Father only
or of the Son only, but is said to be
the Spirit of Father and Son at once;
for he does not proceed from the Father into
the Son, nor from the Son for the sanctification
of creation; rather, he is seen to proceed
from both at the same time, for he is to be
acknowledged as the love and holiness of both.
The Holy Spirit, therefore, is believed to be
sent from both Father and Son just as the Son
is sent from the Father. But the Spirit is
not less than the Father and the Son, in the

[7] *Ibid.,* #374, 375, 376, 377, 387, author's translation.

sense that the Son testified himself to be less than the Father and the Spirit on account of his taking on human flesh.[8]

Creed of the Council of Ferrara-Florence (1439)

Now in the name of the holy trinity, Father, Son and Holy Spirit, in agreement with this sacred and ecumenical Florentine council, we define the following truth of faith to be believed and received by all Christians: that the Holy Spirit is eternally from the Father and the Son, and that he has his essence and subsisting being alike from the Father and the Son, and that he proceeds eternally from both as from one source and by a single spiration. We declare that the teaching of the holy doctors and fathers, that the Holy Spirit proceeds from the Father through the Son, is to be understood in this way: as intending to signify that also the Son is, according to the Greeks, the cause and, according to the Latins, the source of the subsistence of the Holy Spirit, in the same way as the Father. And because all things which are the Father's, the Father himself has given to the Son in begetting him—with the exception of fatherhood—then the Son, himself, who is eternally begotten by the Father, has this as well from the Father: that the Holy Spirit proceeds from the Son. We define, furthermore, that the "filioque" as an explication of these words serves as a declaration of the truth and on account of the needs of the time was rightly and reasonably added to the Creed.[9]

Council of Trent (1545–1563)

The Church of Rome responded to the Protestant onslaught with the decrees of the Council of Trent. The fathers of the council attempted to find a middle ground on the subject of grace and the influence of the Holy Spirit that would maintain the Augustinian tradition of God's direct intervention in human life without, at the same time, denying the human's ability, under the Spirit and that grace, to cooperate with God in working out salvation:

Decree on Justification (13 January 1547)

Canon 3: If anyone says, that without the prevenient inspiration of the Holy Spirit, and without his help, humans can believe, hope, love, or be penitent as they ought, so that the grace of justification may

---

[8] *Ibid.,* #527, author's translation.
[9] *Ibid.,* #1300-1302, author's translation.

be conferred on them, let that one be anathema.

Canon 4: If any one says, that a human's free will moved and excited by God, by assenting to God's exciting and call, in no way cooperates towards disposing and preparing itself for obtaining the grace of justification; or that it cannot refuse its consent, if it wishes, but that, like something inanimate, it does nothing whatever and is merely passive, let that one be anathema.[10]

Catechism of the Council of Trent (1566)

... When the faithful attentively consider that everything they possess is theirs thanks to the generosity and goodness of the Holy Spirit, they gain as a special fruit of this knowledge a greater humility and modesty, and become motivated to place their entire hope on God's help. But is this not the first step for every Christian towards highest wisdom and eternal life? . . .

It must further be taught, moreover, that there are wonderful workings and glorious gifts of the Holy Spirit, which the Faith attributes to him and which flow out from him as out of an uncapable well of goodness. . . .

With devout and thankful feelings, we must therefore recognize that all the blessings and graces vouchsafed us by God—"What do we have," the Apostle states, "that we did not receive from God?" [I Cor. 4:7] are granted through the generosity and gift of the Holy Spirit.

The workings of the Holy Spirit are manifold. In addition to the creation of the world, the maintenance of creation, and the management of everything there is, concerning which we spoke in the first article, furthermore it needs to be pointed out that it is especially the property of the Holy Spirit to give life, which the witness of Ezekiel (37:14) sustains, when he says: "I will give you my Spirit, that you may live." Isaiah lists the works which most outstandingly and above all belong to the property of the Holy Spirit (Isa. 11:2). . . . They are called "gifts" of the Holy Spirit; indeed, sometimes they are given the name "Holy Spirit" itself. . . .

This grace unites our heart through the most indestructible bond of love with God. Its effect is that we are animated by the highest zeal to

[10] *Ibid.,* #1553, 1554, author's translation.

virtue; we begin a new life; and, having become partakers of the divine nature, we are both called and truly are children of God.[11]

(Chapter 9, sections 2, 3)

Swiss Confessions

The Protestant Reformation credited itself with a rediscovery of Paul's and Augustine's doctrine of grace. Especially the Reformed Tradition—the spiritual children of Zwingli and Calvin—put out a lot of energy to try to maintain a balance between the preaching of the external word of Scripture and the internal guiding and illumination and grace-giving activity of the Holy Spirit.

Second Helvetic Confession (1566)

CHAPTER I: Neither do we think that the outward preaching is to be thought as fruitless because the instruction in true religion depends on the inward illumination of the Spirit. . . . For albeit "No one can come to me unless the Father who sent me draws him" (John 6:44), and unless he is inwardly lightened by the Holy Spirit, yet we know undoubtedly that it is the will of God that his word should be preached even outwardly. God could indeed, by his Holy Spirit, or by the ministry of an angel, without the ministry of St. Peter, have taught Cornelius in the Acts; but, nevertheless, he refers him to Peter, of whom the angel speaking says, "He shall tell you what you ought to do" (Acts 10:6).

For he that illuminates inwardly by giving men the Holy Spirit, the self-same, by way of commandment, said unto his disciples, "Go into all the world, and preach the Gospel. . . ."

We know, in the meantime, that God can illuminate whom and when he will, even without the external ministry, which is a thing appertaining to his power; but we speak of the usual way of instructing men, delivered unto us from God, both by commandment and examples.[12]

Helvetic Concensus Formula (1675)

Canon XXI: They who are called unto salvation through the preaching of the Gospel can neither believe nor obey the call, unless

---

[11] Author's translation.

[12] John H. Leith, *Creeds of the Churches* (Garden City, N.Y.: Doubleday Publishing Company/Anchor, 1963), pp. 133-134.

they are raised up out of spiritual death by that very power whereby God commanded the light to shine out of darkness, and God shines into their hearts with the soul-swaying grace of His Spirit . . . this utter inability [of the natural man to receive the things of the Spirit] the Scripture demonstrates by so many direct testimonies and under so many emblems that scarcely in any other point is it surer: . . . it can be shaken off in no way except by the omnipotent heart-turning grace of the Holy Spirit.[13]

Vatican II (1963–1965)

The "prayer of the council fathers" of the second ecumenical council of the Vatican is believed to have been composed by Isidore of Seville (c. 560–636) for use at the second council of Seville, Spain, in 619. It was also used at the fourth council of Toledo (633) and at Vatican I (1869). It was prayed at the beginning of every meeting of preparatory commissions and conciliar commissions of Vatican II.

We are here before You, O Holy Spirit, conscious of our innumerable sins, but united in a special way in Your Holy Name. Come and abide with us. Deign to penetrate our hearts.

Be the guide of our actions, indicate the path we should take, and show us what we must do so that, with Your help, our work may be in all things pleasing to You.

May You be our only inspiration and the overseer of our intentions, for You alone possess a glorious name together with the Father and the Son.

May You, who are infinite justice, never permit that we be disturbers of justice. Let not our ignorance induce us to evil, nor flattery sway us, nor moral and material interest corrupt us. But unite our hearts to You alone, and do it strongly, so that, with the gift of Your grace, we may be one in You and may in nothing depart from the truth.

Thus, united in Your name, may we in our every action follow the dictates of your mercy and justice, so that today and always our judgments may not be alien to You and in eternity we may obtain the unending reward of our actions. Amen.[14]

---

[13] *Ibid.,* pp. 319-320.
[14] *The Documents of Vatican II,* ed. W. M. Abbott (New York: Guild Press, America Press, Association Press, 1966) p. xxii.

HERETICS,
HYMNS,
MYSTICS,
REFORMERS

24

The Qur'an

(Seventh Century)

Muhammad (c. 570–629), the writer of the Qur'an, the holy book of Islam, is generally described as the infidel founder of one of the "world religions" which have nothing to do with the Judeo-Christian faith. In an historical sense, this is not the case. Islam is a blend of Arabic, Jewish, Christian, and Gnostic elements which were fused in the mind and spiritual experience of this sixth- and seventh-century charismatic prophet to the Arabs. It is, in traditional theological language, a "heresy," a deviation from the Christian faith, retaining some original aspects while mixing other foreign matter in. It is a reversion to pre-Christian prophetic religion, seen in one way; it is a nationalistic, somewhat overenthusiastic outburst of "Arabian Pentecostalism," from another point of view. Many of the concepts and doctrines expressed in the Qur'an reflect the state of development of some kinds of Christian thought—especially Jewish-Christian and Gnostic-Christian—contemporary to Muhammad. For example, the classification of the Spirit with the angels in the "first stage" or Meccan period, the identification of Jesus with the Spirit in the "second stage," and the idea of the Spirit being sent by Allah (Jehovah) to strengthen and inspire Jesus and Mary or to reveal scripture (the Qur'an)—are all elements of a Jewish-Christian understanding of the Spirit.

The "stages" identified with these excerpts refer to the periods in the prophet's life during which the several parts of the Qur'an were written—three periods at Mecca and the fourth at Medina. These quotations of the Qur'an are adapted from A. J. Arberry, The Koran Interpreted *(New York: The Macmillan Company, 1955).* © *George Allen & Unwin Ltd. 1955. Reprinted by permission of Macmillan.*

FIRST STAGE

. . .to Him [to God, the Lord of the Stairways] the angels and the
Spirit mount up in a day, whereof the measure is fifty thousand
years.   (70:4)

Upon the day when the Spirit and the angels stand in ranks
they [the God-fearing] shall not speak, save to him to whom
the All-merciful has given leave, and who speaks aright.
                                                            (78:38)

The Night of Power is better than a thousand months;
in it the angels and the Spirit descend,
by the leave of their Lord, upon every command.
Peace it is, till the rising of dawn.
                                                            (97:4)

SECOND STAGE

The Messiah, Jesus son of Mary, was only the Messenger of God,
and His Word which He committed to Mary,
and a Spirit from Him.
So, believe in God and His Messengers,
but do not say: "Three." Refrain! It is better for you.
God is only One God. Glory be to Him!
That he should have a son!
. . . The Messiah will not disdain to be a servant of God,
neither the angels who are stationed near to Him.
                                                        (4:168-170)

Surely We [God] created man of a clay of moulded mud,
and We created the jinn [spirits] beforehand of flaming fire.
And when thy Lord [God] said to the angels:
"See, I am creating a mortal of a clay of moulded mud;
when I have shaped him,

and breathed my Spirit into him,
fall you down,
bowing before him!"
Then the angels bowed themselves, all together.

(15:25-30)
(cf. 38:72)

Then We [God] sent our Spirit unto her [Mary];
who presented himself to her, a man without fault.
She said: "I take refuge in the All-merciful from thee!
If thou fearest God. . . !"
He said: "I am but a messenger come from thy Lord,
to give thee a boy most pure."

(19:17-20)

She who guarded her virginity [Mary],
We breathed of our Spirit into her
and appointed her and her son to be a sign
unto all beings.

(21:91)
(cf. 66:12)

And He [God] originated the creation of man out of clay,
then He fashioned His offspring from an extraction of mere water,
then He shaped him, and breathed His Spirit into him.

(32:8)

THIRD STAGE

Highly exalted be He [God] above those who associate with Him!
He sends down the angels with the Spirit of His command
upon whomsoever He will among His servants, saying:
"Give you warning: there is no God but I. Fear me!"

(16:2)
(cf. 40:15)

They will question you concerning the Spirit.
Say: "The Spirit comes at the bidding of my Lord.
You have been given nothing of knowledge, except a little."
If We [God] willed, We could take away that which We have
revealed to you. . . .

(17:87)

It belongs to no mortal that God should speak to him,
except by revelation,

or from behind a veil,
or that He should send a messenger. . . .
Even so We [God] have revealed to you
  a Spirit of Our counsel.
You did not know what the Book was, or belief;
but We made it a light whereby We guide whom We will of Our
servants.

                     (42:50-52)

FOURTH STAGE

And We gave the Book to Moses,
  and after him sent succeeding Messengers;
And We gave the clear signs to Jesus son of Mary,
  and confirmed him with the Holy Spirit.

                  (2:81)
                (cf. 2:254)

God said: "Jesus son of Mary,
        remember My blessing upon thee and upon thy mother,
        when I confirmed thee with the Holy Spirit,
        to speak to men in the cradle, and of age;
        and when I taught thee the Book, the Wisdom,
        the Torah, the Gospel;
        and when thou createst out of clay—by My leave—
        the likeness of a bird and thou breathest into it
        and it became a bird—by My leave;
        and thou healest the blind and the leper—by My leave—
        and thou bringest the dead forth—by My leave. . . .
        O Jesus son of Mary, didst thou say unto men:
          'Take me and my mother as gods, apart from God?'"

Jesus said: "Glory be to Thee! It is not mine to say what I
        have no right to say. . . ."

               (5:109-116)

You will not find any people who believe
  in God and the Last Day
  who are loving to anyone
  who opposes God and His Messenger. . . .

He has written faith upon their hearts,
    and He has confirmed them with a Spirit from Himself;
    and He shall admit them into gardens underneath which rivers
    flow,
        therein to dwell forever. . . .

(58:22)

25

"Veni Creator Spiritus"

(Ninth Century)

The invocation hymn to the Holy Spirit has been traditionally ascribed to the pen both of Ambrose and Gregory the Great, but was more likely composed either by Rhabanus Maurus (d. 856), whose chapter on the Holy Spirit closely resembles the theology of the hymn (see Migne, Patrologia Latina *111:23-26), or even by the Emperor Charlemagne (d. 814), whose support of the "filioque" assured the inclusion in the creed of the West. This doctrinal point is underscored in the sixth stanza of the hymn. The hymn is not only the most widely used devotional outpouring to the Third Person of the Godhead but is also a liturgical creed, comprising in brief detail the high points of a biblical theology of the Spirit, each stanza being the reflection of some choice chapter in scripture where the functions of the Spirit are described.*

Come, Creator Spirit
Visit the minds and
Fill up with heavenly grace
The hearts of those you have created.

We name you Paraclete,

The gift of the Most High God,
The gushing spring, fire, love
And spiritual anointing.

You, the sevenfold
Down-payment of everlasting life,
The finger of God's right hand
The promise of the Father,
The one whose word gives new tongues.

Kindle the light of our senses
Pour out love in our hearts
Form and shape our bodies
Strengthen our will with your strength.

Drive the Enemy away
Give us peace in our time
So that by your leading
We may avoid all evil.

Through your gift we come to know the Father
And we come to know the Son as well
You are, as we believe, the Spirit of them both
From time out of mind.

[*One of three or four
traditional endings runs:*]

Glory be to the Father
With the Son
And also to the Holy Paraclete
May the Son give us
from the Father
The charisma of the Holy Spirit.

Amen.

(Author's Translation)

26

Hildegard of Bingen

(1098–1180)

Hildegard was a monumental woman: seeress of visions and revelations, tongues-speaker, and the voice of God to twelfth-century Germany. She rebuked emperors and taught popes. She invented new music for hymns, dabbled in the sciences, and ran her religious community with a rigorous and energetic hand. She became a living shrine, sought out by pilgrims, and was listened to as a prophetess of God. In all this she relied on God alone, never answering a query until God told her what to say. Her call as prophetess came while she was still a teenager.

Behold, in the fourteenth year of my life, I saw a heavenly apparition; I fastened my entire attention upon it, shaking, and with great fear. I saw a very great gleaming. A heavenly voice called out from within it. It spoke to me: "O fragile human, ashes from ashes, rottenness from rottenness, say and write what you see and hear! But because you are timid at speaking, simple in the interpretation, and unlearned in the description of what you have seen, speak and describe it not in the eloquence of humans nor in the understanding of human cleverness nor in a human style, but speak rather out of the gift which is made yours in heavenly visions, just as you see and hear it in the wonders of God. . . ."

In the year 1141 of the incarnation of the Son of God, Jesus Christ, when I was forty-two years, seven months old, a fiery light with flashes of lightning came down from the open heaven. It streamed through my brain and burned through my heart and breast like a flame which however does not burn but rather warms—as the sun warms an object on which it pours out its beams. Then, immediately, the sense of scripture—of the Psalter, the Gospel and the other catholic books of the Old and New Testament—was opened to me. Not that I received the ability in this to translate individual words, nor the knowledge of syllabification nor of grammatical declensions and tenses. . . .

The visions which I saw I received neither in a dreamlike state, nor in sleep, nor in a state of spiritual upheaval, nor with bodily eyes, nor in external ears, nor even in secret places. Rather, I perceived them awake, aware and with clarity of mind, with the eyes and ears of the inner person, in common and public places—wherever it pleased God. How all this happened is difficult for a person wrapped up in the flesh to understand.

But having passed my youth and arrived at maturity, I heard a voice from heaven which said: "I am the living Light which enlightens the darkness. . . ." [1]

The love of the Saviour and the motherly concern of the Mother of all the faithful was greatly increased in the sending of the "Power from On High" on the first Pentecost. The Holy Spirit, who strengthened the young church then, remains with the church until the end of the world. The Spirit inspired the water (of baptism) with the divine life, which the church gives to her children. He both beautifies and steels their souls in the anointing with chrism, so that they will become capable of attaining heaven and bringing forth the fullness of the fruit of righteousness. Through this building-up of souls, the church also grows in beauty and power, until she in all her members attains to Perfection on the day of the return of Christ.

This work of the Holy Spirit in the church and in individual souls is portrayed in the fourth vision. . . .

[*The Father's voice from heaven interprets Hildegard's vision of a tower:*]

The tower which you saw represents the flaming fire of the gifts of

---

[1] Hildegard of Bingen, *Wisse der Wegel/ Scivias,* ed. Maura Boeckeler (Berlin: Sankt Augustinus Verlag, 1928), pp. 23-24, author's translation.

grace of the Holy Spirit. The Father, because of his love for his Son, sent the Holy Spirit into the world. He came down in fiery tongues and kindled the hearts of the disciples, so that they became strong in the name of the holy and true trinity. Before the coming of this Spirit of Fire, they sat behind closed doors. This points out how closed up in themselves they were, and as a result were too afraid to preach the righteousness of God; they did not find the courage to withstand the persecution of their opponents. They had indeed seen my Son in the flesh and loved him as well according to the flesh. But their inner eyes were not yet opened, so that they did not understand his teaching clearly enough, which they later would pour out on the whole world. Then they became strong through the descent of the Holy Spirit, and they became so solid that they no longer shrank back from any suffering. This is the strength of this tower, which the very wrath of devilish fury cannot overpower in the church thus strengthened in the Holy Spirit. . . .

The tower is big and round. It stands there, quarried from a single white stone. For so unmeasurable is the sweetness of the Holy Spirit. His grace embraces every creature. No corruption can bring to nothing the fullness of righteousness in them. Grace flows in to them like a river of fire. Grace sends forth every little rivulet of holiness in the lightsome clarity of its power, which not even the slightest smudge can darken. For the Holy Spirit himself is burning, lightening clarity. Grace powerfully kindles glowing virtues. Grace is never quenched, and all darkness flees before it.

. . . the indescribable trinity reveals itself through the pouring out of the lordly gifts of the Holy Spirit.[2]

I saw a fair human form and its countenance was of such beauty and brightness that it would have been easier to gaze into the sun. Its head was ringed with a golden circle through which appeared another face, as of an old man. From the neck of the figure wings on either side swept upwards above the circle and met above. . . . The figure was clothed in brightness like the sun; its hands held a lamb shining with light. Beneath, the feet trampled a horrible black monster of revolting shape, on whose right ear a writhing serpent had fastened itself. . . .
Life, the fiery Spirit of holiness speaks:

I am the fiery life of the substance of God who kindled all living

---

[2] *Ibid.,* pp. 141-144, author's translation.

sparks. Death has no part in me, and yet I parcel it out; therefore I am girded with wisdom as with wings. I am that living and fiery essence of the divine substance that flows in the beauty of the fields. I shine in the water; I burn in the sun and the moon and the stars. The mysterious force of the invisible wind is mine. I sustain the breath of all living beings. I breathe in grass and in the flowers; and when the waters flow like living things, it is I. . . . I formed the columns that support the whole earth. . . . I am the force that lies hidden in the winds; they take their source from me, as a man may move because he breathes; fire burns by my blast. All these live because I am in them and am their life. I am Wisdom. The blaring thunder of the Word by which all things were made is mine. I permeate all things that they may not die, I am Life.[3]

[3] Hildegard of Bingen, *Liber Divinorum Operum,* Migne; *Patrologia Latina* v. 197, col. 741-743, author's translation.

27

"Veni Sancte Spiritus"

(Twelfth Century)

*The "golden" sequential hymn for Pentecost "Come, Holy Spirit"
is one of the most perfect, most sublime of the Latin hymns. It has
been translated more than four hundred times, though in this
translation poetic elegance has been sacrificed to literal clarity. The
traditional author, Pope Innocent III (d. 1216), who was also the
chief benefactor at the founding of the Hospital of the Holy Spirit by
Guy of Montpellier, quite likely learned the hymn from his fellow
student and friend from university days in Paris, Stephen Langton (d.
1228), later archbishop of Canterbury. Innocent's use of the hymn in
passing it on to Ulric, abbot of Sanct Gallen, gained him the
reputation of having composed it. The hymn is less dogmatic than the
"Veni Creator Spiritus" but more devotional. It focuses on what the
Spirit does for us and pours out a litany of names and activities in
praise and description of the Spirit's work.*

> Come, Holy Spirit,
> And send forth from heaven
> The beam of Thy light.
> Come, Father of the poor.
> Come, Giver of the gifts.
> Come, Lamp of our hearts.

Best of comforters,
Sweet Guest of the soul,
Sweet Calm;
Rest in labor,
Cool Breeze in summer's heat,
Consolation in tears.

O Light, most blessed,
Fill the inmost heart
Of your faithful ones.
Apart from your majesty
There is nothing in man,
There is nothing innocent.

Wash what is dirty.
Water what is dry.
Heal what is hurt.
Bend what is stiff.
Warm what is cold.
Guide what is astray.

Give the sacred sevenfold gifts
To Thy faithful ones
Who put their trust in Thee.
Give the merit of virtue.
Give a death that leads to salvation.
Give never-ending joy.

Amen.

(Author's translation)

28

Joachim of Flora

(c. 1132–1202)

Peter John Olivi

(c. 1248–1298)

The prophecies of the Calabrian abbot Joachim of Flora fired the medieval church with eschatological expectation unmatched by any since the days of the original apostles. The heart of his system was a division of world history into three ages: the age of the Father, the age of the Son, and the age of the Holy Spirit. His description of the future church in the age of the Holy Spirit has continued to inspire all kinds of forward-looking Christian movements from the Franciscans to late-medieval and Reformation spiritual and Anabaptist groups, even to the German hope for a "Third Reich" and Communist and other utopian dreams of an earthly paradise of equality, fraternity, and liberty. Joachim's wedding of interest in the Holy Spirit with futuristic eschatology and predictions about the imminent return of Christ has been a lasting union; very often, individuals and movements which experience the gifts of the Spirit become inflamed with apocalyptic dreams and visions.[1] The Franciscans were the charismatic Jesus-People of the thirteenth century. Peter John Olivi brought the prophetic drive of Joachim together with the inspiration

---

[1]See Marjorie Reeves, *The Influence of Prophecy in the Later Middle Ages: A Study in Joachimism* (Oxford: Clarendon Press, 1969).

of the "second Christ" from Assisi, the stigmatic St. Francis. Olivi believed that Francis, coming during the sixth stage of the church's history and just at the beginning of the Joachite third world-age of the Holy Spirit, was, in fact, the second coming of Christ "in the Spirit." The third and final coming would be Christ's advent in judgment at the end of the Third Age of the Spirit. During the Third Age, the church would be transformed into the image of Francis: a democratic, charismatic, nonhierarchical, poor, peace-loving "ecclesia spiritualis"—a Church of the Spirit. The implied judgment against the medieval Church of Rome and its Bishop was part of Olivi's polemic: the pope was in the pay of the Antichrist and the Church was the "Whore of Rome," the adulterous Bride of Christ, who would be replaced by a "new bride," the Church of the Holy Spirit during the Third Age. Olivi speculated that the Third Age would begin approximately in 1300, would last seven hundred years, and thus would end with Christ's physical return around the year 2000. The following excerpts from Olivi's commentary on the Apocalypse or Book of Revelation are based directly on Joachim's theory of the three ages of the world.

Understanding the Apocalypse elucidates the obscurity of the Old Testament by distinguishing three goals or three advents of Christ, which are indistinctly wrapped up in the prophets. It is like a man standing a long distance from a big mountain; the mountain has two great valleys or plains within it and, as a consequence, is triple peaked. The man does not see the mountain as triple, but only as a single mountain; nor are the valleys distinct. But then, when the man stands on the first peak, he sees the first valley and the two peaks on either side of the valley; and then, when he stands on the second or middle peak, he sees the two valleys and the trinity of mountains surrounding them.

The man is like the Jews who lived before the first advent of Christ, as it were, before the first peak. They did not distinguish between the first and the others behind, but took the whole thing for one. And Christians who lived before the sixth stage of the Church distinguished, at least, between the first and last, as if situated on the first and as seeing the space in between—the conversion of the Gentiles, which is and was between the first and last advent. But they do not, however, commonly distinguish between the advent which will be in final judgement, and the one which will be in the sixth stage, when, according to the Apostle, Christ will destroy the Antichrist "with the brightness of his coming" [2 Thessalonians 2:8; cf. Apocalypse 19:20].

But whoever stands in the sixth stage, or "in the Spirit," sees the middle advent and distinguishes it from the first and the last. And then they see this distinction in the prophetical books and even in what Christ and the Apostles said regarding the final advent of Christ and the final state of the world. [end of the "Prologue"][2]

Olivi is interpreting the "key of David" in Apoc. 3:7: By this is signified the proper gift and the special property of the third state of the world, which is inchoate during the sixth stage of the Church, and which, in a certain way of speaking, can be said to be the property of the Holy Spirit. For, just as in the first state of the world before Christ, the patriarchs tried to recount in detail the great works of the Lord which had their beginning from the origin of the world, but in the second state—from Christ up to the third state—it has been the business of the sons to seek the wisdom of mystical things and the hidden mysteries from the beginnings of the ages, so in the third state nothing remains to be done except for us to sing psalms and to jubilate in God, praising his great works and his manifold wisdom and goodness, clearly manifested in his works and in the words of scripture.

And just as God the Father showed himself in the first time as terrible and fearful, wherefore the fear of him was then set forth; so in the second time God the Son showed himself as teacher and preserver and as the express word of his Father; but in the third time the Holy Spirit shall show himself as a flame and a furnace of divine love and as a wine-cellar full of spiritual inebriation and as a warehouse full of divine fragrances and spiritual oils and unguents and as a dance of spiritual jubilation and delight.

Through the Spirit the whole truth of the wisdom of the word of God-incarnate and of the power of God the Father will be seen not only by simple understanding but even by the tasting and touching of experience.[3]

[2] *Peter John Olivi, O.F.M. (1248–1298): Prophet of the Year 2000/Ecclesiology and Eschatology in the Lectura super Apocalipsim (1297/Introduction to a Critical Edition of the Text,* ed. Warren Lewis (University of Tübingen, W. Germany, doctoral dissertation, to be published by Collegio S. Bonaventura, Grottaferrata, Rome), vol. 2., pp. 100-102.

[3] *Ibid.,* pp. 229-231, author's translation.

29

Angela of Foligno

(c. 1248–1309)

Angela lived a life of worldliness until she was forty years old, at which time she experienced a sudden conversion. She joined the Franciscan movement, and when she discovered that she could not attain mystical perfection so long as her husband and children were alive, she prayed for their deaths. Her prayer was heard. She had a Franciscan passion for the crucified Christ and for poverty. She describes her eighteen steps toward mystical spirituality, which she summarizes as "whether walking or sleeping, a divine sweetness in my soul." Her direct communion with the Holy Spirit occurred only after she had gotten beyond these usual steps on the mystic's ladder. After taking these steps of reflection on sin, shame, penance, consideration of God's mercy, tearful self-condemnation, constant prayer, gazing upon the cross, grief for sins having crucified Christ, and going the way of the cross, she experienced the following:

The eighteenth was that I did at last begin to have the understanding and the visions and the words of God, and I so greatly delighted in prayer and I did forget to eat. Wherefore did I wish that there were no need for eating, in order that I might ever be at prayer. This desire did occasion a certain temptation not to eat, or, if I did eat, that I should eat but a small quantity. But I perceived this to be a snare; and there was such a great fire of love in my heart that I never wearied of being on my knees, or of doing other penance. After this I was filled with a yet greater fire and fervour of Divine love, in such a degree that if I heard any man speaking of God, I did cry aloud, and even had there been one with an axe ready to kill me, I could not have refrained. . . . It did often happen that, hearing God spoken of, I did cry aloud, even though I was in the company of other persons, no matter who they might be. And when those persons did say unto me that I was disordered, in that I should do such a thing, I did answer that I was sick and overwhelmed, and that I could not do otherwise. Neither could I convince those who spoke evil against me because of this thing, but I did feel greatly ashamed. When I beheld the Passion of Christ painted in a picture, I could scarce contain myself, but was seized with a fever and fell into a sickness; for the which reason my companion did hide such pictures of the Passion from me whenever it was possible, in order that I might not behold them. During the times of these cryings, I had many illuminations, understandings, visions and consolations. . . .[1]

It must be known that God cometh sometimes unto the soul when it hath neither called nor prayed unto nor summoned Him. And He doth instill into the soul a fire and a love and a sweetness not customary, wherein it doth greatly delight and rejoice, and it doth believe that this hath been wrought by God Himself there present, but this is not certain. Presently the soul doth perceive that God is inwardly within itself, because—albeit it cannot behold Him within—it doth nevertheless perceive that His grace is present with it, wherein it doth greatly delight. Yet is not even this certain. Presently it doth further perceive that God cometh unto it with most sweet words, wherein it delighteth yet more, and with much rejoicing doth it feel God within it. . . . Thus hath it happened divers times unto me, that, out of my burning desire to work the salvation of my neighbour, I did speak things for which I was reproved, and it was said unto me: "Sister, turn thee again unto the Holy Scriptures, for they say not thus, and therefore we do not understand thee." But with that feeling whereby it is certified unto the soul that God dwelleth within it, there

[1]*The Book of Divine Consolation of Blessed Angela of Foligno*, trans. Mary G. Steegmann (London: Chatto and Windus; New York: Duffield and Co., 1909), pp. 12, 13.

is given unto it a disposition so perfect that it doth most entirely and verily agree with the soul in all things, and in every way do all the members of the body agree with the soul and do truly form one cause together with it. . . . Thus doth the soul feel that God is mingled with it and hath made companionship with it.[2]

All who desire to receive the Holy Spirit must pray; for on the day of Pentecost the Holy Spirit descended not upon the disciples save when they were at prayer.[3]

Angela offered a prayer to St. Francis, after which she received reply from another Spirit:
"You have prayed to My servant Francis, and I have not willed to send you another messenger. I am the Holy Spirit who am come to you to bring you such consolation as you have never before tasted. And I will go with you even to St. Francis; I shall be within you and but few of those who are with you will perceive it. I will bear you company and will speak with you all the way. I will make no end to my speaking and you will not be able to attend to any save to Me, for I have bound you and will not depart from you till you come for the second time to St. Francis [to the Church of St. Francis in Assisi]. Then I will depart from you insofar as this present consolation is concerned, but in no other manner will I ever leave you, and you shall love Me."

Then He began to speak the following words to me, which persuaded me to love:
"My daughter who art sweet to Me, my daughter who art My temple; my beloved daughter, do love Me, for I greatly love you and much more than you love Me."

And very often He said to me:
"Bride and daughter, you are sweet to Me, I love you better than any other who is in the valley of Spoleto. Now that I have rested and reposed in you, rest yourself and repose in Me. I have been with the apostles, who beheld Me with their bodily eyes, but they did not feel Me as you feel Me. . . .

"You have seen that as my servant Francis greatly loved Me, I have

<hr>

[2]*Ibid.,* pp. 24-26.
[3]*Ibid.,* p. 105.

done many things for him. If there were today any person who loved
Me more, much more would I do for them. . . . My beloved and My
bride, love Me! All your life, your eating and drinking and sleeping
and all that you do is pleasing to Me, if only you love Me. I will do
great things through you in the sight of all the people; you shall be
known and glorified, so that many shall praise My name in you."

My soul said to Him who had spoken to it: "If You were truly the
Holy Spirit, You would not speak this way to me, for it is neither right
nor seemly, seeing how I am weak and frail and might grow
vainglorious."

He answered me: "Reflect and see if you can be vainglorious because
of all these things for which you are now grown proud. . . ." So I did
try to grow vainglorious, that I might prove if what He had said were
true; and I began to gaze at the vineyards, that I might learn the folly
of my words. And wherever I looked, He said to me: "Behold and see,
this is My creation." And at that I felt the most ineffable
sweetness. . . .

Then He departed with great gentleness; not suddenly, but slowly and
gradually. . . . And at His departure He would not allow me to
prostrate myself before Him, but had me stand upon my feet. . . . So
was I left with the certainty that it was God who had spoken with me;
and because of His sweetness and the grief of His departure did I cry
aloud, desiring to die.[4]

Since He hath left me I have remained as contented as an angel; for I
love toads and serpents, and even fools and demons, and nothing that
I see them do, even sins committed against others, can displease me,
inasmuch as I believe that God doth justly permit it and desire that it
should be done. And when I am in this state I should take no heed if
dogs were to bite me, neither should I seem to suffer any pain.

In this state, therefore, there can be no thought or grievous
remembrance of the Passion of Christ, or any tears, albeit there was
at one time added unto this love the remembrance of the inestimable
worth of the precious Blood through which the world was redeemed.
Wherefore do I marvel how they can exist together. Nevertheless,
there was none of the suffering of the Passion, for the Passion

[4]*Ibid.,* pp. 160-167.

showeth us the way that we have to go and teacheth us what we have
to do. And this state is greater than that of standing ever at the foot of
Christ's Cross, in continual remembrance, as did the Blessed Francis,
albeit the soul frequenteth both the one and the other state.[5]

[5] *Ibid.*, p. 181.

30

Dame Julian of Norwich

(1342–1416/1423)

Margery Kempe

(c. 1373–post 1439)

The lady Julian was a devout, mystical English woman who, after having received visions of Christ, lived in a tiny apartment or "anchorhold" near a church in Norwich for more than fifteen years giving spiritual counsel to those who sought her out. Her experiences revealed to her the totally loving care of God for humankind and especially the motherly qualities of Christ who tenderly embraces and nourishes the soul. Margery Kempe was a similarly spiritual woman who experienced the mystical marriage with Christ typical of the tradition in which Angela of Foligno, Catherine of Siena, and Mother Ann Lee stand. Among other charismations, Margery was given a gift of "boisterous crying" which unsettled especially the male clergy of her time, who brought her to trial for her eccentric behavior. On one occasion, Margery visited Dame Julian to hear her spiritual counsel. "This creature" is Margery's humble way of referring to herself:

Then she [Margery] was bidden by Our Lord to go to an anchoress in Norwich, named Dame Jelyan, and so she did, and showed her the grace that God put into her soul, of compunction, contrition, sweetness and devotion, compassion with holy meditation and high

contemplation, and full many holy speeches and dalliance that Our
Lord spoke to her soul; and many wonderful revelations, which she
shewed to the anchoress to find out if there were any deceit in them,
for the anchoress was expert in such things and could give good
counsel.

The anchoress, hearing the marvellous goodness of Our Lord, highly
thanked God with all her heart for His visitation, counselling this
creature to be obedient to the will of Our Lord God and to fulfil with
all her might whatever He put into her soul, if it were not against the
worship of God, and profit of her fellow Christians, for if it were, then
it were not the moving of a good spirit, but rather of an evil spirit.
[Said she:]
"The Holy Ghost moveth ne'er a thing against charity, for if He did,
he would be contrary to His own self for He is all charity. Also He
moveth a soul to all chasteness, for chaste livers are called the Temple
of the Holy Ghost, and the Holy Ghost maketh a soul stable and
steadfast in the right faith, and the right belief.

"And a double man in soul is ever unstable and unsteadfast in all
his ways. He that is ever doubting is like the flood of the sea which is
moved and born about with the wind, and that man is not likely to
receive the gifts of God.

"Any creature that hath these tokens may steadfastly believe that the
Holy Ghost dwelleth in his soul. And much more when God visiteth a
creature with tears of contrition, devotion, and compassion, he may
and ought to believe that the Holy Ghost is in his soul. Saint Paul
saith that the Holy Ghost asketh for us with mourning and weeping
unspeakable, that is to say, he maketh us to ask and pray with
mourning and weeping so plenteously that the tears may not be
numbered. No evil spirit may give these tokens, for Saint Jerome
saith that tears torment more the devil than do the pains of Hell. God
and the devil are ever at odds and they shall never dwell together in
one place, and the devil has no power in a man's soul.

"Holy Writ saith that the soul of a rightful man is the seat of God,
and so I trust, sister, that ye be. I pray God grant you perseverance.
Set all your trust in God and fear not the language of the world, for
the more despite, shame and reproof that ye have in the world, the
more is your merit in the sight of God. Patience is necessary to you,
for in that ye shall keep your soul."

Much was the holy dalliance that the anchoress and this creature had by communing in the love of Our Lord Jesus Christ the many days that they were together.[1]

---

[1]Margery Kempe, *The Book of Margery Kempe, 1436,* ed. W. Butler-Bowden (London: Jonathan Cape, 1936; Worlds Classics edition, 1954), cap. 18, pp. 72-74; see also Julian of Norwich, *The Revelations of Divine Love,* trans. J. Walsh (New York: Harper & Row, Publishers, 1961).

31

Martin Luther

(1483–1546)

The most famous of the German Reformers, Luther waged one of his many wars of theological polemic against his former friend, Andreas Karlstadt, who had followed the lead of their teacher Johann Staupitz and Augustine's doctrine of grace and the Spirit to "spiritualist" conclusions. Karlstadt pushed the Reformation further, faster, insisting on ending devotion to the saints, breaking the images, spiritualizing the Eucharist, and crushing the human will into nothingness before the irresistible grace of the Spirit. Luther strongly reacted against these tendencies, arguing in favor of external sacraments and the preached/heard Word as the necessary means of the Spirit's coming. Luther saw Karlstadt's rigorism as a new legalism, as bad as that of Rome so recently rejected. Luther's firm stand on the word-only (parallel to the other watchwords of Protestantism: faith-only, Scripture-only, and grace-only) as the exclusive means used by God to give his Spirit became hardened by Protestant scholasticism into an understanding that the Spirit can be given only as a person hears or reads the Bible.

Everyone should know that he [Karlstadt] has a perverted spirit that thinks only of murdering the conscience with laws, sin, and works. . . .

something higher must be there to absolve and comfort the conscience. This is the Holy Spirit, who is not acquired through breaking images or any other works, but only through the gospel and faith. . . . Dr. Karlstadt and his spirits replace the highest with the lowest, the best with the least, the first with the last. Yet he would be considered the greatest spirit of all, he who has devoured the Holy Spirit feathers and all.[1]

Now when God sends forth his holy gospel he deals with us in a twofold manner, first outwardly, then inwardly. Outwardly he deals with us through the oral word of the gospel and through material signs, that is, baptism and the sacrament of the altar. Inwardly he deals with us through the Holy Spirit, faith, and other gifts. But whatever their measure or order the outward factors should and must precede. The inward experience follows and is effected by the outward. God has determined to give the inward to no one except through the outward. For he wants to give no one the Spirit or faith outside the outward word and sign instituted by him, as he says in Luke 16 (:29), "Let them hear Moses and the prophets." . . . the oral gospel is "the power of God for salvation to every one who has faith" (Rom. 1 [:16]).

Observe carefully, my brother, this order, for everything depends on it. However cleverly this factious spirit makes believe that he regards the word and Spirit of God and declaims passionately about love and zeal for the truth and righteousness of God, he nevertheless has as his purpose to reverse this order. His insolence leads him to set up a contrary order and, as we have said, seeks to subordinate God's outward order to an inner spiritual one. Casting this order to the wind with ridicule and scorn, he wants to get to the Spirit first. Will a handful of water [in baptism], he says, make me clean from sin? The Spirit, the Spirit, the Spirit must do this inwardly. Can bread and wine profit me? Will breathing over the bread bring Christ into the sacrament? No, no, one must eat the flesh of Christ spiritually. The Wittenbergers are ignorant of this. They make faith depend on the letter. Whoever does not know the devil might be misled by these many splendid words to think that five holy spirits were in the possession of Karlstadt and his followers.

But should you ask how one gains access to this same lofty spirit,

[1] Martin Luther, *Against the Heavenly Prophets in the Matter of Images and Sacraments* (1525) *Luther's Works* (Philadelphia: Muhlenberg Press, 1958), vol. 40, pp. 82-83. Used by permission of Fortress Press.

they do not refer you to the outward gospel but to some imaginary realm, saying: Remain in "self abstraction" where I now am and you will have the same experience. A heavenly voice will come, and God himself will speak to you. If you inquire further as to the nature of this "self abstraction," you will find that they know as much about it as Dr. Karlstadt knows of Greek and Hebrew. Do you not see here the devil, the enemy of God's order? With all his mouthing of the words "Spirit, Spirit, Spirit," he tears down the bridge, the path, the way, the ladder and all the means by which the Spirit might come to you. Instead of the outward order of God in the material sign of baptism and the oral proclamation of the word of God, he wants to teach you not how the Spirit comes to you but how you come to the Spirit. They would have you learn how to journey on the clouds and ride on the wind. They do not tell you how or when, whither or what, but you are to experience what they do. . . . They pay no attention to God's design of inward things, such as faith. . . . That which God has made a matter of inward faith and spirit they convert into a human work. But what God has ordained as an outward word and sign and work they convert into an inner spirit. . . . Before all other works and acts you hear the word of God, through which the Spirit convinces the world of its sin (John 16 [:8]). When we acknowledge our sin, we hear of the grace of Christ. In this word the Spirit comes and gives faith where and to whom he wills.[2]

The Holy Spirit is sent forth in two ways. In the primitive church he was sent forth in a manifest and visible form. Thus He descended upon Christ at the Jordan in the form of a dove (Matt. 3:16), and upon the apostles and other believers in the form of fire (Acts 2:3). This was the first sending forth of the Holy Spirit; it was necessary in the primitive church, which had to be established with visible signs on account of the unbelievers, as Paul testifies. I Cor. 14:22: "Tongues are a sign, not for believers but for unbelievers." But later on, when the church had been gathered and confirmed by these signs, it was not necessary for this visible sending forth of the Holy Spirit to continue.

The second sending is that by which the Holy Spirit, through the word, is sent into the hearts of believers, as is said here: "God has sent the Spirit of his Son into your hearts." [Galatians 4:6] This happens without a visible form, namely, when through the spoken word we receive fire and light, by which we are made new and different, and by

[2] *Ibid.,* pp. 146-149.

which a new judgment, new sensations, and new drives arise in us. This change and new judgment are not the work of human reason or power; they are the gift and accomplishment of the Holy Spirit, who comes with the preached word, purifies our heart by faith, and produces spiritual motivation in us. . . . So far as the flesh is concerned, then, we are sinners even after we have received the Holy Spirit. Externally there is not much difference between the Christian and another socially upright human being. . . . Therefore there is nothing that the world believes less than that we have the Holy Spirit. But in a time of tribulation or of the cross and the confession of faith (which is the proper and principal work of believers), when one must either forsake wife, children, property and life or deny Christ, then it becomes evident that by the power of the Holy Spirit we confess the faith, Christ and his word.

Therefore we must not doubt that the Holy Spirit dwells in us. . . . For if someone experiences love toward the word, and if he enjoys hearing, speaking, thinking, lecturing and writing about Christ, he should know that this is not a work of human will or reason but a gift of the Holy Spirit. For it is impossible for these things to happen without the Holy Spirit. . . .

We must by all means believe for a certainty that we are in a state of grace, that we are pleasing to God for the sake of Christ, and that we have the Holy Spirit. . . . Therefore anyone who exercises a position of authority in the church or in the government should believe for a certainty that his office is pleasing to God. But he would never be able to believe this if he did not have the Holy Spirit. . . .

We should believe for a certainty that not only our office but also our person is pleasing to God. Whatever our person says, does, or thinks in private is pleasing to God, not indeed on our account but on account of Christ. . . . Christ, that mighty giant, has abolished the Law, condemned sin, and destroyed death and every evil. So long as He is at the right hand of God interceding for us, we cannot have any doubts about the grace of God toward us.

In addition, God has also sent the Spirit of his Son into our hearts as Paul says here. Now Christ is completely certain that in His Spirit He is pleasing to God. Since we have the same Spirit of Christ, we, too, should be certain that we are in a state of grace, on account of him who is certain. So much for the internal testimony, by which the heart should believe with complete certainty that it is in a state of grace and that it has the Holy Spirit. But the external signs, as I have said earlier, are these: to enjoy hearing about Christ; to teach, give thanks, praise, and confess him, even at the cost of property and life; to do one's duty according to one's calling in a manly way, in faith and joy; not to take delight in sin; not to invade someone else's calling but to serve one's own; to help a needy brother, comfort the sorrowful, etc. By these signs we are assured and confirmed a posteriori that we are in a state of grace. The wicked have these signs too, but not in a pure way. . . .

The Holy Spirit is sent into our hearts. He does not whisper and does not pray but cries very loudly: "Abba! Father!" and intercedes for us, in accordance with the will of God, with sighs too deep for words.

How? In deep terrors and conflicts of conscience we do indeed take hold of Christ. . . . Meanwhile, however, the Holy Spirit is helping us in our weakness. . . . Thus the mind is strengthened amid these terrors; it sighs to its Saviour and High Priest, Jesus Christ; it overcomes the weakness of the flesh, regains its comfort, and says: "Abba! Father!" This sighing, of which we are hardly aware, Paul calls a cry and a sigh too deep for words—a sigh that fills heaven and earth. He also calls it a cry and a sigh of the Spirit, because when we are weak and tempted, then the Spirit sets up this cry in our heart. . . .[3]

"Then the eyes of the blind shall be opened." [Isaiah 35:5] In that time when the church will flourish in the midst of drought and will be cultivated in the desert, the blind will see plainly, etc. This is taken literally with reference to the miracles of Christ and the church, as we read in the last chapter of Mark (Mark 16:17, 18), signs that were necessary to confirm the new Word, signs that were added to the glory of the church, signs that are not done physically in the last time of the church, now that Christ is no longer weak. They were necessary then as a witness to the Jews, who ought to have recognized the church of God.[4]

[3] Martin Luther, *Lectures on Galatians* (1535), chapters 1-4; *Luther's Works* (St. Louis: Concordia Publishing House, 1963), vol. 26, pp. 374-382. Reprinted by permission.
[4] Martin Luther, *Lectures on Isaiah,* chapters 1-39 (*ca.* 1528), in *ibid.* (1969), vol. 16, p. 302.

32

The Anabaptists

(Sixteenth Century)

*The third force in the sixteenth-century Reformation, the
Anabaptists, carried reliance on Scripture alone some steps beyond
Luther, Zwingli, and Calvin to rediscover the New Testament
teaching of "believer's baptism." Their understanding of the Holy
Spirit tended to be a restatement of traditional theology supported by
biblical proof-texts but developed in areas particularly dear to the
Anabaptists: the Spirit in relation to the word, baptism, congregational discipline, and unity. Three representatives from this tradition
demonstrate the spectrum of their theological diversity while at the
same time giving evidence of spiritual oneness: Balthasar Hubmaier,
theological opponent of Zwingli's teaching on infant baptism, who
with his wife Elisabeth was martyred by the forces of the other part of
the Reformation both for his theology and his participation in the
Peasant Revolt; Hans Denck, a spiritualist among the Anabaptists
and opponent of Luther's teaching of salvation by faith only; and
Menno Simons, dominant theologian and spiritual father of the
Mennonites, who derive their name from his.*

Balthasar Hubmaier (1480?–1528)

Concerning the Christian Baptism of Believers (1525)

To baptize in water in or towards the changing of life is to cover
over the confessing, self-admitted sinner with external water

according to the divine command and to enroll him in the number of those who know they are willful sinners, and to aim him into a new life according to the rule of Christ.

To baptize in the Spirit and fire is to quicken anew and heal the confessing sinner with the fire of the divine word through the Spirit of God. That takes place thus in the forgiveness of his sins already promised in the life-giving word of God. The Spirit of God acts internally within the human being to make him alive. Apart from this, all is empty of the word, a death-dealing letter.[1]

The Twelve Articles of Christian Belief (1526)

I believe in God . . .

I believe also in Jesus Christ . . .

I also believe and confess, my Lord Jesus Christ, that you were conceived of the Holy Spirit, without any male seed, born out of Mary the pure and ever-chaste virgin, so that you restore to me and to all believers the grace of the Holy Spirit which you earned from your heavenly Father; which grace was taken away from me on account of my sins. I believe and trust that the Holy Spirit has come into me and that the power of the most high God has overshadowed my soul, as it did Mary's, so that I have received a new humanity and am therefore in your living, indestructible word and in the Spirit newly born again, and may see the kingdom of God. . . .

I also believe in the Holy Spirit, who proceeds from the Father and the Son and is nevertheless with them one and true God, who makes all things holy and without whom nothing is holy; in him also I place all my trust, that he will teach me all truth, will increase my faith in me, and will inflame my heart with the fire of his love through his holy inspiration and will actually kindle it so that it burns with true, authentic and Christian love for God and my neighbour. All this I heartfully pray thee, my God, my Lord, my Comforter.[2]

How to Baptize (1527)

The bishop stands before his church, exhorts all the brothers and sisters to fall upon their knees, to cry out to God with heartful devotion, that he may graciously impart the grace and power of his Holy Spirit to this person, that he will complete what he has begun in

---

[1] *Balthasar Hubmaier: Schriften,* ed. G. Westin and T. Bergsten in *Quellen zur Geschichte der Taufer* (Gütersloh: Mohn, 1962), vol. 9, p. 121, author's translation.
[2] *Ibid.,* pp. 216, 218, author's translation.

him through his Holy Spirit and divine word.

[Then pray:] "Come, Holy Spirit, fill the hearts of your believers and kindle the fire of your love in them, you who through the multitude of tongues have gathered the peoples into the unity of believing. Hallelujah! Hallelujah! God be praised! God be praised!"[3]

Hans Denck (*c.* 1500–1527)

Confession for the Council at Nürnberg (1525)

Moreover now for centuries, as soon as the apostles had passed away, there have come so many divisions and sects, who have all armed themselves with misunderstood scripture. Why misunderstood? Because they have come to it following their presumption and have taken for themselves a false faith, instead of desiring a right one from God. Thus Peter says further that scripture is not to be understood according to one's own interpretation, but one is to interpret it having listened to the Holy Spirit, who gave scripture in the first place (II Pet. 1:20). Each one must be sure of this interpretation from the Spirit within themselves ahead of time. Where this is not the case, so will it be false and nothing. Whatever is false and nothing can be stricken down with another testimony from the scripture.

Where the agreement between God and people in baptism is (I Pet. 3:21, Rom. 6:4), there the Spirit of Christ also comes and kindles the fire of love, which consumes totally whatever defects are still left, and completes the work of Christ. After this is the sabbath, the everlasting peacefulness of God, when all tongues cease from speaking. Where outward baptism takes place according to the aforementioned agreement, it is good. Where not, it serves no one in any way to cause the indicated results. Outward baptism is not necessary for salvation; therefore Paul says that he was not sent to baptize, since it is not necessary, but to preach the gospel, since it is necessary (I Cor. 1:17). Inward baptism, however, of which we have spoken above, is necessary. Therefore it is written: "Whoever believes and is baptized will be saved" (Mark 16:16).[4]

---

[3] *Ibid.,* p. 349, author's translation.
[4] Hans Denck, *Schriften,* ed. Walter Fellmann in *Quellen und Forschingen zur Reformationsgeschichte* (Gütersloh: Bertelsmann, 1955), Band XXIV, Quellen zur Geschichte der Täufer VI, 2. Teil., pp. 22 and 24, author's translation.

Scripture Means What It Says (1526)

All Christians are in many ways like Christ. For just as he offered himself up to the Father, they are therefore also ready to offer themselves. I do not say that they are therefore perfect as Christ was, but that they seek the perfection which Christ never lost. Just as earthly fire and elemental fire are one and the same in their warming, drying, burning and lighting, but yet the elemental fire is inexpressibly more subtle than the earthly, so Christ calls himself the light of the world and calls his disciples—that is, all Christians—the light of the world as well. Again, Christ came to kindle a fire, which Jeremiah also kindled, as the Holy Spirit told him: "Behold, I will make my words a fire in your mouth; and this people, wood; and it will devour them," etc. (Jer. 5:14). The conclusion is this: all Christians, that is, all those who have received the Holy Spirit, are one with Christ in God and are like Christ. Therefore, what pertains to one pertains to the other also; as Christ acted, so do they also act and have Christ therefore as their one lord and master.[5]

Concerning the Law of God (1526)

Whoever has received the new agreement with God, that is, whoever has the Law written in their heart through the Holy Spirit, that person is truly righteous. Whoever thinks they can bring that about out of the Book, because they are keeping the rules, that person is counting on the dead letters which belong, rather, to the living Spirit. Whoever does not have the Spirit and presumes to find him in the scriptures, that person seeks light and finds darkness, seeks life and finds empty death—and that, not only in the Old Testament but also in the New. This is the reason why the best-educated people of all times are mostly scandalized at the truth, for they think that their understanding will not fail them, since they have so fondly and cleverly studied the holy scriptures. But then should a carpenter's son come along, who has not gone to school, and gives them the lie, they ask: "What! Does he want to teach us?" They think that he has thrown the Law away because he will not put up with their literalistic misunderstanding.[6]

Denck's Final Confession Before Oecolampadius (1527)

I, Johann Denck, confess that as far as my hereditary nature is

[5] *Ibid.,* p. 24, author's translation.
[6] *Ibid.,* p. 59, author's translation.

concerned, I am a poor soul, subject to every sickness of body and spirit. . . . For a time I prided myself as possessing faith . . . but it was a false faith, because this faith did not overcome my spiritual poverty, my inclination to sin, my weaknesses and my sickness; on the contrary, the more I polished and adorned myself when I had such a nominal faith, the more severe became my spiritual sickness. . . . When Christ the sun of righteousness arises in our hearts, then the darkness of unbelief is overcome for the first time. That has not yet taken place in me. . . . He who does not hearken to the revelation of God in his own breast (i.e., who does not receive illumination from God's Spirit), but undertakes of himself to give an exposition of the Scripture—which only the divine Spirit is able to do—makes of God's secrets which are contained in scripture a desolate abomination, and misuses the grace which he has received from God.[7]

Menno Simons (1496–1561)
Confession of the Triune God (1550)

As we have now indicated and confessed our faith in confession of the true deity of Jesus Christ, so we will also by the grace of God set forth in few words our faith and confession of the Holy Ghost. Let the God-fearing judge. We believe and confess the Holy Ghost to be a true, real, and personal Holy Ghost, as the fathers called Him; and that in a divine fashion, even as the Father is a true Father and the Son a true Son. Which Holy Ghost is a mystery to all mankind, incomprehensible, ineffable, and indescribable (as we have shown above of the Father and the Son); divine with His divine attributes, proceeding from the Father through the Son, although he ever remains with God and in God, and is never separated from the being of the Father and the Son.

He guides us into all truth; He justifies us. He cleanses, sanctifies, reconciles, comforts, reproves, cheers, and assures us. He testifies with our spirit that we are the children of God. This Spirit all they receive who believe on Christ.

Dear brethren, from these plain Scriptures, testimonies, and references, and a great many other tests which are too lengthy to mention and which may be found in abundance in the Scriptures, we believe the Holy Spirit to be the true, essential Holy Spirit of God,

[7] *Mennonite Encyclopedia*, II (1956), p. 33.

who adorns us with His heavenly and divine gifts, and through His influence, according to the good pleasure of the Father, frees us from sin, gives us boldness, and makes us cheerful, peaceful, pious, and holy.[8]

Instruction on Excommunication (1558)

Where the attitude is not pure nor true love, there the understanding is generally partial and the interpretation unjust, as alas I have often experienced in my days. Ah, that some of them might obtain grace. Besides, I know that preferences, judgements, affections, and minds are varied, and that the consistent grasp of the truth and the fear, the Spirit, and the unction of the Lord are not possessed by everyone in the same fullness. . . .

The stiff-necked, bold, and perverse scorners I do not serve. Neither the inflexible partisans or embittered agitators. But those I serve who with an impartial, renewed, and Christian mind allow themselves to be instructed by the Holy Spirit, the fear of God and pure love, men who have received the Lord's holy Word and truth in pure mind, who obediently follow it through the received unction, and so are free from all bitter partisanship, vain honor, hatred, and envy. For with such we find the lovely spirit of peace, a pious and sincere disposition, and unleavened, pure heart and love. . . . They subject themselves to all men, are humble, opposed to all unscriptural contention and strife.[9]

---

[8] Menno Simons, *The Complete Writings of Menno Simons,* ed. H. S. Bender, L. Verduin, and J. C. Wenger (Scottdale, Pa.: Herald Press, 1956), pp. 495-496.
[9] *Ibid.,* p. 965.

33

John Calvin

(1509–1564)

The Institutes *are Calvin's formidable systematic statement of Reformed Protestant theology. The Spirit, for the "master of Geneva," functions as the guardian of the central fortress of the Protestant position. The "inner witness of the Spirit" serves on one hand to authenticate Scripture, instead of appealing to the church and its tradition, and on the other hand to create faith in Christ through the Word in the heart of the predestinated elect person. But when Calvin comes to speak of the Spirit's creative work, he sidetracks into a debate with Rome over the nature of faith (III 2-5). Neither is the Spirit a controlling motif in Calvin's discussion of the Christian life (III 6s). He does accord the Spirit a central role in making the sacraments effective (IV 14:9-10; 16:21-22; 17:8-10, 31-34).*

But a most pernicious error widely prevails that Scripture has only so much weight as is conceded to it by the consent of the church. As if the eternal and inviolable truth of God depended upon the decision of men! For they mock the Holy Spirit when they ask: Who can convince us that these writings came from God? Who can assure us that Scripture has come down whole and intact even to our very day?

Who can persuade us to receive one book in reverence but to exclude another, unless the church prescribe a sure rule for all these matters? . . .

The highest proof of Scripture derives in general from the fact that God in person speaks in it. . . . If we desire to provide in the best way for our consciences . . . we ought to seek our conviction in a higher place than human reasons, judgments, or conjectures, that is, in the secret testimony of the Spirit. . . .

They who strive to build up firm faith in Scripture through disputation are doing things backwards. . . . The testimony of the Spirit is more excellent than all reason. For as God alone is a fit witness of himself in his Word, so also the Word will not find acceptance in men's hearts before it is sealed by the inward testimony of the Spirit. The same Spirit, therefore, who has spoken through the mouths of the prophets must penetrate into our hearts to persuade us that they faithfully proclaimed what had been divinely commanded. . . . Let this point therefore stand: that those whom the Holy Spirit has inwardly taught truly rest upon Scripture, and that Scripture indeed is self-authenticated; hence, it is not right to subject it to proof and reasoning. And the certainty it deserves with us, it attains by the testimony of the Spirit. For even if it wins reverence for itself by its own majesty, it seriously affects us only when it is sealed upon our hearts through the Spirit. . . . the only true faith is that which the Spirit of God seals in our hearts. . . . God deems worthy of singular privilege only his elect, whom he distinguishes from the human race as a whole. . . . Whenever, then, the fewness of believers disturbs us, let the converse come to mind, that only those to whom it is given can comprehend the mysteries of God. (I 7)[1]

. . . as long as Christ remains outside of us, and we are separated from him, all that he has suffered and done for the salvation of the human race remains useless and of no value for us. . . . There is good reason for the repeated mention of the "testimony of the Spirit," a testimony we feel engraved like a seal upon our hearts. . . . By these

[1] John Calvin, *Institutes of the Christian Religion,* Volumes XX and XII, The Library of Christian Classics, ed. John T. McNeill and trans. Ford Lewis Battles (Philadelphia: The Westminster Press, 1960), pp. 74-81. Copyright © MCMLX by W. L. Jenkins. Used by permission.

words [1 Peter 1:2], he explains that, in order that the shedding of Christ's sacred blood may not be nullified, our souls are cleansed by the secret watering of the Spirit. . . . To sum up, the Holy Spirit is the bond by which Christ effectually unites us to himself. . . . By his secret watering the Spirit makes us fruitful to bring forth the buds of righteousness. . . . For by the inspiration of his power he so breathes divine life into us that we are no longer actuated by ourselves, but are ruled by his action and prompting . . . until our minds become intent upon the Spirit, Christ, so to speak, lies idle because we coldly contemplate him as outside ourselves.

Faith is the principal work of the Holy Spirit. . . . Paul shows the Spirit to be the inner teacher by whose effort the promise of salvation penetrates into our minds, a promise that would otherwise only strike the air or beat upon our ears. . . . he is briefly warning us [2 Thessalonians 2:13] that faith itself has no other source than the Spirit. . . . The same Word is the basis whereby faith is supported and sustained; if it turns away from the Word, it falls. Therefore, take away the Word and no faith will then remain. . . . Now we shall possess a right definition of faith if we call it a firm and certain knowledge of God's benevolence toward us, founded upon the truth of the freely given promise in Christ, both revealed to our minds and sealed upon our hearts through the Holy Spirit.

Though only those predestined to salvation receive the light of faith and truly feel the power of the gospel, yet experience shows that the reprobate are sometimes affected by almost the same feeling as the elect. . . . Therefore it is not at all absurd that the apostle should attribute to them a taste of the heavenly gifts (Heb. 6:4-6)—and Christ, faith for a time (Luke 8:13); not because they firmly grasp the force of spiritual grace and the sure light of faith, but because the Lord, to render them more convicted and inexcusable, steals into their minds to the extent that his goodness may be tasted without the Spirit of adoption. . . . For, the Spirit, strictly speaking, seals forgiveness of sins in the elect alone, so that they apply it by special faith to their own use. . . . however deficient or weak faith may be in the elect, still, because the Spirit of God is for them the sure guarantee and seal of their adoption [Eph. 1:14; cf. II Cor. 1:22], the mark he has engraved can never be erased from their hearts; but on the wicked such light is shed as may afterward pass away. . . . the knowledge of faith consists in assurance rather than in comprehension.[2]

And this bare and external proof of the Word of God should have been amply sufficient to engender faith, did not our blindness and perversity prevent it. But our mind has such an inclination to vanity that it can never cleave fast to the truth of God; and it has such a dullness that it is always blind to the light of God's truth. Accordingly, without the illumination of the Holy Spirit, the Word can do nothing. . . . And it will not be enough for the mind to be illumined by the Spirit of God unless the heart is also strengthened and supported by his power. . . . For the Spirit is not only the initiator of faith, but increases it by degrees, until by it he leads us to the Kingdom of Heaven. . . . Therefore, as we cannot come to Christ unless we be drawn by the Spirit of God, so when we are drawn we are lifted up in mind and heart above our understanding. For the soul, illumined by him, takes on a new keenness, as it were, to contemplate the heavenly mysteries, whose splendor had previously blinded it. . . . Indeed, the Word of God is like the sun, shining upon all those to whom it is proclaimed, but with no effect among the blind. Now, all of us are blind by nature in this respect. Accordingly, it cannot penetrate into our minds unless the Spirit, as the inner teacher, through his illumination makes entry for it. . . . Thus Paul denies that man himself initiates faith, and not satisfied with this, he adds that it is a manifestation of God's power. . . . And God, to show forth his liberality more fully in such a glorious gift, does not bestow it upon all indiscriminately, but by a singular privilege gives it to those to whom he will. . . . But why one and not the other? This means much to me. It is an abyss, the depth of the cross. I can exclaim in wonder; I cannot demonstrate it through disputation. To sum up: Christ, when he illumines us into faith by the power of his Spirit, at the same time so engrafts us into his body that we become partakers of every good. (III 2)[3]

I make such a division between Spirit and sacraments that the power to act rests with the former, and the ministry alone is left to the latter—a ministry empty and trifling, apart from the action of the Spirit, but charged with great effect when the Spirit works within and manifests his power . . . the sacraments profit not a whit without the power of the Holy Spirit, and nothing prevents them from

[2] *Ibid.,* pp. 537-560.
[3] *Ibid.,* pp. 580-583.

strengthening and enlarging faith in hearts already taught by that Schoolmaster. (IV 14:8-9)[4]

Infants are baptized into future repentance and faith, and even though these have not yet been formed in them, the seed of both lies hidden within them by the secret working of the Spirit. (IV 16:20)[5]

To summarize: our souls are fed by the flesh and blood of Christ in the same way that bread and wine keep and sustain physical life. For the analogy of the sign applies only if souls find their nourishment in Christ—which cannot happen unless Christ truly grows into one with us, and refreshes us by the eating of his flesh and the drinking of his blood.

Even though it seems unbelievable that Christ's flesh, separated from us by such great distance, penetrates to us, so that it becomes our food, let us remember how far the secret power of the Holy Spirit towers above all our senses, and how foolish it is to wish to measure his immeasurableness by our measure. What, then, our mind does not comprehend, let faith conceive: that the Spirit truly unites things separated in space. . . . Scripture, in speaking of our participation with Christ, relates its whole power to the Spirit. But one passage will suffice for many. For Paul . . . states that Christ dwells in us only through his Spirit (Rom. 8:9). Yet he does not take away that communion of his flesh and blood which we are now discussing (Rom. 8:9), but teaches that the Spirit alone causes us to possess Christ completely and have him dwelling in us. (IV 17:10, 12)[6]

But greatly mistaken are those who conceive no presence of flesh in the Supper unless it lies in the bread. For thus they leave nothing to the secret working of the Spirit, which unites Christ himself to us. To them Christ does not seem present unless he comes down to us. As though, if he should lift us to himself, we should not just as much enjoy his presence! (IV 17:31)[7]

---

[4] *Ibid.,* pp. 1284-1285.
[5] *Ibid.,* p. 1343.
[6] *Ibid.,* pp. 1370, 1373.
[7] *Ibid.,* p. 1403.

34

John of the Cross

(1542–1591)

Spanish mystic and monastic reformer, John of the Cross, was the co-founder, with Teresa of Avila, of the Order of Discalced Carmelites. Part of Catholicism's "counter-reformation," he urged greater devotion for people following the religious life and became the recognized teacher of mystical spirituality in the Roman Catholic Church. "The Living Flame of Love" is a poem written by him, with doctrinal commentary.

Stanzas Which the Soul Recites
in the intimate union with God, its beloved Bridegroom

O living flame of love
   That tenderly wounds my soul
In its deepest center! Since
   Now You are not oppressive,
Now Consummate! if it be Your will:
   Tear through the veil of this sweet encounter!

O sweet cautery,
   O delightful wound!
O gentle hand! O delicate touch
   That tastes of eternal life

And pays every debt!
In killing You changed death to life.

O lamps of fire!
In whose splendors
The deep caverns of feeling,
Once obscure and blind,
Now give forth, so rarely, so exquisitely,
Both warmth and light to their Beloved.

How gently and lovingly
You wake in my heart,
Where in secret You dwell alone;
And in Your sweet breathing,
Filled with good and glory,
How tenderly You swell my heart with love.[1]

Hence, we can compare the soul in its ordinary condition in its state of transformation of love to the log of wood that is ever immersed in fire, and the acts of this soul to the flame that blazes up from the fire of love. The more intense the fire of union, the more vehemently does this fire burst into flames. The acts of the will are united to this flame and ascend, carried away and absorbed in the flame of the Holy Spirit, just as the angel mounted to God in the flame of Manoah's sacrifice (Judges 13:20).

Thus in this state the soul cannot make acts because the Holy Spirit makes them all and moves the soul towards them. As a result all the acts of the soul are divine, since the movement toward these acts and their execution stem from God. Hence it seems to a person that every time this flame shoots up making him love with delight and divine quality, it is giving him eternal life, since it raises him up to the activity of God in God. . . .

But the delight which that flaring of the Holy Spirit generates in the soul is so sublime that it makes it know that which savors of eternal life. Thus it refers to this flame as living, not because the flame is not always living, but because of this effect; it makes the soul live in God spiritually and experience the life of God in the manner David

[1] *The Living Flame of Love* in *The Collected Works of St. John of the Cross,* trans. Kieran Kavanaugh and Otilio Rodriguez (Washington, D.C.: ICS Publications, paperback edition), pp. 578-579. Copyright © 1964 by Washington Province of Discalced Carmelites, Inc.

mentions: *My heart and my flesh rejoiced in the living God* (Psa. 83:3). . . . Thus in this flame the soul experiences God so vividly and tastes him with such delight and sweetness that it exclaims: O living flame of love![2]

The Blessed Trinity inhabits the soul by divinely illuminating its intellect with the wisdom of the Son, delighting its will in the Holy Spirit, and by absorbing it powerfully and mightily in the delightful embrace of the Father's sweetness . . . what we are explaining about the activity of the Holy Spirit within [the soul] is something far greater than what occurs in the communication and transformation of love. This latter resembles the glowing embers, whereas the former is similar to embers not merely glowing but embers that have become so hot they shoot forth a living flame . . . a union of inflaming love.[3]

Before the divine fire is introduced into and united to the substance of the soul through a person's perfect and complete purgation and purity, its flame, which is the Holy Spirit, wounds it by destroying and consuming the imperfections of its bad habits. And this is the work of the Holy Spirit, in which He disposes it for the divine union and transformation in God through love . . . just as the fire that penetrates a log of wood is the same that first makes an assault upon it, wounding it with its flame, drying it out, and stripping it of its unsightly qualities until it is so disposed that it can be penetrated and transformed into the fire.

Spiritual writers call this activity the purgative way. In it a person suffers great deprivation and feels heavy afflictions in his spirit, which ordinarily overflow into the senses, for this flame is extremely oppressive. . . .[4]

The cautery is the Holy Spirit; the hand is the Father; and the touch is the Son. . . . The first is the delightful wound. This the soul attributes to the Holy Spirit and hence calls him a sweet cautery. . . . a fire of love, which being of infinite power, can inestimably consume and transform into itself the soul it touches. Yet He burns each soul according to its preparation: He will burn one more, another less, and this He does insofar as He desires, and how and when He desires.

[2] *Ibid.*, pp. 580-581.
[3] *Ibid.*, p. 585.
[4] *Ibid.*, p. 586.

When He wills to touch somewhat vehemently, the soul's burning reaches such a high degree of love that it seems to surpass that of all the fires of all the world; for He is an infinite fire of love. . . . Oh, the great glory of you who have merited this supreme fire! It is certain that, though it does not destroy you (for it has the infinite force to consume and annihilate you), it does consume you immensely in glory.[5]

Sometimes the unction of the Holy Spirit overflows into the body and all the sensory substance, all the members and bones and marrow rejoice, not in so slight a fashion as is customary, but with the feeling of great delight and glory, even in the outermost joints of the hands and feet. The body experiences so much glory in that of the soul that in its own way it magnifies God, feeling in its bones something similar to what David declares: *All my bones shall say: God, who is like to you?* (Psa. 34:10)[6]

The movements of these divine flames, which are the flickering and flaring up we have mentioned, are not alone produced by the soul that is transformed in the flames of the Holy Spirit, nor does the Holy Spirit produce them alone, but they are the work of both the soul and Him, since He moves the soul in the manner that fire moves the enkindled air. Thus these movements of both God and the soul are not only splendors but also glorifications of the soul.

This activity of the flames and these flares are happy festivals and games which . . . the Holy Spirit inspires in the soul.[7]

[5] *Ibid.*, pp. 595-597.
[6] *Ibid.*, p. 603.
[7] *Ibid.*, p. 614.

35

"Audi Coelum"

(before 1610)

*Claudio Monteverdi (1567–1643), the "maestro di cappella" at St.
Mark's in Venice, was an illustrious composer of sacred music in the
style of the late-Renaissance and Italian baroque. His church music
included elements of secular trends. He was a master of madrigal and
opera, but a genius at church music. In his "Vespers of 1610," he used
the "Audi coelum," a fifteenth-century poem, composing music for it
which bespeaks a love song in honor of Lady Mary in the tradition of
medieval courtly love and in Monteverdi's secular-religious style. The
surprise comes in the closing benediction, where, in place of the
expected trinitarian doxology, Mary's name is substituted for the
Holy Spirit.*

Heaven, hear my words full of desire and filled with joy!
Tell me, I ask you: Who is she, who dawns like the
   rise of morning, that I may praise her?
Tell me, for, beautiful as the moon, choice as the sun,
   Mary fills the lands and heavens with happiness.
The sweet virgin, Mary, Gate of the East predicted by
   the prophet Ezekiel,
That sacred and happy portal through which

death was driven out and eternal life brought in;
Who is always the safe link between men and God
    for the cure of guilt.
Let us all therefore follow after that which,
    with grace, we may merit, and attain eternal life.
God be with us: the Father, Son, and Mother be with us.
The Father and Son and Mother, on whose sweet name we call,
    the consolation of the miserable.
You are blessed, Virgin Mary, you are blessed forever,
    unto all ages.

(Author's translation)

36

Miguel of Molinos

(1628–1696)

Spanish mystic and author of A Spiritual Guide, *Molinos was a very popular guide of souls until severe opposition from the Vatican brought him into disrepute. He ended his days after nine years of penitential imprisonment, during which time he lived out what he had preached: a totally passive acquiescence to whatever humiliation the sovereign grace of God may send. Molinos's system of contemplation was nicknamed "Quietism" due to his teaching that the self must be totally abandoned to God's will and operation in the soul in order to rid oneself of all efforts either to act virtuously or repel temptations, to form thoughts or desires.*

Mystical knowledge proceeds not from Wit, but from Experience; it is not invented, but proved; not read, but received; and is therefore most secure and effective, of great help and plentiful in fruit. It enters not into the Soul by the ears, nor by the continual Reading of Books, but by the abundant Infusion of the Holy Spirit, Whose Grace with most delightful intimacy, is communicated to the meek and lowly.[1] The Soul is a pure Spirit and does not feel herself, and thus the

[1] Miguel de Molinos, *The Spiritual Guide Which Disentangles the Soul,* ed. Kathleen Lyttelton (London: Methuen and Co., Ltd., 1907), p. 50.

internal acts, and the acts of the will, being the acts of the Soul and spiritual, are not perceptible. Hence the Soul knoweth not if she loveth, nor, for the most part, if she acteth.

From this thou mayest infer, that Devotion and sensible Pleasure, is not God, nor Spirit, but the bait of Nature; that therefore thou oughtest to set light by it, and despise it, and persevere firmly in Prayer, leaving thy self to the guidance of God, Who will be to thee light in aridity and in darkness.

Think not that when thou art dry and darksome in the presence of God, in faith and silence, that thou doest nothing, that thou losest time, and that thou art idle. . . .

It must not be said that the Soul is idle; for though she works not actively, yet the Holy Spirit works in her. Besides, she is not without all activity, because she operates, although spiritually, simply, and intimately.[2]

Thou wilt never attain to the Mountain of Perfection, nor to the high Throne of Internal Peace, if thou governest thyself according to thy own Will. This cruel and fierce Enemy of God, and of thy Soul, must be conquered, thy own Direction, thy own Judgment must be subjugated and deposed as Rebels, and reduced to Ashes in the Fire of Obedience. There thou wilt learn as by a Touch-stone, whether thou followest self love or the Divine Love, there in that Holocaust must thine own Judgment, and thine own Will be entirely Annihilated even to the last substance.[3]

There are many Souls dedicated to God who receive from the Divine Hand great Thoughts, Visions, and mental Elevations. And yet, for all that, the Lord has not granted to them the Grace of working Miracles, understanding hidden Secrets, foretelling future events, as He has done to other Souls which have constantly gone through Tribulations and Temptations, in perfect Humility, Obedience and Subjection. . . .

But what a grief is this, that scarce is there one Soul which despises spiritual pleasures and is willing to be denied for Christ. . . .[4]

Good fortune consists not in enjoying, but in suffering with quiet and resignation. St. Teresa appeared after her death to a certain Soul and

[2] *Ibid.,* p. 83.
[3] *Ibid.,* p. 121.
[4] *Ibid.,* pp. 145-146.

said that she had been rewarded only for her pain, but had not received one drachm of reward for the many Extasies and Revelations and Comforts which she had here enjoyed in this World.[5]

Thou wilt see that God make greater account of a Soul that lives in inner resignation, than of another that worketh miracles, even to the raising of the dead.[6]

Simple, pure, infused, and perfect Contemplation therefore is a known and inner manifestation which God gives of Himself, of His Goodness, of His Peace, and of His Sweetness, whose object is God, pure, ineffable, abstracted from all particular thoughts, within an inward Silence. But it is God Who delights us, God Who draws us, God Who sweetly raises us in a spiritual and pure manner; and all this is an admirable gift, which the Divine Majesty bestows on whom He wills, as He wills, and when He wills, and for what time He wills, even though the state of this Life be rather a state of the Cross, of patience, of humility, and of suffering, than of enjoyment.[7]

Till the mind is purged, the affection purified, the memory bared, the understanding enlightened, the will disciplined and set on fire, the Soul can never arrive at the intimate and absolute union with God. Because the Spirit of God is purity It self, and light and rest, the Soul wherein He intends to abide must have great Purity, Peace and Quiet. Finally, the precious Gift of a purified Mind belongs only to those who with continual diligence do seek Love, and hold themselves, and desire to be held the most vile in the world.[8]

Many seek God and find Him not and because they are more moved by curiosity than by sincere, pure and upright intention: they rather desire Spiritual Comforts than God himself.

He that does not seek for complete self abnegation . . . can never receive the truth, and the light of the Spirit. . . . Rare are the men who set a higher value upon hearing than upon speaking. But the wise and truly mystical Man never speaks but when he cannot help it. . . . The Spirit of Divine Wisdom fills men with sweetness, rules them with firmness, and enlightens with fulness those who subject themselves to Its direction. Where the Divine Spirit dwells, there is always found Simplicity and a holy Liberty.[9]

[5] *Ibid.,* p. 156.
[6] *Ibid.,* p. 165.
[7] *Ibid.,* pp. 176-177.
[8] *Ibid.,* p. 185.
[9] *Ibid.,* pp. 190-191.

37

Robert Barclay

(1648–1690)

The spiritual impact of the people called Quakers has been one out of all proportion to their numbers. Beginning with the classical spiritual autobiography of their founder, the Journal *of George Fox (1624–1691), their story was retold a thousand times in terms of a rigorously individual, internal witness of the Spirit. Never ones to boast external wonders or pentecostal extravagances, Quaker theology is, nevertheless, perhaps the most consistently pneumato-logical statement of Christian thought. Their miracles were, rather, the quiet worship of the Silent Meetings, the inner light, uncompro-mising peaceableness, and the respectful disrespect of their Thees and Thous and their undoffed hats in the presence of persons who measured their own importance in terms of the subservience of other people.*

Robert Barclay was the outstanding systematic theologian of the first generation Quakers. He came to his spiritual "convincement" by way of strict Calvinism in his youth followed by Jesuit schooling in Latin, theology, and patristics. His Catechism and Confession of Faith *(1673) was adopted by the Friends as a more or less official teaching instrument, and his* Apology *(first published in 1692) is the most thorough statement of Quaker thought and experience.*

PROPOSITION 2—INWARD AND UNMEDIATED REVELA-
TION

. . . It was by the revelation of the same Spirit that [God] has always manifested himself to the sons of men, whether they were patriarchs, prophets, or apostles.

These revelations of God by the Spirit, whether by outward voices and appearances, dreams, or inward objective manifestations in the heart, were formerly the main purpose of faith. This should continue to be so, since the object of faith is the same in all ages regardless of the variations in form by which it is administered. Moreover, these divine inward revelations are considered by us to be absolutely necessary for the building up of true faith. But, this does not mean that they can or ever do contradict the outward testimony of the scriptures, or proper and sound judgment.

Nevertheless, it does not follow that these divine revelations should be subjected either to the outward testimony of the scriptures, or of the natural reason of man, as more positive or more noble rules or touchstones. These divine revelations and inward illuminations possess their own clarity and serve as their own evidence. They force the well-disposed mind to assent and they inevitably move it in that direction in the same way that the common principles of natural truths move and incline the mind toward a natural agreement.[1]

PROPOSITION 3—THE SCRIPTURES

. . . Because the scriptures are only a declaration of the source, and not the source itself, they are not to be considered the principal foundation of all truth and knowledge. They are not even to be considered as the adequate primary rule of all faith and practice . . . they are and may be regarded as a secondary rule that is subordinate to the Spirit, from which they obtain all their excellence and certainty.[2]

. . . Even though the things of the gospel are true in themselves, they are as lies if they are not uttered in and by that principle and Spirit which should properly activate and direct the mind in such matters. When they are uttered without the Spirit, they are like the words of

[1] Dean Freiday, *Barclay's Apology in Modern English* (Philadelphia: Friends Book Store, 1967), pp. 4-5. Note that the biblical quotations in this edition are taken from the modern language versions as indicated in the text. Permission to quote is granted by the editor, Dean Freiday, and by the prime distributor, Friends Book Store, 156 N. 15th St., Philadelphia, PA 19102.

[2] *Ibid.,* p. 405.

actors upon a stage or the prattling of a parrot who has been taught a few words. A parrot can even learn to utter a rational sentence, just as the intellect of man can learn the words or writings of spiritual men. But these words are not true unless they come from the spiritual rather than the rational principle.

Take away the Spirit and Christianity is no more Christianity than a corpse is a man, once the soul and spirit have departed. And a corpse is a noisome and a useless thing which the living can no longer stand and bury out of sight, no matter how acceptable it was when it was actuated and moved by the soul.

The nature of the New Covenant is expressed in [Isaiah 59:21]. The latter part certainly expresses the perpetuity and continuance of the promises that the Spirit of God is upon them and that the words of God will be put in their mouths.

This was to be a direct experience. No mention is made of any medium. God does not say that by means of such and such books he will convey such and such words into your mouths, but "my words that I have put into your mouth." He does not say he will enlighten your understanding and assent only to words which you will see written, but: you will have my words which I have put into your mouths.

From which it is argued that the righteous man, upon whom the Spirit will remain forever, is taught by the Spirit—directly, objectively and continually.[3]

Finally nothing can be the only, the principal, or the chief rule which does not universally reach every individual who needs it. Many who are handicapped by some physical defect, or those who are mentally retarded, or even children are excluded from the benefit of the scriptures in spite of the fact that they are members of the visible church. . . . No one will deny that they are included in the dispensation under the new covenant. Therefore, there must be some rule and some means of knowledge provided for them. In fact, this is expressly stated in John 6:45, RSV . . . "And they shall all be taught of God.". . . But even if we did not have this difficulty, how many good but illiterate men belong to the church of God. Even though illiteracy is inconvenient, we can hardly consider it sinful. Since these

[3] *Ibid.,* pp. 25, 32, 37.

people have no direct knowledge of the scriptures, their faith necessarily depends upon what is read to them or what others tell them. Even the alteration, addition, or omission of a single word could be the beginning of a very dangerous mistake. They might ignorantly continue some iniquity or they might be very confident in believing a lie.

Even if every one could read the scriptures in his own language, there would still be only one in a thousand who had a thorough enough knowledge of the original languages. . . . What an uncertain basis for a rule of faith this is. . . . We may safely conclude that Jesus Christ . . . did not leave [his children] dependent upon anything which included so many uncertainties. He gave them his Spirit as their principal guide and neither moths nor time can wear it out. Neither transcribers nor translators can corrupt it. And there is no one so young, or so illiterate, or in such a remote place, that he cannot be reached or properly informed by it.

The clarity of the Spirit is in contrast to the difficulties which occur in connection with the scriptures. I myself have been a witness of the dispensation of Christ's Spirit. I have seen the real and unquestionable experience of the great love of God for his children in these latter days. Some of my friends who profess the same faith as I do, and who are faithful servants of the Most High God, are full of the divine knowledge of his truth. This was directly and inwardly revealed to them by the Spirit in a true and living experience. They are not only ignorant of Greek and Hebrew, but some cannot even read their own language. Yet when pressed by some of their adversaries with certain citations from the English translations they have boldly asserted that God never said so. They were sure that the cited passages were wrong because they disagreed with the manifestation of truth in their own hearts. . . . When I seriously examined these passages because of their doubts, I found that they were right. . . .[4]

When we speak of the seed or light we understand a spiritual, celestial, and invisible principle, a principle in which God dwells as Father, Son and Spirit. A measure of this divine and glorious principle exists as a seed in all men which by its nature draws, invites, and inclines the individual toward God. Some call this the *vehiculum Dei,* or the spiritual body of Christ, the flesh and blood of Christ, which came down from heaven, and on which all who have faith are

[4] *Ibid.,* pp. 55-57.

fed and nourished with eternal life. . . . This seed, light, or grace is not an accident . . . but a real spiritual substance which the soul of man can feel and apprehend. It is from this substance that the new man arises in the heart of the believer. . . . It is difficult for a man to comprehend this with his mind until he himself has experienced it, and merely understanding it in the mind would be of little value if that were as far as it went. But we know that it is true, and that our belief is not without solid ground. As the inward and substantial seed in our hearts is nourished and grows we become capable of tasting, smelling, seeing and handling the things of God, for these things are beyond our ordinary spirit and senses.

We know that it is a substance, because it exists in the hearts of wicked men, even while they are in wickedness. This seed of holy substance often lies in men's hearts like a naked grain in stony ground, or like medicine in an unhealthy body. When the divine medicine begins its work in a man's heart, part of him may become cured and good, and part may remain sick and evil.[5]

What makes a man a minister, pastor, or teacher in the Church of Christ? How does he come to be one? We answer: "By the inward power and virtue of the Spirit of God which will not only call him but will in some measure purify and sanctify him." Since the things of the spirit can only be truly known by the aid of the Spirit of God, it is by this same Spirit that a man is called and moved to minister to others. Thus he is able to speak from a living experience of the things to which he is a witness. . . . His words and ministry come from the inward power and virtue of the Spirit of God. By the same power they reach the hearts of his hearers and persuade them to approve of him and to be subject to him. . . . He who gathers Christians also provides ministers and teachers among them by the inward unmediated operation of his own Spirit, to watch over and instruct them and maintain them in an animated, refreshed, and powerful condition. Their call is verified in the hearts of their brethren, and the seals of their apostleship are the awareness of the life and power passing through them which daily and inwardly reinforces them in the most holy faith. . . . For such ministers, the outward ceremony of ordination, or the laying on of hands, is unnecessary. We cannot see what purpose it serves, since those who employ this ceremony admit that the power of conveying the Holy Spirit by these means has

[5] *Ibid.,* pp. 85, 87-88.

ceased. Isn't it a bit ridiculous to keep up the shadow by ape-like imitation if the substance is lacking? If it is possible to bring the Holy Spirit to them in that way, by the same rule they ought to be able to bid the blind to see and the lame to walk, in imitation of Christ and the apostles. They mock both God and men when they put their hands on men and tell them to receive the Holy Spirit when they believe that it is impossible and that the ceremony has no real effect. . . .

In a true church of Christ, gathered together by God, not only into belief in the principles of truth but also into the power and life and Spirit of Christ, it is the Spirit of God that is the orderer, ruler, and governor, not only in general, but in each particular matter. Whenever the believers are assembled together to wait upon God, and for adoration and worship, those whom the Spirit sets apart for the ministry are thus ordained by God and admitted to the ministry. Their mouths are opened by the divine power and influence of the Spirit and words are given to them by which they exhort, reprove and instruct with virtue and with power. Their brethren cannot do otherwise than hear them, receive them, and also give them honor for the sake of their work.

The ministry is not monopolized by a certain kind of men, set aside as clergy (who are educated and brought up for that purpose like people in any other profession), while the rest are despised as laymen. Instead, it is left to the free gift of God to choose anyone he may deem appropriate. . . . yes, even male or female.[6]

When assembled, it should be the common task of one and all to wait upon God. It should be a time for turning away from one's own thoughts and for suspending the imagination in order to feel the Presence of the Lord in the midst and to know a true gathering in his name according to his promise. Then, when everyone is thus gathered, and all meet together inwardly in their spirits, as well as outwardly in their persons, the secret power and the virtue of life are known to refresh the soul. It is there that the pure motions and breathings of God's Spirit are felt to arise.

As words of declaration, prayers or praises arise from these promptings of the Spirit, the acceptable worship is known which edifies the church and is pleasing to God. No one limits the Spirit of

[6] *Ibid.,* pp. 178-179, 191-192, 210.

God in such worship or brings forth his own laboriously assembled ideas. But everyone will state whatever the Lord has placed in his heart. And it will not be uttered from man's own will or wisdom, but in the evidence and demonstration of the Spirit and of power.

Yes, even when a word has not been spoken, true spiritual worship has been performed and the body of Christ has been edified. Indeed it can and often does happen that many of our meetings take place without the utterance of a single word. Yet our souls have been greatly edified and refreshed, and our hearts wonderfully overcome with the secret sense of God's power and Spirit, which has been ministered without words from one vessel to another.[7]

If it should happen that several of those who are meeting together should begin to stray in mind and depart from the grace that is in them, even though they are outwardly silent, and someone comes in, or is present, who is watchful and in whom the life has been raised to a great measure, he will feel a secret travail for the others. It will be a sympathetic response to the seed which is oppressed in them and kept from rising by their meandering thoughts. If he remains faithful and waits in the light, continuing this divine work, God often answers this hidden travail and works through the breathings of his own seed in such persons. Then the rest find themselves secretly smitten without words. The faithful person becomes like a midwife whose inward travail brings forth the life in them. He is like a pump which brings up water by the bucketful when it has been primed with a cup or two. The useless wandering of the imagination is discontinued and the life becomes raised in all. Those who have been helped are aware that such a person has ministered life to them without words.

In part, this is how I came to be a true witness. For it was not by the strength of arguments, or by the formal discussion of each doctrine in order to convince my understanding, that I came to receive and bear witness to the truth. Rather it was by being mysteriously reached by this life. For when I came into the silent assemblies of God's people, I felt a secret power among them, which touched my heart. And as I gave way to it, I found the evil in me weakening, and the good lifted up. Thus it was that I was knit into them and united with them. And I hungered more and more for the increase of this power and life until I

[7] *Ibid.,* pp. 248-249.

could feel myself perfectly redeemed. Indeed, this is the surest way to become a Christian.[8]

[In regard to] the singing of the psalms. For the case is the same as that for preaching and for prayer. This is part of God's worship, and it is very sweet and refreshing when it proceeds from a true sense of God's love in the heart. If it arises from the divine influence of the Spirit, that can just as suitably lead souls to breathe forth sweet harmony as to provide words suitable for the occasion. . . .

But the formal and customary way of singing has no foundation in scripture and no basis in true Christianity. And there is no precept or example for artificial music either by organs or other instruments in the New Testament. . . .

The greatest advantage of this true worship of God which we profess and practice is that it does not consist of man's wisdom, arts, or skills. Nor does it require the glory, pomp, riches, or splendor of the world to beautify it. Being of a spiritual and celestial nature it is too simple and despicable for the natural mind and will of man.[9]

The "one baptism" in Eph. 4:5 which acknowledges "one Lord," "one faith," and so forth, is the baptism of Christ. . . .

It is frequently alleged in explanation of this text that the baptism of water and the Spirit together make up one baptism by virtue of the sacramental union. But the origin of this exposition is not in scripture. . . . We have John's own testimony that water baptism is not properly and distinctively the baptism of Christ. Mat 3:11 NEB says very definitely: "I baptize you with water . . .; but the one who comes after me . . . will baptize you with the Holy Spirit and with fire.". . .

It is apparent from 1 Pet 3:21 RSV that the one baptism of Christ is not a cleansing with water . . . [It is, he says:] "an appeal to God for a clear conscience, through the resurrection of Jesus Christ." . . . How can this be achieved if it is not through the purifying action of the Holy Spirit on the soul, and the cauterizing of our unrighteous nature by the fire of his judgement? Those in whom this has been done can truly be said to have been baptized with the baptism of Christ—the baptism of the Spirit and of fire.[10]

The body of Christ of which the believers partake is one of the Spirit

[8] *Ibid.,* pp. 253-255.
[9] *Ibid.,* pp. 297-299.
[10] *Ibid.,* pp. 305-306, 308.

and not of the flesh. His blood which they drink is pure and celestial and is not composed of human and earthly elements. . . . But the communion or participation in the flesh and blood of Christ has no necessary relationship to the breaking of bread and drinking of wine . . . , because partaking of the flesh and blood of Christ is a spiritual exercise. Everyone agrees that it is by the soul and spirit that we truly partake of communion, for it is the soul and not the body that is nourished by it. But eating bread and drinking wine are physical acts which of themselves add nothing to the soul and there is nothing spiritual about them. The most worldly of men can just as easily eat the bread and drink the wine and do it just as well as the most spiritual of men. . . . everyone acknowledges that many who eat the bread and drink the wine nevertheless do not have life eternal. Even though they say that the elements are consecrated and transubstantiated into the very body of Christ, they do not have Christ dwelling in them. Nor do they live by him as all of those do who truly partake of the flesh and blood of Christ even though they do not use this ceremony. . . . Since the washing of feet has justly been laid aside (as being merely a ceremony), the breaking of bread and drinking of wine should also be discontinued. . . .[11]

For we are certain that the day has dawned in which God has risen and has dismissed all those ceremonies and rites. He is to be worshipped only in Spirit. He appears to those who wait upon him. To seek God in these things is, like Mary at the sepulchre, seeking the living among the dead. For we know that he has risen and has been revealed in Spirit. He is leading his children out of these rudiments, that they may walk with him in his light, to whom be glory forever. Amen.[12]

[11] *Ibid.*, pp. 327, 339, 348.
[12] *Ibid.*, p. 361.

38

Quaker and Ranter Experiences

(Seventeenth Century)

The following examples of Quaker experiences dispel somewhat the usual image of them as "silent." While their Meetings are conducted in pregnant quietness, their nickname is no misnomer, for they did quake. A Ranter can be described as a violent Quaker. Whereas the Quakers were consistently pacifistic, the Ranters, who shared the Quaker spiritual perspective, nevertheless allowed themselves to take up arms in execution of the Spirit's leading. The last example given here is of a Ranter and not, as asserted in the first line, a true Quaker.

Thomas Holme was the apostle of Quakerism to South Wales; the first excerpt is from a letter to Margaret Fell, written during a time of imprisonment. The second selection gives his account of his marriage.

Upon the 5 day of the 2 month [1654] at evening, the word of the Lord came unto me and commanded me to deny the bed which I had lain in, and to ask for a free prison. And they put me into the place where I had lain before. But I obeyed the word of the Lord, and lay upon the floor. And a little before midnight, the power of the Lord came upon me, and sweet melody was within me. And about midnight I was compelled to sing; and the power was so great, it made all my fellow-prisoners amazed, and some were shaken, for the power was exceeding great. And I scarcely know whether I was in the body, yea or no. And there appeared light in the prison and astonished me. And I was afraid, and trembled at the appearance of the light; my legs shook under me. And my fellow-prisoners beheld the light, and wondered. And the light was so glorious, it dazzled my eyes.

And the next night likewise, I was put in there again, and I lay upon the floor. And in like manner the power of the Lord came upon me, and made me to sing about midnight, as I did before, in much power; and light appeared, as did before. And I greatly feared the Lord, for his appearance was glorious, glory and honour for ever be to him! And in the morning I was made to sing. And I was brought to shed many tears, to see the unspeakable love of God, the height, the depth, the breadth, and length of the love of God.[1]

Upon the 16 day of the 8 month [1654], being the same day we were set free from outward bonds, being in Chester at Edward Morgan's house, and she with me, and many more other friends, I was immediately commanded of the Lord to take her to wife that day, having before seen it clear in the light eternal, and had a vision of it long before, as likewise she had. So in obedience to the command of the Lord, I took her to wife, contrary to my will.[2]

A contemporary account, published in three anti-Quaker books, records these events:

Anno Christi 1653, about the month of October, came some Quakers out of the North of Wales, about Wrexham. . . . At meetings after long silence, sometimes one, sometimes more, fell into a great and dreadfull shaking and trembling in their whole bodies, and all their joynts, with such risings and swellings in their bellies and bowels, sending forth such shreekings, yellings, howlings and roarings, as not

---

[1] Geoffrey F. Nuttall, *Studies in Christian Enthusiasm: Illustrated from Early Quakerism* (Wallingford, Pa.: Pendle Hill, 1948), pp. 55-56.
[2] *Ibid.,* p. 54.

only affrighted the spectaters, but caused the dogs to bark, the swine to cry, and the cattel (sic!) to run about.[3]

From B. Whitelocke's Journal *(30 December 1654):*

A Quaker came to the door of the parliament, and drawing his sword, fell to slashing those near him, and knocked at the door aloud: he was laid hold on, and committed to prison. . . . The Quaker being examined by a committee why he drew his sword, and hurt divers at the parliament door, answered, that he was inspired by the Holy Spirit to kill every man that sat in the house.[4]

---

[3] *Ibid.,* p. 61.
[4] *Ibid.,* p. 81.

THEOLOGIANS, CHARISMATICS, POPES

39

John Wesley

(1703–1791)

Charles Wesley

(1707–1788)

John Wesley, the founder of Methodism, tells of his troubled path to spirituality in his Journal, *describing his talks with Quakers, the Moravian followers of Count Zinzendorf, and the Brethren of Herrnhut, and especially Peter Boehler. He resisted the Lutheran/ Moravian notions of justification by faith only and the Quaker emphasis on instantaneous effects of the "new birth," coming to a position of spiritual gradualism, cooperation with God, and the "second work of grace." According to the latter, the effects of original sin are removed so that as long as the Spirit is at work, the Christian no longer sins. With Charles, who composed more than seven thousand hymns, John was a tireless preacher who worked out his original insight of the "Aldersgate experience" in his sermons and especially his hymns.*

In the evening I went very unwillingly to a society in Aldersgate Street, where one was reading Luther's preface to the Epistle to the Romans. About a quarter before nine, while he was describing the change which God works in the heart through faith in Christ, I felt my heart strangely warmed. I felt I did trust in Christ, Christ alone, for salvation: and an assurance was given me, that He had taken away my sins, even mine, and saved me from the law of sin and death. I began to pray with all my might for those who had in a more especial manner despitefully used me and persecuted me. I then testified openly to all there, what I now first felt in my heart.[1]

Whether these gifts of the Holy Ghost [1 Corinthians 12:9-10] were designed to remain in the Church throughout all ages, and whether or no they will be restored at the nearer approach of the "restitution of all things," are questions which it is not needful to decide. But it is needful to observe this, that, even in the infancy of the Church, God divided them with a sparing hand. . . . Did all speak with tongues? No, in no wise. Perhaps not one in a thousand. Probably none but the Teachers in the Church, and only some of them. (I Cor. xii:28-30) It was, therefore, for a more excellent purpose than this that "they were all filled with the Holy Ghost." . . .

Without busying ourselves, then, in curious, needless inquiries, touching those *extraordinary* gifts of the Spirit, let us take a nearer view of these his *ordinary* fruits, which we are assured will remain throughout all ages.[2]

But what is that testimony of God's Spirit, which is superadded to, and conjoined with [the testimony of our own spirit]? [cf. Romans 8:16] How does he "bear witness . . ."? Indeed, there are [no words] in the language of men that will adequately express what the children of God experience. But perhaps one might say (desiring any who are taught of God to correct, to soften, or strengthen the expression), the testimony of the Spirit is an inward impression on the soul, whereby the Spirit of God directly witnesses to my spirit, that I am a child of God; that Jesus Christ hath loved me, and given himself for me; and that all my sins are blotted out, and I, even I, am reconciled to God. . . .

The soul as intimately and evidently perceives when it loves, delights, and rejoices in God, as when it loves, and delights in anything on earth. And it can no more doubt, whether it loves, delights, and rejoices or no, than whether it exists or no. If, therefore, this be just reasoning, he that now loves God, that delights and rejoices in him

John Wesley, *Journal,* Wednesday, May 24, 1738, *The Works of the Rev. John Wesley* (London: Wesleyan Conference Office, 1872), vol. 1, p. 103.
[2]"Scriptural Christianity," *The Works of the Rev. John Wesley* (London: Wesleyan Conference Office, 1872), vol. 5, p. 38.

with an humble joy, and holy delight, and an obedient love, is a child of God:

But I thus love, delight, and rejoice in God;

Therefore, I am a child of God:—

Then a Christian can in no wise doubt of his being a child of God. Of the former proposition he has as full an assurance as he has that the Scriptures are of God; and of his thus loving God, he has an inward proof, which is nothing short of self-evidence. Thus, the testimony of our own spirit is with the most intimate conviction manifested to our hearts, in such a manner, as beyond all reasonable doubt to evince the reality of our sonship.[3]

(Twenty years later, Wesley returned to this text in another sermon by the same name:)

Meantime, let it be observed, I do not mean hereby, that the Spirit of God testifies this by any outward voice; no, nor always by an inward voice, although he may do this sometimes. Neither do I suppose, that he always applies to the heart (though he often may) one or more texts of Scripture. But he so works upon the soul by his immediate influence, and by a strong, though inexplicable operation, that the stormy wind and troubled waves subside, and there is a sweet calm; the heart resting as in the arms of Jesus, and the sinner being clearly satisfied that God is reconciled, that all his "iniquities are forgiven, and his sins covered."

But the point in question is, whether there be any *direct* testimony of the Spirit at all; whether there be any other testimony of the Spirit, than that which arises from a consciousness of the fruit.

I believe there is; because that is the plain, natural meaning of the text [Romans 8:16]. . . .

And here properly comes in, to confirm this scriptural doctrine, the experience of the children of God; the experience not of two or three, not of a few, but of a great multitude which no man can number. It has been confirmed both in this and in all ages by "a cloud" of living and dying "witnesses." It is confirmed by *your* experience and *mine*. . . .

But this is confirmed, not only by the experience of the children of God;—thousands of whom can declare that they never did know

[3]The Witness of the Spirit," I in *ibid.,* pp. 115-117.

themselves to be in the favour of God till it was directly witnessed to them by his Spirit;—but by all those who are convinced of sin, who feel the wrath of God abiding on them. These cannot be satisfied with anything less than a direct testimony from his Spirit. . . . Tell any of these, "You are to know you are a child, by reflecting on what he has wrought in you, on your love, joy, and peace;" and will he not immediately reply, "By all this I know I am a child of the devil! I have no more love to God than the devil has; my carnal mind is enmity against God. I have no joy in the Holy Ghost; my soul is sorrowful even unto death. I have no peace; my heart is a troubled sea; I am all storm and tempest." And which way can these souls possibly be comforted but by a divine testimony (not that they are good, or sincere, or conformable to the Scripture in heart and life, but) that God *justifieth the ungodly?*—him that, till the moment he is justified, is all ungodly, void of all true holiness. . . . Every one, therefore, who denies the existence of such a testimony does in effect deny justification by faith. It follows, that either he never experienced this, either he never was justified, or that he has forgotten. . . .[4]

Now one who is so born of God, as hath been above described, who continually receives into his soul the breath of life from God, the gracious influence of his Spirit, and continually renders it back; one who thus believes and loves, who by faith perceives the continual actings of God upon his spirit, and by a kind of spiritual re-action returns the grace he receives, in unceasing love, and praise, and prayer; not only doth not commit sin, while he thus keepeth himself, but so long as this "seed remaineth in him, he cannot sin, because he is born of God." [1 John 3:4-9]

By sin, I here understand outward sin, according to the plain, common acceptation of the word; an actual, voluntary transgression of the law; of the revealed, written law of God. . . .
(But, admits John Wesley, some who have received the Holy Spirit do, in fact, sin; he answers how this comes about:)
You see the unquestionable progress from grace to sin: Thus it goes on, from step to step. (1.) The divine seed of loving, conquering faith, remains in him that is born of God. "He keepeth himself," by the grace of God, and "cannot commit sin." (2.) A temptation arises; whether from the world, the flesh, or the devil, it matters not. (3.) The Spirit of God gives him warning that sin is near, and bids

[4]"The Witness of the Spirit," II in *ibid.,* pp. 125-129.

him more abundantly watch unto prayer. (4.) He gives way, in some degree, to the temptation, which now begins to grow pleasing to him. (5.) The Holy Spirit is grieved; his faith is weakened; and his love of God grows cold. (6.) The Spirit reproves him more sharply, and saith, "This is the way; walk thou in it." (7.) He turns away from the painful voice of God, and listens to the pleasing voice of the tempter. (8.) Evil desire begins and spreads in his soul, till faith and love vanish away: He is then capable of committing outward sin, the power of the Lord being departed from him.[5]

The First sort of enthusiasm . . . is that of those who imagine they have the grace which they have not. . . . [For instance,] the fiery zealot for religion; or, more properly, for the opinions and modes of worship which he dignifies with that name. . . .

A Second sort of enthusiasm is that of those who imagine they have such gifts from God as they have not. Thus some have imagined themselves to be endued with a power of working miracles, of healing the sick by a word or a touch, of restoring sight to the blind; yea, even of raising the dead,—a notorious instance of which is still fresh in our own history. Others have undertaken to prophesy, to foretell things to come, and that with the utmost certainty and exactness. But a little time usually convinces these enthusiasts. When plain facts run counter to their predictions, experience performs what reason could not, and sinks them down into their senses. . . . They may likewise imagine themselves to be influenced or directed by the Spirit when they are not. . . . Such are they who imagine, they either do or shall receive *particular directions* from God, not only in points of importance, but in things of no moment; in the most trifling circumstances of life. Whereas in these cases God has given us our own reason for a guide; though never excluding the secret assistance of his Spirit.

To this kind of enthusiasm they are peculiarly exposed, who expect to be directed of God, either in spiritual things or in common life, in what is justly called an *extraordinary* manner: I mean, by visions or dreams, by strong impressions or sudden impulses on the mind. I do not deny, that God has, of old times, manifested his will in this manner; or, that he can do so now: Nay, I believe he does, in some very rare instances. But how frequently do men mistake herein! . . .

A Third very common sort of enthusiasm (if it does not coincide

[5]"The Great Privilege of Those that are Born of God," in *ibid.,* pp. 227-228.

with the former) is that of those who think to attain the end without using the means, by the immediate power of God. . . . Such are they who expect to understand the Holy Scriptures, without reading them, and meditating thereon; yea, without using all such helps as are in their power, and may probably conduce to that end. Such are they who designedly speak in the public assembly without any premeditation.

Beware you do not run with the common herd of enthusiasts, fancying you are a Christian when you are not. . . .

Beware you do not fall into the second sort of enthusiasm—fancying you have those gifts from God which you have not. Trust not in visions or dreams; in sudden impressions, or strong impulses of any kind. Remember, it is not by these you are to know what is the will of God on any particular occasion; but by applying the plain scripture rule, with the help of experience and reason, and the ordinary assistance of the Spirit of God.[6]

Some hymns to the Holy Spirit by Charles Wesley, taken from Hymnal with Tunes *of the Methodist Episcopal Church (1878)*

> Granted is the Saviour's prayer,
> Sent the gracious Comforter;
> Promise of our parting Lord,
> Jesus, to his heaven restored;
>
> Christ, who now gone up on high,
> Captive leads captivity,
> While his foes from him receive
> Grace, that God with man may live.
>
> God, the everlasting God,
> Makes with mortals his abode;
> Whom the heavens cannot contain,
> He vouchsafes to dwell in man.
>
> Never will he thence depart,
> Inmate of a humble heart;
> Carrying on his work within,
> Striving till he cast out sin.
>
> There he helps our feeble moans,
> Deepens our imperfect groans,

6"The Nature of Enthusiasm," in *ibid.,* pp. 471-473, 475, 478.

Intercedes in silence there,
Sighs the unutterable prayer.

Come, divine and peaceful Guest,
Enter our devoted breast:
Holy Ghost, our hearts inspire,
Kindle there the gospel fire.

Crown the agonizing strife,
Principle and Lord of life:
Life divine in us renew,
Thou the Gift and Giver too! (264)

• • •

Come, Holy Spirit, raise our songs
To reach the wonders of that day,
When, with thy fiery cloven tongues
Thou didst such glorious scenes display.

Lord, we believe to us and ours,
The apostolic promise given;
We wait the pentecostal powers,
The Holy Ghost sent down from heaven.

Assembled here with one accord,
Calmly we wait the promised grace,
The purchase of our dying Lord;
Come, Holy Ghost, and fill the place.

If every one that asks, may find,
If still thou dost on sinners fall,
Come as a mighty rushing wind;
Great grace be now upon us all.

O leave us not to mourn below,
Or long for thy return to pine;
Now, Lord, the Comforter bestow,
And fix in us the Guest divine. (275)

• • •

Spirit of faith, come down,
Reveal the things of God;
And make to us the Godhead known,
And witness with the blood:

'Tis thine the blood to apply,
And give us eyes to see,
That he who did for sinners die,
Hath surely died for me.

No man can truly say
That Jesus is the Lord,
Unless thou take the veil away,
And breathe the living Word:
Then, only then, we feel
Our interest in his blood;
And cry, with joy unspeakable,
"Thou art my Lord, my God!"

O that the world might know
The all-atoning Lamb!
Spirit of faith, descend and show
The virtue of his name:
The grace which all may find,
The saving power, impart;
And testify to all mankind,
And speak in every heart. (435)*

● ● ●

Love divine, all loves excelling,
Joy of heaven, to earth come down!
Fix in us thy humble dwelling;
All thy faithful mercies crown.
Jesus, thou art all compassion,
Pure, unbounded love thou art;
Visit us with thy salvation;
Enter every trembling heart.

Breathe, O breathe thy loving Spirit
Into every troubled breast!
Let us all in thee inherit,
Let us find thy promised rest.
Take away our bent to sinning;
Alpha and Omega be;
End of faith, as its beginning.
Set our hearts at liberty.

Compare these with the better-known hymn "Love Divine, All Loves Excelling."

Come, almighty to deliver,
Let us all thy life receive;
Suddenly return, and never,
Nevermore thy temples leave:
Thee we would be always blessing,
Serve thee as thy hosts above,
Pray, and praise thee without ceasing,
Glory in thy perfect love.

40

Jonathan Edwards

(1703–1758)

Jonathan Edwards was the Calvinist Congregational preacher at Northampton, Massachusetts, under whose ministry the "Great Awakening" spread. His Faithful Narrative of the Surprising Works of God *(1737) chronicles this movement of the Spirit. After the revival's effects had been fully felt, Edwards attempted to distinguish between the "true affections" of spiritual regeneration as manifested in twelve signs, and the "miracles" which he considered unreliable: vivid imaginations, voices, Scripture passages which seem to be intended especially for a single individual, revelation of secret information, etc.* Religious Affections *(1746) is his great work of spiritual psychology.*

True religion, in great part, consists in holy affections. . . . These affections we see to be the springs that set men agoing, in all the affairs of life, and engage them in all their pursuits. . . . I am bold to assert, that there never was any considerable change wrought in the mind or conversation of any one person, by anything of a religious nature, that ever he read, heard or saw, that had not his affections moved. . . .

The Holy Scriptures do everywhere place religion very much in the affections; such as fear, hope, love, hatred, desire, joy, sorrow, gratitude, compassion and zeal . . . even the Lord Jesus Christ was a person who was remarkably of a tender and affectionate heart; and his virtue was expressed very much in the exercise of holy affections. He was the greatest instance of ardency, vigor and strength of love, to both God and man, that ever was. . . .

And the duty of singing praises to God, seems to be appointed wholly to excite and express religious affections. No other reason can be assigned, why we should express ourselves to God in verse, rather than in prose, and do it with music, but only, that such is our nature and frame, that these things have a tendency to move our affections.[1]

'Tis no sign one way or the other, that religious affections are very great, or raised very high, . . . [or] that they have great effects on the body, . . . [or that they cause those who have them,] to be fluent, fervent and abundant, in talking of the things of religion, . . . [or] that persons did not make 'em themselves, or excite 'em of their own contrivance, and by their own strength, . . . [or] that they are not purposely produced by those who are the subjects of them, or that they arise in their minds in a manner they can't account for, . . . [or] that they come with texts of Scripture, remarkably brought to the mind, . . . [or] that there is an appearance of love in them, . . . [or] that comforts and joys seem to follow awakenings and convictions of conscience, . . . [or] that they dispose persons to spend much time in religion, and to be zealously engaged in the external duties of worship, . . . [or] that they much dispose persons with their mouths to praise and glorify God, . . . [or] that they make persons that have them, exceeding confident that what they experience is divine, and that they are in a good estate, . . . or that the outward manifestations of them, and the relation persons give of them, are very affecting and pleasing to the truly godly, and such as greatly gain their charity, and win their hearts. . . .[2]

There are some who make this an argument in their own favor . . . : "I am sure I did not make it myself: it was a fruit of no contrivance or endeavor of mine; it came when I thought nothing of it; if I might have the world for it, I can't make it again when I please." And hence

[1]Jonathan Edwards, *Religious Affections,* ed. John E. Smith (New Haven: Yale University Press, 1959), pp. 95, 101, 102, 111, 115.

[2]*Ibid.,* pp. 127-190, major topics of discussion under "Part II. Showing No Certain Signs of Truly Gracious Affections."

they determine, that what they have experienced must be from the mighty influence of the Spirit of God, and is of a saving nature; but very ignorantly, and without grounds. What they have been the subjects of, may indeed, not be from themselves directly, but may be from the operation of an invisible agent, some spirit besides their own: but it does not thence follow, that it was from the Spirit of God. There are other spirits who have influence on the minds of men, besides the Holy Ghost. . . .'Tis not in men's power to put themselves into such raptures, as the Anabaptists in Germany, and many other raving enthusiasts like them, have been the subjects of.

And besides, it is to be considered, that persons may have those impressions on their minds, which may not be of their own producing, nor from an evil spirit, but from the Spirit of God, and yet not be from any saving, but a common influence of the Spirit of God.[3]

[Some mention] that their experience came with the Word, and will say: "There were such and such sweet promises brought to my mind: they came suddenly, as if they were spoke to me: I had no hand in bringing such a text to my own mind; I was not thinking of anything leading to it; it came all at once, so that I was surprised. I had not thought of it a long time before; I did not know at first that it was Scripture; I did not remember that ever I had read it." And it may be, they will add: "One Scripture came flowing in after another, and so texts all over the Bible, the most sweet and pleasant, and the most apt and suitable, which could be devised; and filled me full as I could hold: I could not but stand and admire; the tears flowed; I was full of joy, and could not doubt any longer." And thus, they think they have undoubted evidence, that their affections must be from God, and of the right kind, and their state good: but without any manner of grounds. How come they by any such rule, as that if any affections or experiences arise with promises, and comfortable texts of Scripture, unaccountably brought to mind, without their recollection, or if a great number of sweet texts follow one another in a chain, that this is a certain evidence their experiences are saving? Where is any such rule to be found in the Bible, the great and only sure directory in things of this nature?

. . . affections may arise on *occasion* of the Scripture, and not *properly come from* the Scripture, as the genuine fruit of the

---

[3] *Ibid.,* pp. 140-142.

Scripture, and by a right use of it; but from an abuse of it. . . . What evidence is there that the devil can't bring texts of Scripture to the mind, and misapply them, to deceive persons?[4]

'Tis to be feared that some have gone too far towards directing the Spirit of the Lord, and marking out his footsteps for him, and limiting him to certain steps and methods. Experience plainly shows, that God's Spirit is unsearchable and untraceable, in some of the best of Christians, in the method of his operations, in their conversion. Nor does the Spirit of God proceed discernibly in the steps of a particular established scheme, one half so often as is imagined. A scheme of what is necessary, and according to a rule already received and established by common opinion, has a vast (though to many a very insensible) influence in forming persons' notions of the steps and method of their own experiences.[5]

If we see a man that boldly calls God his Father, and commonly speaks in the most bold, familiar and appropriating language in prayer, "My Father, my dear Redeemer, my sweet Saviour, my Beloved," and the like, and it is a common thing for him to use the most confident expressions before men, about the goodness of his state; such as: "I know certainly that God is my Father; I know so surely as there is a God in heaven, that he is my God; I know I shall go to heaven, as well as if I were there; I know that God is now manifesting himself to my soul, and is now smiling upon me": and seems to have done forever with my inquiry or examination into his state, as a thing sufficiently known, and out of doubt, and to condemn all that so much as intimate or suggest that there is some reason to doubt or fear whether all is right; such things are no signs at all that it is indeed so as he is confident it is. Such an overbearing, high-handed and violent sort of confidence as this, so affecting to declare itself with a most glaring show, in the sight of men, which is to be seen in many, has not the countenance of a true Christian assurance: it savors more of the spirit of the Pharisees, who never doubted but that they were saints, and the most eminent of saints, and were bold to go to God, and come up near to him, and lift up their eyes, and thank him for the great distinction he had made between them and other men. . . . A hypocrite may retain his hope without

4 *Ibid.*, pp. 143-144.
5 *Ibid.*, pp. 161-162.

opposition, as long as he lives, the devil never disturbing it, nor attempting to disturb it. But there is perhaps no true Christian but what has his hope assaulted by him.[6]

Affections that are truly spiritual and gracious, do arise from those influences and operations on the heart, which are *spiritual, supernatural* and *divine.* . . . The epithet "spiritual" [is used] with relation to the Holy Ghost, or Spirit of God. . . . Thus Christians are called spiritual persons, because they are born of the Spirit, and because of the indwelling and holy influences of the Spirit of God in them. And things are called spiritual as related to the Spirit of God . . . yet not all those persons who are subject to any kind of influence of the Spirit of God, are ordinarily called spiritual in the New Testament. . . . spiritually minded, Rom 8:6, means graciously minded. And though the extraordinary gifts of the Spirit, which natural men might have, are sometimes called spiritual, because they are from the Spirit; yet natural men, whatever gifts of the Spirit they had, were not, in the usual language of the New Testament, called spiritual persons. For it was not by men's having the gifts of the Spirit, but by their having the virtues of the Spirit, that they were called spiritual . . . though the Spirit of God may many ways influence natural men; yet because it is not thus communicated to them, as an indwelling principle, they don't derive any denomination or character from it; for there being no union it is not their own. . . .

Another reason why the saints and their virtues are called spiritual (which is the principal thing), is that the Spirit of God, dwelling as a vital principle in their souls, there produces those effects wherein he exerts and communicates himself in his own proper nature. Holiness is the nature of the Spirit of God . . . , which is as it were the beauty and sweetness of the divine nature. . . . Not that the saints are made partakers of the essence of God, and so are "Godded" with God, and "Christed" with Christ, according to the abominable and blasphemous language and notions of some heretics; but, to use the Scripture phrase, they are made partakers of God's fullness (Eph. 3:17-19; John 1:16), that is, of God's spiritual beauty and happiness, according to the measure and capacity of a creature. . . .

In those gracious exercises and affections which are wrought in the minds of the saints, through the saving influences of the Spirit of God, there is a new inward perception or sensation of their minds,

[6] *Ibid.,* pp. 171-172.

entirely different in its nature and kind, from anything that ever their minds were the subjects of before they were sanctified. . . . In the more ordinary influences of the Spirit of God on the hearts of sinners, he only assists natural principles to do the same work to a greater degree, which they do of themselves by nature. Thus the Spirit of God by his common influences may assist men's natural ingeniosity, as he assisted Bezaleel and Aholiab in the curious works of the tabernacle: so he may assist men's natural abilities in political affairs, and improve their courage, and other natural qualifications; as he is said to have put his Spirit on the seventy elders, and on Saul, so as to give him another heart. . . .[7]

It appears that spiritual understanding does not consist in any new doctrinal knowledge, or in having suggested to the mind any new proposition; . . . don't consist in opening to the mind the mystical meaning of the Scripture, in its parables, types and allegories; for this is only a doctrinal explication of Scripture. . . . And many men can explain these types, who have no spiritual knowledge. 'Tis possible that a man might know how to interpret all the types, parables, enigmas, and allegories in the Bible, and not have one beam of spiritual light in his mind; because he mayn't have the least degree of that spiritual sense of the holy beauty of divine things which has been spoken of. . . .[8]

If persons have the will of God concerning their actions, suggested to them by some text of Scripture, suddenly and extraordinarily brought to their minds, which text, as the words lay in the Bible before they came to their minds, related to the action and behavior of some other person, but they suppose, as God sent the words to them, he intended something further by them, and meant such a particular action of theirs; I say . . . the suggestion being accompanied with an apt text of Scripture, don't make the suggestion to be of the nature of spiritual instruction. As for instance, if a person in New England, on some occasion, were at a loss whether it was his duty to go into some popish or heathenish land, where he was like to be exposed to many difficulties and dangers, and should pray to God that he would show him the way of his duty; and after earnest prayer, should have those words which God spake to Jacob, Gen. 46, suddenly and

---

[7] *Ibid.,* pp. 197-207.
[8] *Ibid.,* p. 278.

extraordinarily brought to his mind, as if they were spoken to him; "Fear not to go down into Egypt . . . and I will go with thee; and I will surely bring thee up again." In which words, though as they lay in the Bible before they came to his mind, they related only to Jacob, and his behavior; yet he supposes that God has a further meaning, as they were brought and applied to him; that thus they are to be understood in a new sense, that by Egypt is to be understood this particular country he has in mind, and that the action intended is his going thither, and that the meaning of the promise is that God would bring him back into New England again. There is nothing of the nature of a spiritual or gracious leading of the Spirit in this; for there is nothing of the nature of spiritual understanding in it. . . . Spiritually to understand the Scripture, is rightly to understand what *is in* the Scripture, and what *was in* it before it was understood: 'tis to understand rightly, what used to be contained in the meaning of it; and not the making a new meaning. . . . This making a new meaning to the Scripture, is the same thing as making a new Scripture: it is properly adding to the Word; which is threatened with so dreadful a curse.

And as to a gracious leading of the Spirit, it consists in two things; partly in *instructing* a person in his duty by the Spirit, and partly in powerfully *inducing* him to comply with that instruction . . . being guided by a spiritual and distinguishing taste of that which has in it true moral beauty.[9]

Truly gracious affections differ from those affections that are false and delusive, in that they tend to, and are attended with the lamblike, dovelike spirit and temper of Jesus Christ; or in other words, they naturally beget and promote such a spirit of love, meekness, quietness, forgiveness and mercy, as appeared in Christ.[10]

Christian practice is the sign of signs, in this sense that it is the great evidence, which confirms and crowns all other signs of godliness. There is no one grace of the Spirit of God, but that Christian practice is the most proper evidence of the truth of it. . . . Christian practice is the chief of all the signs of saving grace. . . . Indeed all Christian experience is not properly called practice; but all Christian practice is properly experience.[11]

[9] *Ibid.,* pp. 279-281.
[10] *Ibid.,* pp. 344-345.
[11] *Ibid.,* pp. 444, 450-451.

41

Emanuel Swedenborg

(1688–1772)

Philosopher, scientist, metallurgist, anatomist, psychologist—
Swedenborg was a man of advanced talents who also suffered from
strange dreams and visions of light. His neoplatonic philosophy
included a place within it for Jesus Christ, but excluded the idea of the
Trinity and the atonement. After his conversion to Christianity, he
claimed to have been in near constant communication with angels
and other beings from the spirit world; the information which he
derived through his conversation with the angels provided authenti-
cation for the theology he had developed.

The Speech of Angels

Angels talk with each other just the way people in the world do,
and they talk of various things—household matters, political
matters, issues of moral life and issues of spiritual life, for example.
There is no noticeable difference, except that they talk with each
other more intelligently than men do, since they talk more
profoundly, from thought.

I have often been allowed to associate with them, to talk with them
as friend with friend—occasionally as stranger with stranger. At such
times, being in a condition like theirs, I had no way of knowing that I
was not talking with people on earth.

Angelic speech, like human speech, is divided into units. Too, it is just as much spoken aloud and heard aloud, for angels have mouths, tongues, and ears. They have an atmosphere in which their speech sounds are pronounced; but it is a spiritual atmosphere, fit for angels who are spiritual. Angels breathe in their atmosphere and use breath to pronounce words just the way men do in theirs.

There is a single language for everyone in all heaven. They all understand each other no matter what community they come from, near or far. The language is not learned there—it is native to everyone. It actually flows from their very affection and thought. The sound of speech corresponds to their affection, and the distinctions of sound—the speech units—to thought concepts stemming from affection. Because the language does correspond to these elements, it too is spiritual, being affection sounding and thought speaking.

. . . we can see how choice and pleasant their conversation is. It actually touches not just the ears, but the more inward reaches of the minds of those who hear it.

There was one particular hard-hearted spirit with whom an angel spoke. Eventually he was so touched by the conversation that he burst into tears, saying that he couldn't help it, love was talking, and he had never cried before.

The concepts of angels' thinking, which are the sources of their words, are changes in heaven's light as well; and the affections which give rise to their tones of voice are changes in heaven's warmth. This is because heaven's light is the Divine-True, or wisdom, and heaven's warmth is the Divine-Good, or love. . . . Angels derive affection from Divine love and thinking from Divine wisdom.

. . . angels can say more in a minute than man can say in half an hour. They can also set down in a few words the contents of many written pages. This too has been demonstrated to me by an abundance of evidence.

There is a kind of harmony in angelic speech that defies description. The source of this harmony is this: the affections and thoughts that give rise to speech pour out and spread in accord with heaven's form,[1]

[1] Emanuel Swedenborg, *Heaven and Hell,* trans. George F. Dole (New York: Swedenborg Foundation, 1976). Sections 234, 235, 236, 238, 239, 240, 242, pp. 148-153.

Angels who talk with man do not talk in their own language, but in the person's language. They also talk in other languages a person knows, but not in languages unfamiliar to him. The reason for this is that when angels are talking with someone, they turn toward him and bond themselves to him. The bond of angel to man brings the two into a similar kind of thinking. And since a person's thought is connected to his memory, where speech comes from, the two are in command of the same language.

Further, when an angel or spirit comes to a person and is bonded to him by turning toward him, he gains entrance to his whole memory— so much so that as far as he is aware, he on his own knows everything the person knows, including languages.[2]

A spirit filled by the Lord with what is Divine has no awareness that he is not the Lord, or that it is not the Divine which is speaking. This lasts until he has finished speaking. Afterward he realizes that he is a spirit, and that he has not spoken on his own, but rather from the Lord.

Since this was the condition of the spirits who spoke with the Prophets, the Prophets say that Jehovah spoke. Even the spirits themselves called themselves "Jehovah," as can be illustrated not only by Prophetic passages, but even by historical passages of the Word.[3]

[2] *Ibid.,* Section 246, p. 154.
[3] *Ibid.,* Section 254, pp. 158-159.

42

The Shakers

(Eighteenth and Nineteenth Centuries)

The United Society of Believers in Christ's Second Appearing, founded c. 1747 in England by the Quakers Jane and James Wardly under the influence of the French Prophets or Camisards, came under the spiritual motherhood of Ann Lee after 1758. Mother Ann was believed to be the incarnation in "these last days" of the eternal feminine in God—the eternal Christ-Spirit or Holy Spirit or Bride of Christ—and thus the spiritual Second Coming of Christ in the feminine form. She led her followers to America in 1774 where, at Watervliet (near Albany), New York, the millennial reign of Christ began under Mother Ann's spiritual rule, accompanied by a remarkable outbreak of spiritual gifts. Ann died in 1784, but the Shakers, as they were known, continued to expand along the American frontier, riding the crest of the general optimistic eschatological expectations in which the Mormons, Millerites and other Adventists, and some Campbellites variously shared. Since, however, the Shakers doctrinally eschewed sexual intercourse and the procreation of children (according to Mother Ann, the outstanding manifestation of original sin), when the social conditions which contributed to their rise and growth changed, the movement declined. They were famous for their technical inventiveness, their ecstatic dancing in worship and their simple life, of which their most famous hymn, "Simple Gifts," is an eloquent expression. Some other Shaker songs follow here. Also included are excerpts from the Testimony of Christ's Second Appearing . . . *etc., published by the United Society of Shakers.*

A spiritual drinking song to accompany the holy dance:

> Drink ye of Mother's wine,
> Drink, drink, drink ye freely,
> Drink ye of Mother's wine
> It will make you limber.
> If it makes you reel around,
> If it makes you fall down,
> If it lays you on the floor,
> Rise and take a little more.
>   (author unknown)[1]

O the simple gifts of God

O the simple gifts of God,
They're flowing like an ocean,
And I will strive with all my might
To gather in my portion.
I love, I love the gifts of God,
I love to be partaker
And I will labor day and night
To be an honest Shaker
          (Polly Champlain)[2]

Vision songs:

Hoo haw hum necatry O necatry O
Hoo haw hum necatry O cum
Ne holium ne-holium necatry O necatry O
Ne holium ne-holium ne hoo haw hum.
          (Hannah Ann Agnew)

O werekin werekin catry catry
Werekin werekin catry coo
O werekin werekin catry catry

[1] Edward D. Andrews, *The Gift to Be Simple: Songs, Dances, and Rituals of the American Shakers* (New York: Dover Publications, Inc., 1940, 1952), p. 124.
[2] *Ibid.*, p. 106.

Werekin werekin catry coo.
(Hannah Ann Agnew)[3]

A tongues song with interpretation:

O sa ri anti va me	O Saviour wilt thou hear me
O sa ri anti va me	O Saviour wilt thou hear me
I co lon se ve re	I am poor and kneedy
I con e lo se va ne	I'll come and bow before thee
I con e lo se va ne	I'll come and bow before thee
Se ran te lo me.	Thy cross I'll take upon me.

(E. D.-East family, New Lebanon)[4]

A tongues song of spiritual delight:

Ine vine violet,
Ene sene vingo pret,
Yfen wafen wane voo,
Ole mole minzy two
Acren wacren waney vo,
Mother's love is even so.
Une ene Ine va,
Now in love we'll dance and play.
(Hannah Ann Agnew)[5]

The idea which so extensively prevails, that all inspired revelation ceased with the canon of Scripture, is inconsistent with both reason and *Scripture*. It is not unreasonable to suppose, that the spiritual work of God should alone remain stationary, whilst all the natural arts and sciences among men, are continually improving and increasing. . . .

In no part of the Scriptures can the least intimation be found that the revelations of the Divine and Holy Spirit to man will ever cease; but many declarations to the contrary. . . . Such as deny those heavenly gifts have not because they ask not. . . . Thus the Saviour and his Apostles show the reason of that general barrenness of spiritual gifts among all denominations. . . . But ancient prophecy

[3] *Ibid.*, p. 78.
[4] *Ibid.*, p. 76.
[5] *Ibid.*, p. 118.

foretells a wonderful influx of spiritual manifestations "in the last days.". . . According to all the movements of Providence, in the civil, political, and ecclesiastical orders of the world, and from the general and earnest expectation of all classes among the human race, of the near approach of some great and marvelous displays of Divine power, which will bring the world to its consummation, it is evident that the "great day of God Almighty," has commenced in the world.

Therefore, in the display of his Divine Providence, He has opened the avenues of correspondence from the spirit-world to mortals on earth, and poured out his Spirit, in various degrees, by which the many wonderful events, both natural and spiritual, have been brought forth in the natural world. And these displays will doubtless continue to increase, in the orders of both Providence and grace, in greater and more spiritual degrees, of higher and higher orders, until the prophecy will be fulfilled, that the Spirit and Divine influence will be "poured out upon all flesh."

And we testify, that all true members of this Society are living witnesses that the great and last dispensation has commenced; and that the marvelous revelations, spiritual gifts, signs, and wonders, predicted to take place "in the last days," have been, and are being, fulfilled in so plain and evident a manner as cannot be disputed by any rational and candid mind.

This order of people originated in spiritual and Divine revelation from the heavenly orders above; and they have been continually supported, and have advanced in various degrees, by an influx of Divine revelations and heavenly ministrations with increasing light, adapted to their state, up to the present time.

But it was foretold by the spirit of prophecy, years before the event began, that a wonderful work of Divine revelation and heavenly gifts, light, and power, would take place in and among this people, in the fiftieth year after the gathering together of their United Society commenced, which would be as an antetype of the ancient Jewish jubilee. Accordingly, during the year 1838, a most wonderful manifestation of Divine revelation and heavenly light and power, simultaneously commenced in the two central societies, and in a few months visited every branch and family of the people called Shakers, throughout the land.

This work was attended with all those operations of Divine light, gifts, and power, enumerated by the Apostle in 1 Cor. xii; particularly verses seven to eleven, inclusive. These heavenly gifts being adapted to all states and circumstances, much new light was revealed by them on many important subjects.[6]

Therefore, it was also necessary, that Christ should make his second appearing in the line of the female, and that in one who was conceived in sin, and lost in the fulness of man's fall; because in the woman the root of sin was first planted, and its final destruction must begin where its foundation was first laid, and from when it first entered the human race.

Therefore, in the fulness of time, according to the unchangeable purpose of God, that same Spirit and word of power, which created man at the beginning—which spake by all the Prophets—which dwelt in the man Jesus—which was given to the Apostles and true witnesses as the holy Spirit and word of promise, which groaned in them, waiting for the day of redemption—and which was spoken of in the language of prophecy, as "a woman travailing with child, and pained to be delivered" [Revelation 12:2], was revealed in a WOMAN.

And that *woman,* in whom was manifested that Spirit and word of power, who was anointed and chosen of God, to reveal the mystery of iniquity, to stand as the first in her order, to accomplish the purpose of God, in the restoration of that which was lost by the transgression of the first woman, and to finish the work of man's final redemption, was ANN LEE.

As a chosen vessel, appointed by Divine wisdom, she, by her faithful obedience to that same anointing, became the temple of the Holy Spirit, and the second heir with Jesus, in the covenant and promise of eternal life. And by her sufferings and travail for a lost world, and her union and subjection to Christ Jesus, her Lord and Head, she became the *first born of many sisters,* and the true MOTHER *of all living* in the new creation. . . . So that by the first and second appearing of Christ, the foundation of God is laid and completed, for the full restoration and redemption of both the man and the woman in Christ. . . .

Then the man who was called JESUS, and the woman who was called ANN, are verily the two first visible foundation pillars of the

[6] *Testimony of Christ's Second Appearing* . . . etc., published by the United Society, called Shakers (Albany: Van Benthuysen, 1856, 4th edition.), Preface, pp. iii-v. See also *A Summary View of the Millennial Church* . . . etc., compiled by Calvin Green and Seth Y. Wells (Albany: Van Benthuysen, 1848), for a more careful history of the early Shakers and several "acts" of Mother Ann. Calvin Green, with Benjamine S. Youngs, is also the author of the "Preface to the Fourth Edition" of the Testimony.

Church of Christ . . . the first *Father* and *Mother* of all the children of regeneration—the two first visible Parents in the work of redemption—and in whom was revealed the invisible joint Parentage in the new creation, for the increase of that seed through which "all the families of the earth shall be blessed."[7]

This paragraph from the Testimony *describes the "year of jubilee."*
In the year 1837, the fiftieth after the gathering of the Church commenced, a remarkable Divine manifestation, as had been previously predicted, began, and shortly spread through all the societies of Believers in the land.

This work was attended with marvelous operations of divine power, accompanied with many extraordinary signs and wonders. Many were exercised in visions of the spiritual world, and of the beautiful order and glories of the heavens; also with revelations and discerning of spirits. Many were endowed with the gift to hear the melodious songs of the angels, and spirits of the just; many beautiful songs were given in this way. Others were exercised by inspired gifts of instruction, warning, reproof, and encouragement, etc. . . .

Many prophetic gifts were given, foretelling future events, which would take place among Believers, and also in the political, providential, and spiritual orders of the world; and likewise many wonderful phenomena and convulsions of nature, which have taken place, were clearly predicted. So that the discerning mind may see that these prophetic revelations were truly emanations from the Divine prescience.[8]

[7] *Testimony, op. cit.,* pp. 383-384.
[8] *Ibid.,* p. 431.

43

Edward Irving

(1792–1834)

After his expulsion from the London Presbytery of the Church of Scotland, Edward Irving formed his charismatic circle, which centered in the pentecostal revival of the Regent Square Church, into the "Catholic Apostolic Church." The new church was fitted out with the full complement of the charismata, including the restored office of "apostle." After Irving's death, Henry Drummond became the predominant spokesman for the church and continued its ministry of proclaiming the imminent coming of Christ's millennial kingdom in preparation for which the primitive fullness of the Holy Spirit had now been poured out afresh upon the people. Irving's teaching was based on two chief points: that Christ had assumed the fallen flesh of humankind, redeeming it by the power of the Holy Spirit (cf. Karl Barth, Church Dogmatics [*Edinburgh: T. & T. Clark, 1956*], *I ii 153-154), and that the Spirit was now pleased to indwell that flesh in men and women, giving the gifts where they might be received. He issued rigorous criticisms of established Christianity for its lack of openness to God's charismatic activity. The gift of tongues was especially prized by the Irvingites; Irving himself called glossolalia the "standing sign" of the presence of the Spirit and praised it as one of the "greater works" promised to Christians by Jesus, who himself had not spoken in tongues. The first person to speak in tongues as a part of the Irvingite movement was Mary Campbell of Fernicarry on the Gareloch in 1830, after she had been healed of consumption. Of her, Irving wrote:*

She saw the truth of our Lord's human nature, which in itself was no other than our own, and derived the virtues of immaculate holiness and superhuman power from no passive quality, but from an active operation thereon of the Son of God by the Holy Ghost. She came to see what for six or seven years I had been preaching in London, that all the works of Christ were done by the man anointed with the Holy Ghost, and not by the God mixing himself up with the man. The person is the Son of God; the bounds which he hath consented to speak and act in are the bounds of mortal manhood; the power by which, when within these narrow bounds, he doth such mighty things, against and above the course of nature, death and hell, is the power of the Holy Ghost; and the end of the whole mystery of his incarnation is to show unto mortal men what every one of them, through faith in his name, shall be able to perform.[1]

Christ, as a creature, was a poor weak mortal; a worm, and no man. This he consented to be; this he was, in the form of a slave; but what power was given to him! what liberty! what Godhead wisdom! what Godhead virtue! . . . To do these things was not man's province, himself mortal, nor Adam's at first, nor angels', nor any creature's, but only God's; and so God exhibited himself in action, through the powers and faculties of the Man Jesus. He revealed the Father in will, in thought, in word, in act. To do this was in his case the baptism with the Holy Ghost. And what is it in ours? The same, the very same.[2]

Mary Campbell's experience began with her healing as a result of the charismatic ministry of James MacDonald, another of the Irving circle. Following these fillings with the Spirit and healings, they began a few days later to speak in tongues; James MacDonald's sister writes concerning Margaret MacDonald, another sister:
For several days Margaret had been so unusually ill that I quite thought her dying, and on appealing to the doctor, he held out no

---

[1] "Facts Connected with Recent Manifestations of Spiritual Gifts," *Fraser's Magazine*, January, 1832, p. 757; see C. Gordon Strachan, *The Pentecostal Theology of Edward Irving* (London: Darton, Longman and Todd, 1973), p. 65.

[2] Edward Irving, *The Day of Pentecost, or the Baptism with the Holy Ghost*, 1831, pp. 31-32.

hope of her recovery unless she were able to go through a course of powerful medicine, which he acknowledged to be in her case impossible. She had scarcely been able even to have her bed made for a week. Mrs. _____ and myself had been sitting quietly at the bedside, when the power of the Spirit came upon her. She said: "There will be a mighty baptism of the Spirit this day," and then broke forth in a most marvellous setting forth of the wonderful works of God, and as if her own weakness had been altogether lost in the strength of the Holy Ghost, continued with little or no intermission for two or three hours, in mingled praise, prayer and exhortation.

At dinner time James and [brother] George came home as usual, whom she then addressed at great length, concluding with a solemn prayer that he might *at that time* be endowed with the power of the Holy Ghost. *Almost instantly* James *calmly* said: "I have got it." He walked to the window and stood silent for a minute or two. I looked at him and almost trembled, there was such a change upon his whole countenance. He then with a step and manner of the most indescribable majesty, walked up to Margaret's bedside and addressed her in those words of the Twentieth Psalm—"Arise and stand upright." He repeated the words, took her by the hand, and she arose; then we all *sat down quietly* and *had our dinner.* . . . After it, my brother went to the building yard as usual, where James wrote over [*across the firth of Clyde from Port Glasgow where the MacDonald family lived to Fernicarry where Mary Campbell lived*] to Miss Campbell commanding her in the name of the Lord to arise.

The next morning, after breakfast, James said: "I am going down to the quay to see if Miss Campbell is coming across the water": at which we expressed our surprise, as he had said nothing to us of having written to her. The result showed how much he knew of what God had done and would do for her, for she came as he expected, declaring herself perfectly whole.[3]

John Cardale visited Port Glasgow the following summer and wrote this report of the tongue-speakers there:
These persons, while uttering the unknown sounds, have every appearance of being under supernatural direction. The manner and voice are (speaking generally) different from what they are at other times. This difference does not consist merely in the peculiar

[3]"Facts . . . ," *op. cit.,* pp. 107-109, as quoted in A. L. Drummond, *Edward Irving and His Circle* (London: James Clark, 1938), p. 140.

solemnity and fervour of manner (which they possess), but their whole deportment gives an impression, not to be conveyed in words, that their organs are made use of by supernatural power. . . . They declare that their organs of speech are made use of by the Spirit of God; and that they utter that which is given to them, and *not* the expressions of their own conceptions.[4]

Irving's understanding of glossolalia was that it is one of the several gifts of the Spirit given to the church by Christ as evidence of God's presence in humanity on earth:
The Church is to be not only the container of the manifested God, but she is the actor of His works and the utterer of His wisdom; and to accomplish this, Christ, when He ascended up on high, received the Seven Spirits, the fulness and completeness of the vital, active Godhead. This is His occupation in heaven, to build the spiritual temple of the Lord out of the materials which He hath impregnated with His own life. And the Church is this temple; we are it; we on earth are it. The idea and the end of the Church is to be such a thing. . . . The Church is this building of God, where God is heard in His manifold wisdom and seen in His various actings: His wisdom, in this membership having the word of wisdom; His knowledge, in this membership having the word of knowledge; His truth, in this membership having the gift of faith; His health, in this membership having the gift of healing; His supremacy of spirits, in this membership having the discernment of spirits; His voice, in this membership having the gift of tongues; and His understanding, in this membership having the interpretation of tongues. [cf. I Cor. 12:8-10][5]

The miracle-workers in the Church are Christ's hand, to show the strength that is in Him: the healers of diseases are His almoners, to show what pity and compassion are in Him; the faith-administrators are His lion-heart, to show how mighty and fearless He is; and the utterers of wisdom and knowledge are His mind, to show how rich and capacious it is. . . .

[4] John B. Cardale, "On the Extraordinary Manifestations in Port Glasgow," *Morning Watch*, vol. 2, December, 1830, pp. 869-873, as quoted in Drummond, *op. cit.*, p. 142.

[5] Edward Irving, "On the Gifts of the Holy Ghost, Commonly Called Supernatural," *Morning Watch*, vols. 2, 3; and Irving, *Collected Writings*, vol. 5, p. 518; Strachan, *op. cit.*, p. 88.

But particularly of tongues, Irving writes that glossolalia is like an ambassador's commission:

And what an assurance to a man's heart, and confirmation to his faith, to have his mission thus ascertained to him, and sealed by the Holy Ghost! Methinks it would be more effectual than a salary of a thousand pounds by the year from the most notable of our missionary societies. . . . Of a truth, when that power is within, (it) doth testify to no other person but to Christ. . . . And thus is the Divinity and the Personality of the Comforter made to appear through this great truth of Christ the inhabiter of His people; which, again, is proved by His using their organs in a way in which they themselves are not able to do. Moreover, this power of Christ in the Spirit to speak all the diversities of speech, shows him to be the fountain-head of speech, the Word, by whose endowment man is a word-speaking creature. . . . Methinks it is altogether equal to the speaking with the trumpet from the thick darkness of the Mount, or with a voice as thunder from the open vault of heaven. The using of man's organs is indeed, a mark of a new dispensation, foretold as to come to pass after Christ ascended up on high, when He would receive gifts and bestow them on men, that the Lord God might dwell, might have an habitation, in them. . . . God . . . is now perfecting His Church, who are His temple, in whom He abideth as in the holy place, and from whom He speaketh forth His oracles in strange tongues. The strange tongues takes away all source of ambiguity, proving that the man himself hath nothing to do with it, and leaves the work and the authority of the word wholly in the hand of God. . . .

It is not in us as men that God speaks; but in us as members of Christ, as the Church and body of Christ, that God speaks. The honour is not to us, but to Christ; not to the Godhead of Christ, which is ever the same, but to the manhood of Christ, which hath been raised from the state of death to the state of being God's temple, God's most holy place, God's shechinah, God's oracle, for ever and ever.[6]

The following personal accounts of glossolalia by a Mr. Erskine of Linlathen, Irving, and an unknown person quoted by Irving show the spiritual effects of the experience. Mr. Erskine wrote:

Whilst I see nothing in Scripture against the re-appearance or rather continuance of miraculous gifts in the Church, but a great deal for it, I

[6] Edward Irving, "The Church, with Her Endowment of Holiness and Power," *Morning Watch*, vol. 2, and *Collected Writings*, vol. 5, pp. 480-499.

must further say that I see a great deal of internal evidence in the West country to prove their genuine miraculous character, especially in the speaking in tongues. . . . The languages are distinct, well-inflected, well-compacted languages; they are not random collections of sounds; they are composed words of various length, with the natural variety, and yet possessing that commonness of character which marks them to be one distinct language. I have heard many people speak gibberish, but this is not gibberish. (Specimens preserved as taken down by hearers: "O Pinitos, Elelastino Halimangotos Dantita, Hampooteni, Farini, Aristos, Ekrampos.")[7]

Of a "gifted person," Irving recounts this sense of the charismatic experience:
When I am praying in my native tongue, however fixed my soul be upon God, and Him alone, I am conscious of other thoughts and desires, *which the very words I use force in before me.* I am like a man holding straightforward to his home full in view, who, though he diverge neither to the right hand nor to the left, is ever solicited by many well-known objects on every hand of him.

But the moment I am visited with the Spirit, and carried out to God in a tongue which I know not, it is as if a deep covering of snow had fallen on all the country round,—and I saw nothing but the object of my desire and the road which leadeth to it. I am more conscious than ever of the presence of God. He and He only is in my soul. *I am filled with some form of the mind of God,* be it joy or grief, desire, love, pity, compassion or indignation; and I am *made* to utter it in words which are full of *power* over my spirit, but not being accessible to my understanding, my devotion is not interrupted by *associations or suggestions from the visible or intellectual world:* I feel myself, as it were, shut in with God into His own pavilion, and hidden close from the invasions of the world, the devil, and the flesh.[8]

Irving records the glossolalia of this person, describing it as: Jesus occupying the speech, and using the tongue of his servant, to speak the things which he desireth at that time to be spoken and heard.[9]

What was actually said was reported by Irving as another had recorded it:

[7] Drummond, *op. cit.,* p. 143.
[8] *Ibid.,* pp. 161-162.
[9] *Ibid.,* p. 162.

Hippo gerosto—Hippo—Booros—Senoote—
"Foorime—Gorin Hoopo Tanto Noostin."
Noostarin—Niparos—Hipanos—Bantos—Boorin—
"O Pinitos, O Fastos Sungor O Fastos Sungor"
Deripangito—Boorinos—Hypen—Eletanteti—Eretini—Menati

Hey amei hassan alla do
hoc alors loore
Has heo massan amor ho
ti prov his aso me[10]

Irving offers this apology for the absence of the gifts in established Christendom:

The true reason why the gifts of tongues hath ceased to be in the Church is, the exaltation of the natural methods of teaching above, or into copartnery with, the teaching of the Holy Ghost, the meanness of our idea, and the weakness of our faith, concerning the oneness of Christ glorified, with His Church on earth; the unworthiness of our doctrine concerning the person and office of the Holy Ghost, to knit up the believer into complete oneness with Christ, every thread and filament of our mortal humanity with His humanity, immortal and glorious; to bring down into the Church a complete Christ, and keep Him there, ever filling her bosom, and working in her members; the shortcoming of our knowledge, in respect to the gifts themselves; our having ceased to lament their absence, and to pray for their return; our want of fasting, and humiliation, and crying unto the Lord; our contentment to be without them; our base and false theories to account for their absence, without taking guilt to ourselves. Any one of these causes were sufficient, all of them are far more than sufficient, to account for their long absence from the bosom of the Church. These are the true reasons; and the commonly given reason, that they were designed only for a short time, is utterly false and most pernicious.[11]

[10] *Ibid.,* p. 170.
[11] "On the Gifts of the Holy Ghost, Commonly Called Supernatural," *Morning Watch,* vols. 2, 3; *Collected Writings,* vol. 5, p. 560; Strachan, *op. cit.,* p. 105.

44

Barton Warren Stone

(1772–1844)

The American "Restoration Movement" arose in the mid-nineteenth century, an ecumenical call to Christian primitivism, as a result of the flowing together of the followers of Alexander Campbell of Bethany, (West) Virginia, and Barton W. Stone of Cane Ridge and Concord, Kentucky. Campbell, the rational thinker and man of the academy, was balanced by Stone, the fiery preacher of God's universal love for all humankind. Stone's position was fought for and won over against his background in "frontier Calvinism," a change in theology which he attributed to the work of the Spirit. Whereas a contemporary Calvinist would have interpreted the "exercises" which Stone describes as the power of God's predestination at work confirming the elect, Stone saw them rather as signs of God's general desire to save everyone who would believe, repent, and be baptized. Stone understood the "exercises" to be not a part of salvation itself but God's way of bringing people to salvation or as effective signs of salvation. These events took place for the most part in 1801. The "churches of Christ," "Christian Churches," and "Disciples of Christ" are the three main bodies of believers descended from the Campbell-Stone movement.

At a religious meeting in Logan County, Kentucky, where Presbyterian James McGready was preaching, Stone describes what he witnessed:

The scene to me was new, and passing strange. It baffled description. Many, very many fell down, as men slain in battle, and continued for hours together in an apparently breathless and motionless state—sometimes for a few moments reviving, and exhibiting symptoms of life by a deep groan, or piercing shriek, or by a prayer for mercy most fervently uttered. After lying thus for hours, they obtained deliverance. The gloomy cloud, which had covered their faces, seemed gradually and visibly to disappear, and hope in smiles brightened into joy—they would rise shouting deliverance, and then would address the surrounding multitude in language truly eloquent and impressive. With astonishment did I hear men, women and children declaring the wonderful works of God, and the glorious mysteries of the gospel. Their appeals were solemn, heart-penetrating, bold and free. Under such addresses many others would fall down into the same state from which the speakers had just been delivered.

Two or three of my particular acquaintances from a distance were struck down. I sat patiently by one of them, whom I knew to be a careless sinner, for hours, and observed with critical attention every thing that passed from the beginning to the end. I noticed the momentary revivings as from death—the humble confession of sins—the fervent prayer, and the ultimate deliverance—then the solemn thanks and praise to God—the affectionate exhortation to companions and to the people around, to repent and come to Jesus. . . . After attending to many such cases, my conviction was complete that it was a good work—the work of God; nor has my mind wavered since on the subject. Much did I then see, and much have I since seen, that I considered to be fanaticism; but this should not condemn the work. The Devil has always tried to ape the works of God, to bring them into disrepute. But that cannot be a Satanic work, which brings men to humble confession and forsaking of sin—to solemn prayer—fervent praise and thanksgiving, and to sincere and affectionate exhortations to sinners to repent and go to Jesus the Saviour.

I am always hurt to hear people speak lightly of this work. I always think they speak of what they know nothing about. Should every thing bearing the impress of imperfection be blasphemously rejected, who amongst us at this time could stand?[1]

Stone returned to Cane Ridge and Concord, bringing both his gospel of God's universal love and his power in the Spirit with him. Quoting Mark 16:15-16 as his text, Stone relates:
On the universality of the gospel, and faith as the condition of salvation, I principally dwelt, and urged the sinner to believe now, and be saved. . . .
At our night meeting at Concord, two little girls were struck down under the preaching of the word, and in every respect were exercised as those were in the south of Kentucky, as already described. . . . [At Cane Ridge] in less than twenty minutes, scores had fallen to the ground—paleness, trembling, and anxiety appeared in all—some attempted to fly from the scene panic stricken, but they either fell, or returned immediately to the crowd, as unable to get away. In the midst of this exercise, an intelligent deist in the neighborhood, stepped up to me, and said: "Mr. Stone, I always thought before that you were an honest man; but now I am convinced you are deceiving the people." I viewed him with pity, and mildly spoke a few words to him—immediately he fell as a dead man, and rose no more till he confessed the Saviour. The meeting continued on that spot in the open air, till late at night, and many found peace in the Lord.

In August, 1801, an extensive camp meeting was held at Cane Ridge:
The roads were literally crowded with wagons, carriages, horsemen, and footmen, moving to the solemn camp. The sight was affecting. It was judged, by military men on the ground, that there were between twenty and thirty thousand collected. Four or five preachers were frequently speaking at the same time, in different parts of the encampment, without confusion. The Methodist and Baptist preachers aided in the work, and all appeared cordially united in it—of one mind and one soul, and the salvation of sinners seemed to be the great object of all. . . . Many things transpired there, which were so much like miracles, that if they were not, they had the same effects as miracles on infidels and unbelievers; for many of them by these were convinced that Jesus was the Christ, and bowed in submission to him. This meeting continued six or seven days and

[1] Barton W. Stone, *The Biography of Elder Barton Warren Stone, written by himself* (Cincinnati: J. A. and U. P. James, 1847), pp. 34-35.

nights, and would have continued longer, but provisions for such a multitude failed in the neighborhood.[2]

The bodily agitations or exercises, attending the excitement in the beginning of this century, were various, and called by various names—as, the falling exercise—the jerks—the dancing exercise—the barking exercise—the laughing and singing exercise, etc. The falling exercise was very common among all classes, the saints and sinners of every age and of every grade, from the philosopher to the clown. The subject of this exercise would, generally, with a piercing scream, fall like a log on the floor, earth, or mud, and appear as dead. Of thousands of similar cases, I will mention one. At a meeting, two gay young ladies, sisters, were standing together attending to the exercises and preaching at the time. Instantly they both fell, with a shriek of distress, and lay for more than an hour apparently in a lifeless state. Their mother, a pious Baptist, was in great distress, fearing they would not revive. At length they began to exhibit symptoms of life, by crying fervently for mercy, and then relapsed into the same death-like state, with an awful gloom on their countenances. After awhile, the gloom on the face of one was succeeded by a heavenly smile, and she cried out: precious Jesus, and rose up and spoke of the love of God—the preciousness of Jesus, and of the glory of the gospel, to the surrounding crowd, in language almost superhuman, and pathetically exhorted all to repentance. In a little while after, the other sister was similarly exercised. From that time they became remarkably pious members of the church.

I have seen very many pious persons fall in the same way, from a sense of the danger of their unconverted children, brothers, or sisters—from a sense of the danger of their neighbors, and of the sinful world. I have heard them agonizing in tears and strong crying for mercy to be shown to sinners, and speaking like angels to all around.

The jerks cannot be so easily described. Sometimes the subject of the jerks would be affected in some one member of the body, and sometimes in the whole system. When the head alone was affected, it would be jerked backward and forward, or from side to side, so quickly that the features of the face could not be distinguished. When the whole system was affected, I have seen the person stand in one place, and jerk backward and forward in quick succession, their head nearly touching the floor behind and before. All classes, saints and

[2] *Ibid.,* pp. 36-38.

sinners, the strong as well as the weak, were thus affected. I have inquired of those thus affected. They could not account for it; but some have told me that those were among the happiest seasons of their lives. I have seen some wicked persons thus affected, and all the time cursing the jerks, while they were thrown to the earth with violence. Though so awful to behold, I do not remember that any one of the thousands I have seen ever sustained an injury in body. This was as strange as the exercise itself.

The dancing exercise. This generally began with the jerks, and was peculiar to professors of religion. The subject, after jerking awhile, began to dance, and then the jerks would cease. Such dancing was indeed heavenly to the spectators; there was nothing in it like levity, nor calculated to excite levity in the beholders. The smile of heaven shone on the countenance of the subject, and assimilated to angels appeared the whole person. Sometimes the motion was quick and sometimes slow. Thus they continued to move forward and backward in the same track or alley till nature seemed exhausted, and they would fall prostrate on the floor or earth, unless caught by those standing by. While thus exercised, I have heard solemn praises and prayers ascending to God.

The barking exercise (as opposers contemptuously called it) was nothing but the jerks. A person affected with the jerks, especially in his head, would often make a grunt, or bark, if you please, from the suddenness of the jerk. This name of barking seems to have had its origin from an old Presbyterian preacher of East Tennessee. He had gone into the woods for private devotion, and was seized with the jerks. Standing near a sapling, he caught hold of it, to prevent his falling, and as his head jerked back, he uttered a grunt or kind of noise similar to a bark, his face being turned upwards. Some wag discovered him in this position, and reported that he found him barking up a tree.

The laughing exercise was frequent, confined solely with the religious. It was a loud, hearty laughter, but one *sui generis;* it excited laughter in none else. The subject appeared rapturously solemn, and his laughter excited solemnity in saints and sinners. It is truly indescribable.

The running exercise was nothing more than, that persons feeling something of these bodily agitations, through fear, attempted to run away, and thus escape from them; but it commonly happened that they ran not far, before they fell, or became so greatly agitated that they could proceed no farther. I knew a young physician of a celebrated family, who came some distance to a big meeting to see the strange things he had heard of. He and a young lady had sportively agreed to watch over, and take care of each other, if either should fall. At length the physician felt something very uncommon, and started from the congregation to run into the woods; he was discovered running as for life, but did not proceed far till he fell down, and there lay till he submitted to the Lord, and afterwards became a zealous member of the church. Such cases were common.

I shall close this chapter with the singing exercise. This is more unaccountable than any thing else I ever saw. The subject in a very happy state of mind would sing most melodiously, not from the mouth or nose, but entirely in the breast, the sounds issuing thence. Such music silenced every thing, and attracted the attention of all. It was most heavenly. None could ever be tired of hearing it. Doctor J. P. Campbell and myself were together at a meeting, and were attending to a pious lady thus exercised, and concluded it to be something surpassing any thing we had known in nature.

Thus have I given a brief account of the wonderful things that appeared in the great excitement in the beginning of this century. That there were many eccentricities, and much fanaticism in this excitement, was acknowledged by its warmest advocates; indeed it would have been a wonder, if such things had not appeared, in the circumstances of that time. Yet the good effects were seen and acknowledged in every neighborhood, and among the different sects it silenced contention, and promoted unity for awhile; and these blessed effects would have continued, had not men put forth their unhallowed hands to hold up their tottering ark, mistaking it for the ark of God. [*Stone refers to the denominational opposition to his unity movement waged especially by his former fellow-Calvinists.*][3]

---

[3] *Ibid.,* pp. 39-42.

45

Joseph Smith

(1805–1844)

The Church of Jesus Christ of Latter-Day Saints, or the Mormons, receive the writings and revelations of Joseph Smith as inspired and canonical alongside the usual Christian canon. As founder and first president of the Mormon Church, Smith taught a fullness of experience of the charismas of the Spirit, including especially tongues, prophecies, and day-to-day revelations according to which he governed the church in the early days. According to the Book of Mormon, Jesus sent the Spirit to twelve pre-Columbian American disciples (descendants of the Twelve Lost Tribes of Israel) in parallel to the Jerusalem Pentecost, leading to the restoration of the church among Smith and his followers. Smith and the Mormons drew a direct line from charismation by the Spirit in receiving revelations to the writing of latter-day scripture.

Do ye not remember that I said unto you that after ye had received the Holy Ghost ye could speak with the tongues of angels? And now, how could ye speak with the tongues of angels save it were by the Holy Ghost? Angels speak by the power of the Holy Ghost; wherefore, they speak the words of Christ. Wherefore, I said unto you, feast upon the words of Christ; for behold, the words of Christ will tell you all things what ye should do. (2 Nephi 32:2-3)

And it came to pass that when Jesus had made an end of these sayings, he touched with his hand the disciples whom he had chosen, one by one, even until he had touched them all, and spake unto them as he touched them. And the multitude heard not the words which he spake, therefore they did not bear record; but the disciples bare record that he gave them power to give the Holy Ghost. . . .

And it came to pass when they were all baptized and had come up out of the water, the Holy Ghost did fall upon them, and they were filled with the Holy Ghost and with fire. And behold, they were encircled about as if it were by fire; and it came down from heaven, and the multitude did witness it, and did bear record; and angels did come down out of heaven and did minister unto them. . . . And . . . Jesus came and stood in the midst and ministered unto them.

[He said:] "Father, I thank thee that thou hast given the Holy Ghost unto these whom I have chosen; and it is because of their belief in me that I have chosen them out of the world. Father, I pray thee that thou wilt give the Holy Ghost unto all them that shall believe in their words. Father, thou hast given them the Holy Ghost because they believe in me. . . . (3 Nephi 18:36-37; 19:13-15, 20-22)

Almost the last page of the last prophecy in the Book of Mormon contains this theology of the Gifts, with the promise that they would never cease:

By the power of the Holy Ghost ye may know the truth of all things: . . . wherefore I would exhort you that ye deny not the power of God; for he worketh by power, according to the faith of the children of men, the same today and tomorrow, and forever. And again, I exhort you, my brethren, that ye deny not the gifts of God, for they are many; and they come from the same God. And there are different ways that these gifts are administered; but it is the same God who worketh all in all; and they are given by the manifestations of the Spirit of God unto men, to profit them. For behold, to one is given by the Spirit of God that he may teach the word of wisdom; and to another, that he may teach the word of knowledge by the same Spirit; and to another, exceeding great faith; and to another, the gifts of healing by the same Spirit; and again, to another, that he may work mighty miracles; and again, to another, that he may prophesy concerning all things; and again, to another, the beholding of angels and ministering spirits; and again, to another, all kinds of tongues;

and again, to another, the interpretation of languages and of divers kinds of tongues. And all these gifts come by the Spirit of Christ; and they come unto every man severally, according as he will. And I would exhort you, my beloved brethren, that ye remember that every good gift cometh of Christ. And I would exhort you, my beloved brethren, that ye remember that he is the same yesterday, today, and forever, and that all these gifts of which I have spoken, which are spiritual, never will be done away, even as long as the world shall stand, only according to the unbelief of the children of men. Wherefore, there must be faith; and if there must be faith there must also be hope; and if there must be hope there must also be charity. (Moroni 10:5-20; cf. *Doctrine and Covenants* 46:6-33; 84:45-47, 64-75)

Revelation given through Joseph Smith the Prophet, to Oliver Cowdery, at Harmony, Pennsylvania, April, 1829. . . . Oliver Cowdery, verily, verily, I [the Lord] say unto you, that assuredly as the Lord liveth, who is your God and your Redeemer, even so surely shall you receive a knowledge of whatsoever things you shall ask in faith, with an honest heart, believing that you shall receive a knowledge concerning the engravings of old records, which are ancient, which contain those parts of my scripture of which has been spoken by the manifestation of my Spirit. Yea, behold, I will tell you in your mind and in your heart, by the Holy Ghost, which shall come upon you and which shall dwell in your heart. Now, behold, this is the spirit of revelation; behold, this is the spirit by which Moses brought the children of Israel through the Red Sea on dry ground. Therefore this is thy gift; apply unto it, and blessed art thou, for it shall deliver you out of the hands of your enemies. . . . (*Doctrine and Covenants* 8)

An apostle is an elder, and it is his calling to baptize; and to ordain other elders, priests, teachers, and deacons; and to administer bread and wine—the emblems of the flesh and blood of Christ—and to confirm those who are baptized into the church, by the laying on of hands for the baptism of fire and the Holy Ghost, according to the scriptures; and to teach, expound, exhort, baptize, and watch over the church; and to confirm the church by the laying on of the hands and the giving of the Holy Ghost; and to take the lead of all meetings. The elders are to conduct the meetings as they are led by the Holy

Ghost, according to the commandments and revelations of God. . . . Every elder, priest, teacher, or deacon is to be ordained according to the gifts and callings of God unto him; and he is to be ordained by the power of the Holy Ghost, which is in the one who ordains him. (*Doctrine and Covenants* 20:38-45, 60)

The oft-repeated "plan of salvation" improves somewhat on Acts 2:38:

I give unto you a commandment that ye go among this people, and say unto them, like unto mine apostle of old, whose name was Peter: Believe on the name of the Lord Jesus, who was on the earth, and is to come, the beginning and the end; repent and be baptized in the name of Jesus Christ, according to the holy commandment, for the remission of sins; And whoso doeth this shall receive the gift of the Holy Ghost, by the laying on of the hands of the elders of the church. (*Doctrine and Covenants* 49:11-14)

And the spirit and the body are the soul of man. And the resurrection from the dead is the redemption of the soul. . . . For man is spirit. The elements are eternal, and spirit and element, inseparably connected, receive a fulness of joy; and when separated, man cannot receive a fulness of joy. . . . The Father has a body of flesh and bones as tangible as man's; the Son also; but the Holy Ghost has not a body of flesh and bones, but is a personage of Spirit. Were it not so, the Holy Ghost could not dwell in us. A man may receive the Holy Ghost, and it may descend upon him and not tarry with him. . . . There is no such thing as immaterial matter. All spirit is matter, but it is more fine or pure, and can only be discerned by purer eyes; we cannot see it; but when our bodies are purified we shall see that it is all matter. . . . When the Savior shall appear we shall see him as he is. We shall see that he is a man like ourselves. And that same sociality which exists among us here will exist among us there, only it will be coupled with eternal glory, which glory we do not now enjoy . . . and the idea that the Father and the Son dwell in a man's heart is an old sectarian notion, and is false. (*Doctrine and Covenants* 88:15-16; 93:33-34; 130:22-23; 131:7-8; 130:1-3)

There are two kinds of beings in heaven, namely: Angels, who are resurrected personages, having bodies of flesh and bones— . . . . Secondly: The spirits of just men made perfect, they who are not resurrected, but inherit the same glory. When a messenger comes saying he has a message from God, offer him your hand and request him to shake hands with you. If he be an angel he will do so, and you will feel his hand. If he be the spirit of a just man made perfect he will come in his glory; for that is the only way he can appear—Ask him to shake hands with you, but he will not move, because it is contrary to the order of heaven for a just man to deceive; but he will still deliver his message. If it be the devil as an angel of light, when you ask him to shake hands he will offer you his hand, and you will not feel anything; you may therefore detect him. These are three grand keys whereby you may know whether any administration is from God. (*Doctrine and Covenants* 129)

He that trembleth under my power shall be made strong, and shall bring forth fruits of praise and wisdom, according to the revelations and truths which I have given you. . . . The Holy Ghost shall be thy constant companion, and thy scepter an unchanging scepter of righteousness and truth; and thy dominion shall be an everlasting dominion, and without compulsory means it shall flow unto thee forever and ever. (*Doctrine and Covenants* 52:17; 121:46)

46

Nat Turner

(1799–1831)

On August 21 and 22, 1831, Nat Turner, a black slave, led a band of what ultimately amounted to more than fifty other slaves to cut a swath across the white population of Southampton County, Virginia, beheading, shooting, and bludgeoning to death fifty-five men and women, including gray heads and infants. A few days before his execution, Turner told his story to Thomas R. Gray in the jail at Jerusalem, Virginia. The introduction to the odyssey of the massacre includes Turner's accounts of how his parents thought him a born prophet, how he knew the alphabet without having learned it, his precocious inventiveness, and his thorough religiousness. After the description of his communications with the Spirit, there follows his recounting of the murders which fulfilled the prophecy of his vision of "white spirits and black spirits engaged in battle." Thus led by the Spirit, his final plea was "not guilty"; because, as he said, he did not feel so.

By this time, having arrived to man's estate, and hearing the scriptures commented on at meetings, I was struck with that particular passage which says: "Seek ye the kingdom of Heaven and all things shall be added unto you." [Matthew 6:33] I reflected much

254

on this passage, and prayed daily for light on this subject—As I was praying one day at my plough, the Spirit spoke to me, saying: "Seek ye the kingdom of Heaven and all things shall be added unto you." *Question* [by Mr. Gray]—what do you mean by the Spirit? *Ans.* The Spirit that spoke to the prophets in former days—and I was greatly astonished, and for two years prayed continually, whenever my duty would permit—and then again I had the same revelation, which fully confirmed me in the impression that I was ordained for some great purpose in the hands of the Almighty. . . . Now finding I had arrived to man's estate, and was a slave, and these revelations being made known to me, I began to direct my attention to this great object, to fulfill the purpose for which, by this time, I felt assured I was intended. Knowing the influence I had obtained over the minds of my fellow servants, (not by the means of conjuring and such like tricks—for to them I always spoke of such things with contempt) but by the communion of the Spirit whose revelations I often communicated to them, and they believed and said my wisdom came from God. I now began to prepare them for my purpose, by telling them something was about to happen that would terminate in fulfilling the great promise that had been made to me—[describes running away and returning]. But the reason of my return was, that the Spirit appeared to me and said I had my wishes directed to the things of this world, and not to the kingdom of Heaven, and that I should return to the service of my earthly master—"For he who knoweth his Master's will, and doeth it not, shall be beaten with many stripes, and thus have I chastened you." [Luke 12:47] And the negroes found fault, and murmured against me, saying that if they had my sense they would not serve any master in the world. And about this time I had a vision—and I saw white spirits and black spirits engaged in battle, and the sun was darkened—the thunder rolled in the Heavens, and blood flowed in streams—and I heard a voice saying: "Such is your luck, such you are called to see, and let it come rough or smooth, you must surely bare [sic] it." I now withdrew myself as much as my situation would permit, from the intercourse of my fellow servants, for the avowed purpose of serving the Spirit more fully—and it appeared to me, and reminded me of the things it had already shown me, and that it would then reveal to me the knowledge of the elements, the revolution of the planets, the operation of tides, and changes of the seasons. After this revelation in the year of 1825, and the knowledge of the elements being made known to me, I sought more than ever to obtain true holiness before the great day of judgment should appear, and then I began to receive the true knowledge of faith. And from the first steps of righteousness until the last, was I made perfect; and the Holy Ghost was with me, and said: "Behold me as I stand in the Heavens"—and I looked and saw the forms of men in different attitudes—and there were lights in the sky to which the children of darkness gave other names than what they really were—for they were the lights of the Savior's hands, stretched forth from east to west, even as they were extended on the cross on Calvary for the redemption of sinners. And I wondered greatly at these miracles, and prayed to be informed of a certainty of the meaning thereof—and shortly afterwards, while laboring in the field, I discovered drops of blood on the corn as though it were dew from heaven—and I communicated it to many, both white and black, in the neighbourhood—and I then found on the leaves in the woods hieroglyphic characters, and numbers, with the forms of men in different attitudes, portrayed in blood, and representing the figures I had seen before in the heavens. And now the Holy Ghost had revealed itself to me, and made plain the miracles it had shown me—For as the blood of Christ had been shed on this earth, and had ascended to heaven for the salvation of sinners, and was now returning to earth again in the form of dew—and as the leaves on the trees bore the impression of the figures I had seen in the heavens, it was plain to me that the Savior was about to lay down the yoke he had borne for the sins of men, and the great day of judgment was at hand. About this time I told these things to a white man (Ethelred T. Brantley), on whom it had a wonderful effect—and he ceased from his wickedness, and was attacked immediately with a cutaneous eruption, and blood oozed from the pores of his skin, and after praying and fasting nine days, he was healed, and the Spirit appeared to me again, and said, as the Savior had been baptised so should we be also—and when the white people would not let us be baptised by the church, we went down into the water together, in the sight of many who reviled us, and were baptised by the Spirit—After this I rejoiced greatly, and gave thanks to God. And on the 12th of May, 1828, I heard a loud noise in the heavens, and the Spirit instantly appeared to me and said the Serpent was loosened, and Christ had laid down the yoke he had borne for the sins of men, and that I should take it on and fight against the Serpent, for the time was fast approaching when the first should be last and the last should be first. *Question* [by Mr. Gray] Do you not find yourself mistaken now?

Ans. Was not Christ crucified? And by signs in the heavens that it [the Spirit] would make known to me when I should commence the great work—and until the first sign appeared, I should conceal it from the knowledge of men—And on the appearance of the sign, (the eclipse of the sun last February) I should arise and prepare myself, and slay my enemies with their own weapons. And immediately on the sign appearing in the heavens, the seal was removed from my lips, and I communicated the great work laid out for me to do, to four in whom I had the greatest confidence (Henry, Hark, Nelson and Sam)—It was intended by us to have begun the work of death on the 4th July last— Many were the plans formed and rejected by us, and it affected my mind to such a degree, that I fell sick, and the time passed without our coming to any determination how to commence—Still forming new schemes and rejecting them, when the sign appeared again, which determined me not to wait longer.[1]

[1] Thomas R. Gray, *The Confessions of Nat Turner* (Baltimore: Lucas and Deaver, 1831) as printed in Herbert Aptheker, *Nat Turner's Slave Rebellion* (New York: Humanities Press, 1966), pp. 135-138, *passim.*

47

Horace Bushnell

(1802–1876)

Horace Bushnell began his treatise on the inspiration of the Spirit in the ripeness of old age, at seventy-five. A year later he died, leaving the manuscript unfinished. Bushnell was the pioneer and preacher of liberal theology in America. Famous for his moral reinterpretation of the atonement and his doctrine of the Trinity as symbol rather than statement about the essential nature of God, Bushnell stressed the immanence of God at work in creation in his analogous "moral" understanding of the Spirit.

Bushnell reasoned that the spirit of God is universally present to all, at work in their moral renovation, and thought to be immediately accessible by all due to the fact that each person has a "faculty of inspiration." This faculty, like a windowpane, is permeable by the light.

"It is the faculty of being permeated or interiorly and receptively visited by the higher nature of God, communicating somewhat of his own quality." *But whereas the sunlight passes through the windowpane without leaving any impression of itself upon the glass,* "the beams of the Holy Spirit shine to beget heat, and to lodge a divine property in moral natures that is akin to itself. . . .

This faculty of inspiration is the summit of our human nature. . . . In a sense, God inhabits the world . . . but in this inhabitation of the Spirit he temples himself socially and morally in our human nature, working it responsively toward himself, imparting his own thought and the very habit in which he lives."[1]

Bushnell emphasizes the personal nature of the Spirit, since the Spirit's moral, social work can be appropriately predicated only of a true person. But this person, like the Father and Son, is everywhere present. Therefore, the scriptural description of the Spirit coming, going, falling, and departing is merely symbolic, the "machineries of language."

But suppose that, dropping out all these instrumentations, [a man] were to begin at the omnipresence of the Spirit and word a prayer for these same gifts or bestowments, how very soon will he be instructed as to their necessity? "Come down"—No, that certainly is not what is wanted. "Draw near"—No, he is near enough already. "Grant us thy presence"—No, we have his presence before we ask it. "Return, O thou departed"—No, we must not ask it, for he is not departed. . . . [The machinery and figures of his prayer] are not meant to set the Spirit moving in space according to their forms, but simply to obtain a consciousness of his presence, who before was unconsciously or less consciously present.[2]

Bushnell rejected the traditional Calvinist teaching regarding the irresistibility of the Spirit's working and reinterpreted the Calvinist idea of the Spirit in the interpretation of the Word. He describes a work proper to the Spirit beyond the work of Christ in that the Spirit is Christ's "successor working by another method."

[Christ's] gospel, gotten into language by his incarnate ministry and teaching, lacked altogether when taken by itself the efficiency needed to make it a great converting power. It does not appear that Christ gained many converts by his preaching; partly for the reason, I suppose, that he was always too much of a problem to be a proper word of salvation. His miracles begot a state of questioning and of idle wonder too curious to be convincingly serious; much as we see now in the levitations and aerial transportations and ghostly oracles

---

[1] Horace Bushnell, "Inspiration by the Holy Spirit," in *The Spirit in Man: Sermons and Selections,* ed. Mary Bushnell Cheney (New York: Charles Scribner's Sons, 1903), pp. 7 and 8.

[2] *Ibid.,* pp. 12 and 13.

of our wizard practitioners. For the time, . . . the promulgations bore a look of extravagance. . . .

Mere revelation, or a word of truth that has gotten form as in language, has by itself no effectually quickening or regenerative power in character. It stands before the mind, glassing truth in a way to act upon it, but it can accomplish nothing save as another kind of power acting in the mind makes it impressible under and by the truth. Hence the necessity of the Paraclete. . . . [to] set you in a state of sensibility toward the truth that will be its glorification, and bring you into it as a new life. . . . The Spirit operates efficiently in the subject to prepare him to the word, convincing him of sin, raising him up, for the time and more or less always, to a state of just sensibility, so that he may apprehend the divine things of Christ in a lively manner, and there stops short, as he must, laying no hand of force on the man that shall break his natural or thrust him out of his chosen liberty.[3]

Citing Emerson's notion of the Oversoul, Bushnell argues for "universal inspiration" in a nutritive, moral, and corrective sense, though not in the sense of the inspiration of Scripture. He seems to limit that "certain special infallibility" to the authors of the canon, promising a fuller statement later in his work, but to which he never returns in the truncated manuscript.

The universal inspiration of which I wished to speak is that which is grounded or supposed in the natural relation of God to souls. . . . At this point two particular facts ask as it were to be named, which as far as I know are never connected with the doctrine of the Spirit at all. I speak of his inspirations in the time of infancy, and in times of lapsed consciousness in the dying. Infancy has no Bible, no language, no capacity for a time of representative instruction. All the form-world of the mind is vacant or empty. But it is a world open to the Spirit and the dear inspirations of God, where, going through as living bible in the sweet effusions of love and gentleness, he may lodge all most beautiful germs of character, probably sometimes never to be effaced. . . . Hence the wondrous and almost divine beauty of childish unconsciousness and guilelessness. It is the sole gift and grace of the Spirit. We call it angelic, finding flavors in it that we cannot impute to any purest motherhood, or to anything but some celestial nutrition.

When the Spirit helps the dying it is in a different manner, but sometimes in a manner scarcely less affecting. He has carried the

3 *Ibid.,* pp. 21-23.

soldier through his war, and now he sleeps. For whole hours or possibly days he has been wholly unconscious and speechless. Is he alone? or is his divine friend with him? How very often we are permitted to see! As when he opens suddenly his eyes to say, looking up and round: "Beautiful angels," "Lord Jesus, I come," "The gates, thank God, are open," "Good-bye all." What is it now that puts it in the soul, shut up for so many hours in the supineness of a block, to break out thus perceptibly into second life and a second world, unless it be the Spirit of God . . . ? As he came to the infant, bible before Bible, so here he comes to the servant lapsing in death as a bible revelation within when the word without is gone by, to put him on thoughts not spoken outwardly, and open to discoveries that can be witnessed only by their own light.[4]

4 *Ibid.,* pp. 14-17.

48

Leo XIII

(1810–1903, pope from 1878)

"Divinum illud munus," Leo's encyclical on the Holy Spirit, was issued toward the close of the pope's long and productive reign. In it, he surrendered his lifelong concerns for unity and social reform to the Source of ethical relations, the Holy Spirit. He emphasizes the unity within the Trinity according to which the Spirit works, stressing that the Spirit does not work separately in sanctification. Leo's treatment of the mission of the Spirit, its role as the "soul" of the Mystical Body of Christ, and his personal presence in the souls of the just, is a summary of catholic teaching on the Spirit, especially according to Augustine and Thomas Aquinas. Leo urges the faithful to a stronger devotion to the Spirit and closely associates the activities of the saints and especially of the Virgin Mary with the charisma of the Holy Spirit.

That divine office which Jesus Christ received from his Father for the welfare of mankind, and most perfectly fulfilled, had for its final object to put men in possession of the eternal life of glory, and proximately during the course of ages to secure to them the life of divine grace, which is destined eventually to blossom into the life of heaven. . . . Nevertheless, according to His inscrutable counsels, he did not will to complete entirely and finish this office Himself on earth, but as He had received it from the Father, so He transmitted it for its completion to the Holy Ghost. . . . He gave as the chief reason of His departure and His return to the Father the advantage which would most certainly accrue to His followers from the coming of the Holy Ghost, and, at the same time, He made it clear that the Holy Ghost is equally sent by—and therefore proceeds from—Himself and the Father; that He would complete, in his office of Intercessor, Consoler and Teacher, the work which Christ Himself had begun in His mortal life. For, in the redemption of the world, the completion of the work was by divine Providence reserved to the manifold power of that Spirit, who, in the creation *adorned the heavens* [Job 26:13] and *filled the whole world* [Wisdom 1:7].

The Church is accustomed most fittingly to attribute to the Father those works of the divinity in which power excels, to the Son those in which wisdom excels, and those in which love excels to the Holy Ghost. Not that all perfections and external operations are not common to the divine persons, for "the operations of the Trinity are indivisible, even as the essence of the Trinity is indivisible." [Augustine, *De Trinitate* 1:1:4-5] . . . The Holy Ghost is the ultimate cause of all things, since, as the will and all other things finally rest in their end, so He, who is the divine goodness and the mutual love of the Father and Son, completes and perfects by his strong yet gentle power the secret work of man's eternal salvation. "In Him are all things": *in Him* referring to the Holy Ghost.

. . . among the external operations of God, the highest of all is the mystery of the Incarnation of the Word. . . . Now this work, although belonging to the whole Trinity, is still appropriated especially to the Holy Ghost. . . . Moreover, human nature was thereby elevated to a *personal* union with the Word; and this dignity is given, not on account of any merits, but entirely and absolutely through grace, and therefore, as it were, through the special gift of the Holy Ghost. . . . By the operation of the Holy Spirit, not only was the conception of Christ accomplished but also the sanctification of His soul, which, in Holy Scripture, is called his *anointing* [Acts 10:38]. Wherefore all His actions were *performed in the Holy Ghost* [Basil, *De Spiritu Sancto* 16], and especially the sacrifice of Himself: *Christ, through the Holy Ghost, offered himself without spot to God*

[Heb. 9:14]. Considering this, no one can be surprised that all the gifts of the Holy Ghost inundated the soul of Christ. In Him resided the absolute fulness of grace, in the greatest and most efficacious manner possible; in Him were all the treasures of wisdom and knowledge, graces *gratis datae,* virtues and all other gifts foretold in the prophecies of Isaias [Isa. 4:1; 11:23], and also signified in that miraculous dove which appeared at the Jordan, when Christ, by His Baptism, consecrated its waters for a new sacrament. . . . At this time, then, at his baptism, He was pleased to prefigure His Church, in which those especially who are baptized receive the Holy Ghost [Augustine, *De Trinitate* 1:15:26]. Therefore, by the conspicuous apparition of the Holy Ghost over Christ and by His invisible power in His soul, the twofold mission of the Spirit is foreshadowed, namely His outward and visible mission in the Church and His secret indwelling in the souls of the just.

The Church which, already conceived, came forth from the side of the Second Adam in His sleep on the cross, first showed herself before the eyes of men on the great day of Pentecost. On that day the Holy Ghost began to manifest His gifts in the mystic body of Christ, by that miraculous outpouring already foreseen by the prophet Joel [2:28, 29], for the Paraclete "sat upon the apostles as though new spiritual crowns were placed upon their heads in tongues of fire" [Cyril of Jerusalem, *Catecheses* 17]. Then the Apostles "descended from the mountain," as St. John Chrysostom writes, "not bearing in their hands tables of stone like Moses, but carrying the Spirit in their mind, and pouring forth the treasure and the fountain of doctrines and graces" [Commentary on Matthew, Homily 1, II Cor. 3:3]. . . . The Spirit of Truth . . . communicates this truth to His Church, guarding her by His all powerful help from ever falling into error and aiding her to foster daily more and more the germs of divine doctrine and to make them fruitful for welfare of the peoples. And since the welfare of the peoples, for which the Church was established, absolutely requires that this office should be continued for all time, the Holy Ghost perpetually supplies life and strength to preserve and increase the church.

By Him the bishops are constituted, and by their ministry are multiplied not only the children but also the fathers—that is, the priests—to rule and feed the Church by that blood wherewith Christ has redeemed her. . . . And both bishops and priests, by the miraculous gift of the Spirit, have the power of absolving sins. . . . That the Church is a divine institution is most clearly proved by the splendor and glory of those gifts and graces with which she is adorned, and whose author and giver is the Holy Spirit. Let it suffice to state that, as Christ is the head of the Church, so the Holy Ghost is her soul. "What the soul is in our body, that the Holy Ghost is in Christ's Body, the Church." [Augustine, Sermon 187, de Temp.] This being so, no further and fuller "manifestation and revelation of the Divine Spirit" may be imagined or expected; for that which now takes place in the Church is the most perfect possible, and will last until that day when the Church herself, having passed through her militant career, shall be taken up into the joy of the saints triumphing in heaven.

The manner and extent of the action of the Holy Ghost in individual souls is no less wonderful, although somewhat more difficult to understand, inasmuch as it is entirely invisible. . . . It is indeed true that in those of the just who lived before Christ, the Holy Ghost resided by grace, as we read in the Scriptures concerning the prophets, Zachary, John the Baptist, Simeon and Anna; so that on Pentecost the Holy Ghost did not communicate Himself in such a way "as then for the first time to begin to dwell in the saints, but by pouring Himself forth more abundantly; crowning, not beginning, His gifts; not commencing a new work, but giving more abundantly" [Leo I, Homily 3, On Pentecost]

God by grace resides in the just soul as in a temple, in a most intimate and peculiar manner. From this proceeds that union of affection by which the soul adheres most closely to God, more so than the friend is united to his most loving and beloved friend, and enjoys God in all fulness and sweetness. Now this wonderful union, which is properly called "indwelling," differing only in degree or state from that with which God beatifies the saints in heaven . . . is attributed in a peculiar manner to the Holy Ghost. For whilst traces of divine power and wisdom appear even in the wicked man, charity, which, as it were, is the special mark of the Holy Ghost, is shared in only by the just. In harmony with this, the same Spirit is called "holy," for He, the first and supreme Love, moves souls and leads them to sanctity, which ultimately consists in the love of God. . . .

The fulness of divine gifts is in many ways a consequence of the indwelling of the Holy Ghost in the souls of the just. . . . . Among these gifts are those secret warnings and invitations, which from time to time are excited in our minds and hearts by the inspiration of the Holy Ghost. Without these there is no beginning of a good life, no progress, no arriving at eternal salvation. And since these words and admonitions are uttered in the soul in an exceedingly secret manner, they are sometimes aptly compared in holy scripture to the breathing of a coming breeze, and the Angelic Doctor [sc. Thomas Aquinas] likens them to the movements of the heart which are wholly hidden in the living body. . . . More than this, the just man, that is to say he who lives the life of divine grace, and acts by the fitting virtues as by means of faculties, has need of those seven *gifts* which are properly attributed to the Holy Ghost. By means of them the soul is furnished and strengthened so as to be able to obey more easily and promptly His voice and impulse. Wherefore these gifts are of such efficacy that they lead the just man to the highest degree of sanctity; and of such excellence that they continue to exist even in heaven, though in a more perfect way. By means of these gifts the soul is excited and encouraged to seek after and attain the evangelical beatitudes, which, like the flowers that come forth in the springtime, are the signs and harbingers of eternal beatitude. Lastly, there are those blessed *fruits,* enumerated by the Apostle [Gal. 5:22], which the Spirit, even in this mortal life, produces and shows forth in the just; fruits filled with all sweetness and joy, inasmuch as they proceed from the Spirit "who is in the Trinity the sweetness of both Father and Son, filling all creatures with infinite fulness and profusion."

Christians . . . will daily strive to know him, to love him and to implore him more earnestly; for which reason may this Our exhortation, flowing spontaneously from a paternal heart, reach their ears. Perchance there are still to be found among them, even nowadays, some, who if asked, as were those of old by St. Paul the Apostle, whether they have received the Holy Ghost, might answer in like manner: *We have not so much as heard whether there be a Holy Ghost.* [Acts 19:2] At least there are certainly many who are very deficient in their knowledge of Him. They frequently use His name in their religious practices, but their faith is involved in much darkness. Wherefore all preachers and those having care of souls should remember that it is their duty to instruct their people more diligently and more fully about the Holy Ghost, avoiding, however, difficult and subtle controversies. . . .

Lastly we ought to pray and to invoke the Holy Spirit, for each one of us greatly needs His protection and His help. The more a man is deficient in wisdom, weak in strength, borne down with trouble, prone to sin, so ought he the more to fly to Him who is the never-ceasing fount of light, strength, consolation and holiness. And chiefly that first requisite of man, the forgiveness of sins, must be sought for from Him: "It is the special character of the Holy Ghost that He is the Gift of the Father and the Son. Now the remission of sins is given by the Holy Ghost as by the Gift of God." [Thomas Aquinas, *Summa Theologica* 3a pars, q. 3, a. 8, ad 3]

Unite, then, Venerable Brethren, your prayers with Ours, and at your exhortation let all Christian peoples add their prayers also, invoking the powerful and ever-acceptable intercession of the Blessed Virgin. You know well the intimate and wonderful relations existing between her and the Holy Ghost, so that she is justly called His spouse. The intercession of the Blessed Virgin was of great avail both in the mystery of the Incarnation and in the coming of the Holy Ghost on the apostles. May she continue to strengthen our prayers with her suffrage, that, in the midst of all the stress and trouble of the nations, those divine prodigies may be happily revived by the Holy Ghost, which were foretold in the words of David: *Send forth thy Spirit and they shall be created, and Thou shalt renew the face of the earth"* [Psa. 103:30].[1]

[1] Leo XIII, *The Great Encyclical Letters of Pope Leo XIII* (New York: Benziger Brothers, 1903), pp. 422-440, *passim.*

49

Rudolf Steiner

(1861–1925)

Rudolf Steiner was the founder of Anthroposophy, a curious blend of Theosophy, the Roman Catholicism of his youth, Christian patristic gnosticism, German folktales, Goethe's romantic individualism, and a highly productive concern for educational, medical, agricultural, and artistic repersonalization during a time when Germany was headed through one world war toward the next. His most influential book, The Philosophy of Freedom *(1896), is not excerpted here in favor of some of his Pentecost speeches because Steiner's actual influence in Europe came as the result of his extensive lecture tours.*

Steiner's controlling interest was to develop each person's inborn faculty of "spirit cognition" and move each one to get in touch with the spirit world around. His gnostic heavens were peopled with a multitude of ethereal and astral oversouls of animal and human species, filling out the heavenly hierarchies above the earthborn mineral and vegetal impulses. Steiner held an idea similar to the thought of William of Auvergne (d. 1249) who, under the influence of Averroist philosophy, identified the universal Agent Intellect with the Holy Spirit. Steiner identified the Holy Spirit with the group soul of all mankind, characterized by intellectual nobility, freedom, and immortality, but seen in continuity with other preternatural, soulish "entities" which inhabit romantic German forests. But Steiner was a Christian and held that it was the Christ-impulse, the eternal Logos, resident on the sun, which through the activity of the Spirit, will be brought to fullness in the future of mankind.

There is a lot of talk these days about the powers of nature, but one does not hear much about the Entities which stand behind these natural forces . . . sylphs . . . salamanders . . . gnomes . . . undines. . . . These elemental spirits, if they were to be left to themselves, would upset the cosmos. It is only right that their realms lie under the authority of men. But it can also come about that man himself be cut off from his group-soul, so that as an individual soul he is no longer able to find his way to further evolution. . . . We go so far these days that each person has his own religion and recommends his own opinion as the highest ideal. But when men interiorize the ideals, then we are on the way again towards unity, towards a common mind. For example, we acknowledge interiorly that 3 x 3 = 9, or that three angles in a triangle comprise 180 degrees. That is interior cognition. It is not necessary to vote about interior cognition. . . . A man discovers through his inner powers what the humanities teach, and these lead him to an absolute unity, to peace and harmony. . . . When humans thus unite in a higher wisdom, then the group-soul descends out of the higher worlds, that is, when free associations arise out of the naturally determined common bonds. . . . We form, as it were, the seed-bed, the context, in which the group-soul can build its body.

The church on the Day of Pentecost is the signal that mankind can find the way to a connecting bond of souls which will offer the common Spirit a place where he can take up his body. It is the discovery of an ardent love inflaming a multitude of men who had gathered to give themselves away to a common task. It is a multitude of men whose souls were still quaking from the same shaking experience through which they had lived together. It was in the flowing together of this one, common feeling that they provided themselves as that in which the higher, common Soul could embody itself. And this can be expressed with the words which say that the Holy Spirit, the Group-soul, fell upon them and imparted itself as fiery tongues. This is the great symbol for the humanity of the future.

Pentecost is not only a memory of that experience in Jerusalem but it will also be thought of as the beginning of that forever-recurring Pentecost of the aspiring together of souls. It will become a symbol for the yet to come great Church of Pentecost when humanity will have come together in a common truth in order to provide the higher Entities the opportunity to embody themselves. It will depend upon men themselves how valuable the earth in the future will be through all of this, and how effective such ideas can be for humanity. When mankind strives onward in this right way towards wisdom, then the higher spirits will unite themselves with men.[1]

The same Spirit which had worked in the power of the Christ-impulse appeared again in a manifold way to make the first confessors of Christianity the bearers and proclaimers of the message of Christ. Thus at the beginning of Christian evolution this powerful signal tells us: Just as each one of the first confessors took up the Christ-impluse and were allowed to take up the fiery tongues as inspiring their own souls, so may all of you, if you go to the trouble to understand the Christ-impulse, individualize these powers and yourselves take up the Christ-impulse into your hearts, take up powers which will enable you in the sense of the Christ-impulse to function always in an ever more perfect way.

An all-encompassing hope can overwhelm us as a result of this signal which was set up at the beginning point of Christianity: a man can feel, the more he develops himself to perfection, that the Holy Spirit is speaking out of his own inner self in the extent to which the thinking, feeling and willing of the human person is shot through with this Holy Spirit, who is through his fission and diversity an individual Spirit even in every individual human being. Because of this, the Holy Spirit is for us men, on our way towards the evolution of the future, the Spirit of that evolution towards being a free man, towards being a free human soul. The Spirit of freedom ruled in the Spirit which poured itself out upon those who were the first to grasp Christianity on the first Christian Pentecost. It was the Spirit whose most telling characteristic Christ Jesus himself had indicated when he said: "You

---

[1] Rudolf Steiner, "The Feast of Pentecost—the Soulish Striving and Work Towards Making the World Spiritual," addresses delivered in Köln, June 7 and 9, 1908 (Dornach, Switzerland: Verlag der Rudolf Steiner—Nachlassverwaltung, 1959), author's translation.

shall know the truth and the truth shall make you free!"[2]

The mystery of Pentecost: . . . The Christ himself has descended upon the earth. His power rises in our hearts as the power which insures immortality for men. . . . And not only at the beginning of our era was the Christ there; he is always there; he speaks to us, when we are willing to listen. But in order to do that, we must learn anew through study of the arts (Geisteswissenschaft) to be able to see something spiritual (ein Geistiges) behind every physical being: something spiritual behind the rock, something spiritual behind the plant, something spiritual behind the animals, something spiritual behind men, something spiritual behind the clouds, something spiritual behind the stars, something spiritual behind the Sun. . . . Anthroposophy is able to affirm that the Spirit is behind all nature. . . . My dear friends, the fate of Anthroposophy and that of Christianity will likely be the same. But to this end it is necessary for men of today to look not on the dead words spoken to them about the Christ, . . . but that they take the way of Anthroposophy to the living Christ and feel that in this way the mystery of Pentecost can be renewed in every Anthroposophist: that to him the recognition of Christ himself rise in his heart and that he feel himself warmed and enlightened by the fiery tongues of the Christian perception of the world. Let us find our way to that which is spiritual through Anthroposophy and at the same time find our way to Christ through the spirit! . . . Then will come that which humanity so verily needs for its healing and health: then the Healing Spirit will bring us to a new understanding of humanity. The Healing Spirit which Christ sent will heal the disease in the souls of humanity and then, my dear friends, will come that which humanity needs: World-Pentecost![3]

---

[2] Rudolf Steiner, "Pentecost, the Feast of Free Individuality," address delivered in Hamburg, May 15, 1910, in *ibid.,* author's translation.

[3] Rudolf Steiner, "World-Pentecost, the Gospel of Anthroposophy," address delivered in Kristiania (Oslo), May 17, 1923 (Dornach, Switzerland: Verlag der Rudolf Steiner—Nachlassverwaltung, 1956), author's translation.

50

Nicolas Berdyaev

(1874–1948)

Nicolas Berdyaev, with many others, fled from Russia to Paris after the Leninists came to power in Russia. His earlier Marxist leanings were modified by a growing affinity for Russian Orthodox Christian ideas which he syncretized with several other elements, among them early Christian gnosticism, medieval exemplarism, Rheinland mysticism, and German idealism. In his own system of "eschatological metaphysics," he forsook the language of logic to prophesy in mystical terms of the ultimate transfiguration of creation and the emergence of the "truly human community" (sobornost) upon which the kingdom of God would come, humanity having used its innate creative and spiritual powers to conform human personality to the universal divine image.

Berdyaev's central purpose is to understand "spirit" as the:

Divine element in man, the spiritual element inherent in him. The spiritual life is the new life for which man is thirsting; the *pneuma* is its principle. All man's loftiest aspirations are spiritual. Therefore we must think of the new life in spiritual rather than in natural or social terms.[1]

[1]Nicolas Berdyaev. *Spirit and Reality* (New York: Charles Scribner's Sons, 1939), p. 198. Used by permission of Collins Publishers.

Since the form of the new life will be that of an eschatalogical sobornost *(community of love), Berdyaev's apocalyptical, anti-authoritarian understanding of the Spirit is finally a statement about spontaneous divine/human creativity that yearns for the oft-promised Age of the Spirit:*

Spirit—the Holy Spirit—is incarnated in human life, but it assumes the form of a *whole humanity* rather than of authority. This is, indeed, the pivotal idea of my book. . . . The agency of the Holy Spirit is not manifest in hierarchy, authority, natural laws, State regulations, or in the determinism of an objective world, but in human existence, creation, inspiration, love and sacrifice.[2]

Objectification is the way in which spirit adapts itself and conforms to the world; it is a failure of spiritual creativeness, a subjection of the personal element to the general, of the human element to the non-human, of inspiration to law. . . .

The tendency to regard the spiritual life as a way of salvation, and Christianity as a religion of personal salvation, has led to spirituality being narrowed, diminished and weakened. The attitude of men to social and historical life was objectified, and they realized spirituality only in a symbolical way. . . . Obedience is pseudo-spirituality. It inevitably involves obedience to evil and a slave mentality. In the name of obedience Christians have suffered evils so long, that others—non-Christians—have at last been forced to rebel against them and to subdue them, but at the price of attacking Christianity itself. Obedience was an instrument of government which more than any other exhausted Christian spirituality.[3]

St. Simon the New Theologian says that illumination can dispense with written laws. There is a profound antagonism between spirit and law. There is a profound difference between inspiration, charismatism and new birth of early Christianity and the later ascetic schools with their disciplines, laws and stages of perfection. . . . There is a gulf between spirit and authority. The agency of the Holy Spirit and spirit is not continuous and evolutionary, but sporadic and catastrophic.

Authority is of paramount importance in the religious life. It is

[2] *Ibid.,* p. 187.
[3] *Ibid.,* pp. 164, 165, 169.

often invested with religious attributes. But actually questions of authority pertain to the sociological rather than to the pneumatological sphere. Authority is purely a product of objectification and, as such, does not exist in the spiritual life. . . . The life of the Church as a social and historical institution is based upon the maxim: Let the powers that be, government, authority, with their guarantees of security, be active whether spirit is active or not. Thus the life of the Church is subject to social determination.[4]

It is inexact to say that man is spirit; but it can be said that he has spirit. The distinction between *being* and *having* is only completely resolved in God. . . . What does it mean to *have* and to *be* spirit? *To be* definitively spirit is theosis or participation in the Divine life. Spirit is from God. And when man *has* spirit, when he is in spirit, then spirit enters into him and inspires him. Hence there is an indissoluble tie between spirit and inspiration or the creative spirit. . . . In essence spirituality is always creativeness, since freedom and activity are the attributes of spirit. In creativeness there are two elements: that of grace, of inspiration coming to man from on high, of genius and talent possessed by man; and that of freedom, having no external cause and determination, but forming the new elements in the creative act. Creativeness implies interaction not only between man and the world, but also between man and God. . . . It is high time that a spirituality—a Christian spirituality—were founded in the world. Whatever name we give it, be it Socialism or Communism, it should be first and foremost a personalistic spirituality, one based upon the relation of one man to another, of one concrete personality to another. This spirituality would defend the human personality against the tyranny of society. . . . When the forms of community and society are admittedly based upon forms of spirituality, then the development of the human character and the improvement of human qualities will become the primary considerations.[5]

Christianity is *pneuma-centric.* The *pneuma* or spirit is the bearer and source of prophetic inspiration in Christianity. The *paracletism* inherent in Christianity has always encouraged Christians to hope for its revelation, for the advent of a new age of the Holy Spirit. S. Bulgakov very rightly maintains that there can be no personal

[4] *Ibid.,* pp. 183-185.
[5] *Ibid.,* pp. 170, 171, 172, 180.

incarnation of the Holy Spirit, that His incarnation must be universal, diffused throughout the world. . . . The workings of the Holy Spirit are manifest in spirit. Spiritual life is communion with Divine life. . . . All charisms, all gifts are the spirit's: those of the prophet, the apostle, the saint as well as those of the poet, the philosopher, the inventor, the reformer. The religion of spirit speaks not of justification or salvation, but of the illumination of human nature, of a real change.[6]

Christian spirituality has assumed the burden of the fallen world as an act of free expiation, as an expression of love and charity. Spirituality disdains obedience, servitude, conformity and compromise with the powers of the world; it looks upon the world in the light of sacrifice and love, of expiation and acceptance of the burden of the world. The new spirituality should appear disincarnate; it should rebel against incarnation as a form of objectification or of historical relativity; but actually it will be a reincarnation, a catastrophic rather than an evolutionary reincarnation. . . . The spiritualization of Christianity is not at an end, it is more than ever necessary. . . . In this context atheism itself is, perhaps, but a dialogical moment in the process of theological purification, spiritualization and humanization. Man's notion of God bears the symbolical imprint of his inhumanity. But the purified spiritual life will also be a revelation of Divine humanity. This purer form of spirituality should do away with the physical torments associated with mysticism, it should liberate man from the phantasmagoric and pathological idea that God is moved by human suffering. In the light of this, the whole character of the spiritual life is transformed. God has no need of human suffering, fear and servitude; He only needs men's ascension, their ecstatic transcendence of their limitations. The new spirituality will be first and foremost an experience of creative energy and inspiration. Hence we can discard the symbolism associated with human slavery and humiliation.[7]

---

[6] *Ibid.,* pp. 181 and 183.
[7] *Ibid.,* pp. 190-193.

51

Pius XII

(1876–1958, pope from 1939)

"Mystici Corporis Christi" (June 29, 1943) continues the orthodox teaching of the Roman Catholic Church in the line of Augustine, Aquinas, and Leo XIII. Promulgated during the Second World War, the pope's understanding of the church as the mystical, spiritual Body of Christ, held together organically and gifted charismatically by the permeation of the Holy Spirit, was his attempt to preach peace and unity to the war-torn world. Along the way, his body-theology allows Pius to cover "the less honorable members of the Body" with "more abundant honor" as he issues a strong polemic against the policy of euthanasia being implemented in Nazi Germany (#106). Pius's teaching is down to earth in the sense that it affirms the earthly, visible nature of the spiritual Body in opposition to false "mysticism" and "quietism"; yet, in its acknowledgment of the charismatic qualities eternally present in the church, the encyclical presages the Catholic pentecostal movment which would flourish twenty years later. This kind of balance is also evident in Pius's other encyclical which touches on the work of the Holy Spirit, "Divino afflante Spiritu" (September 30, 1943), in which he affirms that the biblical exegete may and ought to consider the historical context and the literary character and style of an inspired writer in establishing the meaning of Scripture.

But after the unhappy fall of Adam, the universal progeny of mankind, infected by a hereditary stain, lost their sharing of the divine nature . . . the Word of the Eternal Father through this same divine love [of God] assumed human nature from the race of Adam—but an innocent and spotless nature it was—so that He, as a new Adam, might be the source whence the grace of the Holy Spirit should flow unto all the children of the first parent.[1]

Just as at the first moment of the Incarnation, the Son of the Eternal Father adorned with the fullness of the Holy Spirit the human nature which was substantially united to Him, that it might be a fitting instrument of the Divinity in the sanguinary task of the Redemption, so at the hour of His precious death He wished that His Church should be enriched with the abundant gifts of the Paraclete in order that in dispensing the divine fruits of the Redemption it might be for the Incarnate Word a powerful instrument that would certainly never fail. For the juridical mission of the Church, and the power to teach, govern and administer the sacraments derive their supernatural efficacy and force for the building up of the Body of Christ from the fact that Jesus Christ hanging on the Cross, opened up to His Church the fountain of divine graces, which protect it from ever teaching men false doctrine, and enable it to rule them for their soul's salvation through supernaturally enlightened pastors and to bestow on them abundant heavenly graces.[2]

The Church which He founded by His Blood, He strengthened on the day of Pentecost by a special power, given from heaven. For, having solemnly installed in his exalted office him whom he had already nominated as His Vicar [i.e., Peter, the first pope], He had ascended into heaven; and sitting now at the right hand of the Father He wished to make known and proclaim His Spouse through the visible coming of the Holy Spirit with the sound of a mighty wind and tongues of fire. For just as He Himself when He began to preach was made known by His Eternal Father through the Holy Spirit descending and remaining on Him, so likewise, as the Apostles were about to enter upon their office of preaching, Christ our Lord sent the Holy Spirit down from heaven, to touch them with tongues of fire and to point

[1] Gerald C. Treacy, *Mystici Corporis Christi by Pope Pius XII: Encyclical Letter on the Mystical Body of Christ* (New York: The Paulist Press, © 1943), #12 on p. 9.
[2] *Ibid.,* #32 on p. 19.

out as by the finger of God the supernatural mission and supernatural office of the Church.[3]

For if not even the smallest act conducive to salvation can be performed except in the Holy Spirit, how can unnumbered multitudes of every people and every race work together harmoniously for the supreme glory of the Triune God, except in the power of Him, Who proceeds from Father and Son in one eternal act of love? . . . Above all, everyone must be able to see the Supreme Head, who gives effective direction to what all are doing in a mutually helpful way towards attaining the desired end, and he is the Vicar on earth of Jesus Christ. As the Divine Redeemer sent a Paraclete, the Spirit of Truth, who in His name should govern the Church in an invisible way; similarly He commissioned Peter and his Successors, to be His personal representatives on earth and to assume the visible government of the Christian community.[4]

We think how grievously they err who arbitrarily picture the Church as something hidden and invisible, as do they also who look upon it as a mere human institution with a certain disciplinary code and external ritual, but lacking power to communicate supernatural life. No; the Mystical Body of Christ is like Christ the Head and Exemplar of the Church, "Who is not complete, if only His visible human nature is considered, or if only His divine, invisible nature . . . but He is one through the union of both and one in both. . . ."
The same reason that led our divine Redeemer to give to the community of men He founded the constitution of a society, perfect of its kind, containing all the juridical and social elements, namely that He might perpetuate on earth the saving work of Redemption, was also the reason why He wished them to be enriched with the heavenly gifts of the Consoling Spirit. . . . There can, then, be no real opposition or conflict between the invisible mission of the Holy Spirit and the juridical commission of Ruler and Teacher received from Christ. Like body and soul in us, they complement and perfect each other, and have their source in our one Redeemer, Who not only said, as He breathed on the Apostles: "Receive ye the Holy Spirit," but also clearly commanded: "As the Father hath sent Me, so I send you," and again: "He who heareth you, heareth Me."[5]

[3] *Ibid.,* #34 on p. 20.
[4] *Ibid.,* #75, 76 on pp. 40 and 41.
[5] *Ibid.,* #69, 70, 71 on pp. 37 and 38.

... To Bishops, more than to the rulers of this world, even those in supreme authority, should be applied the sentence: "Touch not my anointed ones!" For Bishops have been anointed with the chrism of the Holy Spirit.[6]

If we examine closely this divine principle of life and power given by Christ, in so far as it constitutes the very source of every gift and created grace, we easily see that it is nothing else than the Holy Spirit, the Paraclete who proceeds from the Father and the Son, and who is called in a special way the "Spirit of Christ" or the "Spirit of the Son." For it was by His breath of grace and truth that the Son made beautiful His soul in the immaculate womb of the Blessed Virgin; this Spirit delights to dwell in the dear soul of our Redeemer as in His most cherished shrine; this Spirit Christ merited for us on the Cross by shedding His own blood; this Spirit He bestowed on the Church for the remission of sins, when He breathed on the Apostles; and while Christ alone received this Spirit without measure, to the members of the Mystical Body He is imparted only according to the measure of the giving of Christ, from Christ's own fullness. But after Christ's glorification on the Cross, His Spirit is communicated to the Church in an abundant outpouring, so that she, and her single members may become daily more and more like to our Saviour. It is the Spirit of Christ that has made us adopted sons of God in order that one day "we all beholding the glory of the Lord with open faces may be transformed into the same image from glory to glory."

To this Spirit of Christ, too, as to an invisible principle, is to be ascribed the fact that all the parts of the Body are joined one with the other and with their exalted Head; for He is entire in the Head, entire in the Body and entire in each of the members. To the members He is present and assists them in proportion to their various tasks and offices and the greater or less grade of spiritual health which they enjoy. It is He Who through His heavenly grace is the principle of every supernatural act in all the parts of the Body. It is He Who while He is personally present and divinely active in all the members, also acts in the inferior members through the ministry of the higher members. Finally, while with His grace He provides for the constant growth of the Church, He yet refuses to dwell with sanctifying grace in members that are wholly severed from the Body. . . . The Church, then, no less than each of her holy members

[6] *Ibid.*, #44 on p. 24.

can make this thought of the Apostle her own: "And I live, now not I; but Christ liveth in me."[7]

. . . from heaven He assisted the evangelists in such a way that as members of Christ they wrote what they had learned at the dictation, as it were, of the Head. And for us today, who still linger on in this earthly exile, He is the author of faith as in our heavenly house He will be its finisher. It is He Who grants the light of faith to believers; it is He Who from His divine riches imparts the supernatural gifts of knowledge, understanding and wisdom to the pastors and teachers and above all to His Vicar on earth, so that they may faithfully preserve the treasury of faith, defend it, with reverence and devotion explain and protect it. It is He Who, though unseen, presides at the Church's Councils and guides them.[8]

One must not think, however, that this ordered or "organic" structure of the Body of the Church contains only hierarchical elements and with them is complete; or, as an opposite opinion holds, that it is composed only of those who enjoy charismatic gifts— though members gifted with miraculous power will never be lacking in the Church. That those who exercise sacred power in this Body are its first and chief members must be maintained uncompromisingly. . . . At the same time, when the Fathers of the Church sing the praises of this Mystical Body of Christ, with its ministries, its variety of ranks, its offices, its conditions, its order, its duties, they are thinking not only of those who have received sacred orders, but of all those, too, who following the evangelical counsels pass their lives either actively among men or in the silence of the cloister, or who aim at combining the active and contemplative life according to their Institute. They were thinking of those who though living in the world consecrate themselves wholeheartedly to spiritual or corporal works of mercy; as well as those who live in the state of holy matrimony. Indeed let this be clearly understood, especially in these our days: the fathers and mothers of families, and those who are spiritual parents through Baptism, and in particular those members of the laity who assist the ecclesiastical hierarchy in spreading the Kingdom of the Divine Redeemer, occupy an honorable, even though often lowly place in the Christian community. Under the impulse of God and with His help they can reach the peak of holiness; and such holiness,

---

[7] *Ibid.,* #60-62 on pp. 32-33.
[8] *Ibid.,* #53 on p. 29.

Jesus Christ has promised, will never be wanting to the Church.[9]

. . . Christ is in us and we are in Christ. . . . Christ is in us through His Spirit, whom He gives to us, and through whom He acts within us in such a way that all divine activity of the Holy Spirit within our souls must also be attributed to Christ. . . .

This communication of the Spirit of Christ is the channel through which flow into all the members of the Church those gifts, powers and extraordinary graces found superabundantly in the Head as in their source, and they are perfected day by day in these members according to the office they may hold in the Mystical Body of Jesus Christ. Thus the Church becomes, as it were, the filling out and complement of the Redeemer, while Christ in a sense attains through the Church a fullness in all things. . . .

We do not censure those who in various ways and with diverse reasonings strain every effort to understand and to clarify the mystery of this our marvelous union with Christ. But let all agree uncompromisingly on this, if they would not err from truth and from the orthodox teaching of the Church: to reject every kind of mystic union, by which the faithful would in any way pass beyond the sphere of creatures and rashly enter the divine, even to the extent of one single attribute of the eternal Godhead being predicated of them as their own. And besides, let all hold this as certain truth, that all these activities are common to the most Blessed Trinity, in so far as they have God as supreme efficient cause.

Let it be observed also that one is treating here of a hidden mystery, which in this earthly exile can never be fully disclosed and grasped, and expressed in human language. The Divine Persons are said to be indwelling in as much as They are present to intellectual creatures in a way that lies beyond human comprehension, and are known and loved by them in a purely supernatural manner alone within the deepest sanctuary of the soul. . . .[10]

False and dangerous is the error of those who try to deduce from the mysterious union of all with Christ a certain unhealthy quietism. They would attribute the whole spiritual life of Christians and their progress in virtue exclusively to the action of the divine Spirit, setting

---

[9] *Ibid.*, #18 on pp. 11 and 12.
[10] *Ibid.*, #84-86 on pp. 44-46.

aside and neglecting the corresponding work and collaboration which we must contribute to this action. . . .

But that men should continue consistently in their good works, that they advance generously in grace and virtue, that they strive earnestly to reach the heights of Christian perfection and at the same time do their best to stimulate others to gain the same goal—all this the Spirit from above does not wish to bring about, unless men contribute their daily share of zealous activity. . . . In our mortal body, the members are strengthened and grow through continued exercise; much more is this true in the social Body of Jesus Christ, in which each member retains his own personal freedom, responsibility and principles of conduct. . . .[11]

Venerable Brothers, may the Virgin Mother of God grant the prayers of Our paternal heart—and they are yours too—and obtain for all a true love of the Church. Her sinless soul was filled with the divine Spirit of Jesus Christ more than all other created souls, and "in the name of the whole human race," she gave her consent for a "spiritual marriage between the Son of God and human nature." . . .

Thus she who corporally was the mother of our Head, through the added title of pain and glory, became spiritually the mother of all His members. She it was who, through her powerful prayers, obtained the grace that the Spirit of our divine Redeemer, already given to the Church on the Cross, should be bestowed through miraculous gifts on the newly founded Hierarchy on Pentecost. . . . and she continued to show for the Mystical Body of Christ, born from the pierced Heart of the Saviour, the same mother's care and ardent love with which she clasped the Infant Jesus to her warm and nourishing breast.

May she, then, most holy mother of all Christ's members . . . never cease to beg from Him that a continuous, copious flow of graces may pass from its glorious Head into all the members of the Mystical Body. May she throw about the Church today, as in times gone by, the mantle of her protection and obtain from God that now at last the Church and all mankind may enjoy more peaceful days.[12]

[11] *Ibid.*, #93 and 94 on pp. 49-50.
[12] *Ibid.*, #127-129 on pp. 64 and 65.

52

Karl Barth

(1886–1968)

In 1919 Barth issued his commentary on Romans which was written in defense of the radical transcendence of God (over against the liberal theology and religion of culture prevalent in Europe at that time.) His immense work, Church Dogmatics, *written between 1932 and 1962, spells out his initial insights. Barth's later theological maturation toward the perspectives of Swiss Anabaptism blended with his basic Calvinism and Augustinianism to enable him to bridge the gap between the catholic and the charismatic traditions. In these two excerpts, he upholds the full personhood of the Spirit as totally other than the human mind and spirit while at the same time allowing for the Spirit's charismating action within the believer, immersing in the Spirit, creating true freedom, and giving the gifts.*

The Holy Ghost as Creator

Man's being in the image of God only becomes actual fact when the Holy Ghost comes on the spot on man's behalf. This likeness to God is, therefore, not, and will not be, a property of the human spirit created, but it is and remains the free work of the Creator upon his creature: a work only to be understood as grace, and never to be comprehended by man.

Christian life is human life that has been made open by the Holy Ghost to receive God's word. Thus the Holy Ghost, by virtue of His being present and at work, is the subjective aspect when revelation occurs. Man's knowledge, which is imparted to him by Scripture and experience, concerning what his Creator demands from him (i. e., "the orders of creation"), *is* not man's own but *becomes* his in the Holy Ghost, when that information has been given through the word.

The Holy Ghost as Reconciler

Being the Spirit of grace, the Holy Spirit strives against man's hostility to grace, in other words, man's seeking to justify himself by works; for this is the characteristic, unique sin which man cannot get rid of, nor escape thinking of. The Holy Spirit strives against this.

Christian life is man's actual life in the Holy Ghost; man is accounted as righteous through the word, or for Christ's sake; man's righteousness is by faith on his part, seen in repentance and trust. Because this righteousness—this being accounted as righteous— attaches to the actual man, it coincides with his sanctification. Man's own obedience to his own true reality as one being sanctified is in the Holy Ghost, and is only actual when it responds to the Holy Ghost.

The Holy Ghost as Redeemer

The Holy Ghost is present to man in God's revelation as Spirit of promise. In the Holy Ghost, i. e., in the finality and futurity of what, in principle, is transcendent of man's existence (on earth), man is a new creature: God's child.

Christian life is the new life in hope, begotten of the Holy Ghost. Seeing that the Christian man is hidden with Christ in God, he has always a conscience that is leading him into all truth: he is always bound to God in thankfulness, and therefore in freedom: he prays and because he prays he is always being heard.[1]

(Excerpts from The Foundation of the Christian Life*)*
A man's turning to faithfulness to God, and consequently to calling upon Him, is the work of this faithful God which, perfectly accomplished in the history of Jesus Christ, in virtue of the awakening, quickening and illuminating power of this history, becomes a new beginning of life as his baptism with the Holy Spirit.

[1] Karl Barth, *The Holy Ghost and the Christian Life* (lecture, Oct. 9, 1929, at Elberfeld; trans. R. Birch Hoyle) (London: Frederick Muller, 1938), pp. 9-10.

The first step of this life of faithfulness to God, the Christian life, is a man's baptism with water, which by his own decision is requested of the community and which is administered by the community, as the binding confession of his obedience, conversion and hope, made in prayer for God's grace, wherein he honors the freedom of this grace.[2]

To put it again in a single sentence: In the work of the Holy Spirit the history manifested to all men in the resurrection of Jesus Christ is manifest and present to a specific man as his own salvation history. . . . In the work of the Holy Spirit that which was truth for all, and hence for [this man] too, even without his acceptance, becomes truth which is affirmed by him. . . . In this work it begins to be genuine intercourse in which the human partner, far from confusing himself with the divine partner or trying to take His place, occupies the place which is appropriate in relation to Him. The work of the Holy Spirit, then, does not entail the paralysing dismissal or absence of the human spirit, mind, knowledge and will. It has often been depicted thus. Attempts have been made to achieve it by strangely resigned twistings of human thought, feeling and effort. . . . There is no more intimate friend of sound human understanding than the Holy Spirit.[3]

Baptism with the Holy Spirit . . . especially does not consist in [a person] donning a uniform and clapping on a helmet and as a member of the community, as one specimen among many others, being subjected to the same regimented spiritual and ethical drill. "Infinite gifts from his rich store, The wondrous hand of God doth pour." The Holy Spirit, being the Spirit of the one, but eternally rich God, is no compactly uniform mass. When he is poured forth, when men are baptized with him, he exists in the fulness of the "charismata" of the one community. Through their distribution each individual Christian—independently of the particularity of his natural character or personal concerns—receives his own special spiritual power and therewith his own special task in the total life and ministry of the community.[4]

Baptism with the Holy Spirit does not exclude baptism with water. It

[2] Karl Barth, *Baptism as the Foundation of Christian Life*, *Church Dogmatics*, IV 4, trans. G. W. Bromiley (Edinburgh: T. & T. Clark, 1969), p. 2.

[3] *Ibid.*, pp. 27 and 28.

[4] *Ibid.*, pp. 37 and 38.

does not render it superfluous. Indeed, it makes it possible and demands it. Again, baptism with water is what it is only in relation to baptism with the Holy Spirit. Whether it looks back to this or forward to it, it presupposes it. . . . On the one side is the word and command of God expressed in His gift, on the other man's obedience of faith required of him and to be rendered by him as a recipient of the divine gift. Without this unity of the two in their distinction there could be no Christian ethics.[5]

[5] *Ibid.,* p. 41.

SOUTHERN CALIFORNIA CEN
Golden Gate Baptist Theological Sem
12311 Chapman Avenue
Garden Grove, California 92040